Evidence-Based
School
Counseling

Carey Dimmitt • John C. Carey • Trish Hatch

Evidence-Based School Counseling

Making a Difference With Data-Driven Practices

CORWIN PRESS
A SAGE Publications Company
Thousand Oaks, CA 91320

For information:

Corwin Press
A Sage Publications Company
2455 Teller Road
Thousand Oaks, California 91320
www.corwinpress.com

Sage Publications Ltd.
1 Oliver's Yard
55 City Road
London EC1Y 1SP
United Kingdom

Sage Publications India Pvt. Ltd.
B 1/I 1 Mohan Cooperative
  Industrial Area
Mathura Road, New Delhi 110 044
India

Sage Publications Asia-Pacific Pte. Ltd.
33 Pekin Street #02-01
Far East Square
Singapore 048763

Printed in the United States of America.

Library of Congress Cataloging-in-Publication Data

Dimmitt, Carey.
Evidence-based school counseling: Making a difference with data-driven practices/Carey Dimmitt, John C. Carey, Trish Hatch.
    p. cm.
Includes bibliographical references and index.
ISBN 978-1-4129-4889-0 (cloth)
ISBN 978-1-4129-4890-6 (pbk.)
    1. Educational counseling. I. Carey, John C. II. Hatch, Trish. III. Title.

LB1027.5.D466 2007
371.4—dc22   2006101268

This book is printed on acid-free paper.

07   08   09   10   11   10   9   8   7   6   5   4   3   2   1

Acquisitions Editor:	Stacy Wagner and Jessica Allan
Editorial Assistant:	Joanna Coelho
Production Editor:	Sarah K. Quesenberry
Copy Editor:	Robert Holm
Typesetter:	C&M Digitals (P) Ltd.
Proofreader:	Sally Jaskold
Indexer:	Sheila Bodell
Cover Designer:	Lisa Miller

Contents

Preface

E vidence-based school counseling can be defined as the intentional use of the best available evidence in planning, implementing, and evaluating school counseling interventions and programs. The primary purpose of this book is to help school counselors develop the data skills that are needed for evidence-based practice in modern public schools.

Public education has gone through dramatic transformations in the past 15 years. Much of this transformation has been driven by a profound and fundamental change in the relationships of state governments to local school districts and by resultant changes in how districts and schools are led and managed. An equally profound shift in the relationship of the federal government to local public schools is evidenced in the No Child Left Behind legislation, which both reinforces a standards-based approach to public school management and accountability and introduces new requirements for public schools to adopt research-based approaches to education. Schools must be capable of demonstrating that their educational practices are supported by empirical evidence. These changes require that all educators become skilled in using data for planning, evaluation, and accountability and in evaluating outcome research.

Few school counselors were drawn to the profession because of the opportunities it affords to read research and work with data. Some school counselors resent the recent push to use data to document the outcomes of their work when every day they can see that they make a difference for students. Over the past quarter century, there have been recommendations to incorporate accountability practices into school counseling programs with little success (Aubrey, 1982; Fairchild, 1993; Fairchild & Seeley, 1995; Fairchild & Zins, 1986; Myrick, 1984; Wiggins, 1985). The predominant message of the accountability movement has been that producing evidence of effectiveness is a necessary condition for job security in public education. However, this message has been ineffective in persuading school counselors to add accountability practices to their already strained workload. This may be due in part to a lack of clarity about the relationship between accountability and the improvement of services for students. Another roadblock is that most school counselors were not trained to use data or program evaluation in their graduate programs and may be intimidated by the prospect.

The Time Is Now

The new message in public education is that evidence-based practice skills and activities are necessary for continuous improvement in all aspects of education, including school counseling. The primary reason that school counselors need evidence-based skills is to increase their effectiveness in helping students. However, moving to an evidence-based approach is not simply a matter of adding accountability practices. It is a paradigm shift that incorporates the collection and use of evidence in all phases of the work of school counseling to support the counselor's professional decision making. In an evidence-based practice mode, the data that are needed to document accountability to stakeholders are generated naturally as a by-product of the school counselor's decision-making processes.

This book provides the information and skills in use of data that school counselors need in order to make the shift to evidence-based school counseling. These practices are linked to work that counselors and educators are doing in schools across the country and are rooted in the belief that evidence-based school counseling practice is the best way for us to determine that what we are doing is effective. The ultimate goal of school counseling is to help all students be successful (ASCA, 2003), and evidence-based practice provides the tools needed to support that objective. Implicit in this goal is a moral imperative to address equity issues by providing the best possible services for all students (Education Trust, 1999, 2001; House & Martin, 1998; Paisley & Hayes, 2003; Stone & Dahir, 2006). Data-based decision making, using existing evidence to identify possible interventions, and evaluating interventions and programs—the skills and processes delineated in this book—create success.

Ways to Use this Book

Throughout the book examples and scenarios are provided for readers as cutting edge ideas about what evidence-based school counseling practice could look like. We hope these will prompt discussion, new ways of thinking, and an expansion of possibility. Beginning with the end in mind is an effective way to approach change, so some readers may want to start with Chapter 9. There is a logical order to the chapters, but given that every reader will have unique experiences and knowledge, moving around in the book may also be valuable.

Acknowledgments

Many people contributed in myriad ways to the development of the ideas in this book and to the writing and editing process. We would like to thank all of the school counselors, administrators, and teachers who have attended our trainings and leadership institutes over the years, as they have consistently provided invaluable information about what is needed, how they are using data, and what works. Tim Poynton, now counselor educator at Suffolk University, helped to develop several ideas contained in this book. Karen Harrington, the Center for School Counseling's senior research fellow, provided stellar editing support throughout the project and contributed in too many ways to count. Julie Hall, future school counselor, helped tremendously with the research appendix. Paul Meyers, the reviewers of early versions of the book, and Stacy Wagner at Corwin Press all provided constructive comments at crucial points in the process.

Corwin Press gratefully acknowledges the contributions of the following reviewers:

Tom Carr, MS, NCC, LPC, Carr Counseling & Consultation, Inc., Hillsborough, NC

Joyce A. DeVoss, PhD, Associate Professor, Northern Arizona University, Statewide Program, Tucson, AZ

Katharine Gray, MD, Director of Student Services, Blackstone Valley Regional Vocational Technical High School, Upton, MA

Shawn Grime, School Counselor, Bryan High School, Bryan, OH

Sylvia R. Jackson, High School Counselor, Adolfo Camarillo High School, Camarillo, CA

Mary Pat McCartney, MEd, Elementary School Counselor, Prince William County Public Schools, Manassas, VA

Graciela L. Orozco, EdD, Assistant Professor and School Counseling Coordinator, Department of Counseling San Francisco State University, San Francisco, CA

Kelli Saginak, Assistant Professor and School Counseling Coordinator, University of Wisconsin, Oshkosh, Oshkosh, WI

About the Authors

 **Carey Dimmitt** is the Associate Director of the Center for School Counseling Outcome Research, an Assistant Professor of School Counseling, and the Clinical Director of the School Counseling Program at the University of Massachusetts, Amherst. She received her PhD in counseling psychology from UMass-Amherst. Prior to her work as a counselor educator, she worked for 14 years with children and families in schools and community mental health settings. Her major scholarly interests are in the areas of outcome research, effective teaching and counseling practices K–16, school counseling curriculum development, clinical training for school counselors, and systemic change in educational institutions. She is a member of the National Panel for Evidence-Based School Counseling and the mother of two children.

 **John C. Carey** is the Director of the National Center for School Counseling Outcome Research, Associate Professor of School Counseling, and the Coordinator for the School Counselor Education Program at the University of Massachusetts, Amherst. He received his PhD in counselor education from the University of Wyoming. He was awarded 2006 Counselor Educator of the Year by the American School Counselor Association. His research interests include school counseling outcome measurement, school counseling program evaluation, standards-based models of school counseling, and the development of research-based interventions to promote career development and eliminate the achievement gap. He is a member of the National Panel for Evidence-Based School Counseling and the coeditor of the text *Multicultural Counseling in Schools: A Practical Handbook*.

 **Trish Hatch** is the Director of the Center for Excellence in School Counseling and Leadership, Assistant Professor and Director of the School Counseling Program at San Diego State University. She received her PhD in education, institutional leadership, and policy studies at University of California, Riverside. She was awarded 2001 Administrator of the Year by the American School Counseling Association (ASCA).
She is a former school counselor, administrator, and vice president of ASCA. Her research interests include the use of data to effect change and the impact of the National Model on the operational efficiency, institutional legitimacy, and political social capital of school counselors. She is a member of the National Panel for Evidence-Based School Counseling. She is coauthor of *The ASCA National Model: A Framework for School Counseling Programs* and the mother of three grown sons.

To the school counseling practitioners who are using data to support the success of all students, and to our students, who are the future of the profession.

1

Moving to Evidence-Based School Counseling Practice

Consider two scenarios:

Scenario 1: *Bob, a high school counselor, is asked by his principal to see what can be done to reduce fights and disciplinary referrals. Bob creates a series of guidance lessons on conflict resolution and implements these in classrooms where teachers typically provide ready access. He also sets up a peer mediation program based on handouts he picked up at a presentation at the last state school counseling association conference. He recruits, selects, trains, and supervises a team of student mediators who help resolve conflicts between peers. The program runs for five years, and during this time over 60 students participate as peer mediators. Bob is very happy with the program's success and even documents his interventions and teaches other counselors how to implement his program at a session at the state conference.*

Scenario 2: *Bob, a high school counselor, notices an increase in disciplinary referrals related to fighting in institutional data and suggests to the principal that something be done to reduce fights and increase school safety. After consultation with the principal and a discussion at a faculty meeting, he organizes* *a team of parents and teachers to find research-based approaches to reducing school violence and fighting. The team in consultation with students, identifies the problem as a lack of student conflict resolution skills, and chooses a research-based conflict resolution curriculum focused on teaching all students these skills. Bob receives training in implementing the curriculum and, serving as a trainer to the social studies teachers, he partners with them to teach the curriculum in the ninth grade social studies classes. Pre- and posttests of student learning indicate that the ninth graders have learned new conflict resolution strategies and skills. Disciplinary referrals drop by 25%. Student school climate surveys show that ninth graders think that the school is now a safer and more orderly environment. Bob and the social studies chair disseminate the results in a PowerPoint presentation to the school board, teachers, school community, and parents in the annual school counseling program report card. The following year, the curriculum is implemented and evaluated in all grade levels.*

These two scenarios reflect two very different paradigms for school counselor functioning. The first paradigm reflects current common practices, perhaps even best practices. Bob is responsive to his principal's request, develops interventions using his own skill in lesson planning, and uses information transmitted through the official channels of his professional community. Bob works hard, delivers many lessons, trains numerous mediators, and gives back to the profession by teaching others how to implement his interventions.

In the second scenario, Bob is actively engaged in monitoring school data (especially data related to achievement, attendance, and safety). He uses this information as *evidence* for what problem needs to be addressed and takes the leadership necessary to get it done. Bob collaborates with teachers in reviewing different approaches to the identified problem and in selecting an approach with evidence of its effectiveness. Again, Bob teams with teachers to integrate the intervention into the academic curriculum, another practice with research-based evidence of its effectiveness. Through pre- and posttests, Bob gathers evidence that students actually learned the intended material. This learning benefits the larger school community through improved school climate and reduced disciplinary referrals. Finally, Bob disseminates the evidence of his intervention to public education stakeholders.

While the first scenario reflects twentieth century best practices, the second scenario reflects twenty-first-century evidence-based practice. We believe that the school counseling profession needs to make the transition from a best practice orientation to an evidence-based practice orientation so that school counselors can maximize their effectiveness, demonstrate their worth, and increase their legitimacy in public schools.

In this chapter, we begin this process by defining *evidence-based school counseling* and identifying specific competencies needed for evidence-based practice. Next we examine the context of evidence-based school counseling practice by (a) looking at the forces driving change in school counseling practice and (b) reviewing the key concepts of ongoing attempts to reform practice (the Education Trust's *Transforming School Counseling Initiative* and the American School Counselor Association's National Model). Subsequent chapters will help counselors acquire this knowledge and build these skills.

Integrating Evidence and Practice

The *evidence-based practice* movement originally evolved in the field of medicine where it has been defined as "the integration of the best evidence with clinical expertise and patient values" (Sackett, Straus, Richardson, Rosenberg, & Haynes, 2000, p. 1). This approach emphasizes medical practitioners' use of best available research to guide practice and the integration of this knowledge with clinical skills. This movement has resulted in significant changes in medical practice and education. Medical educators now recognize that their students need to learn how to integrate research literature into their practice. In recent years, many human service professions have incorporated evidence-based practice principles in both professional practice and education. For example, evidence-based practice concepts are being applied in counseling psychology (Chwalisz, 2003), school psychology (Kratochwill & Shernoff, 2003), nursing (Deaton, 2001), and public health (Bronson, Gurney, & Land, 1999).

Sexton, Schofield, and Whiston (1997) have argued that adopting an evidence-based practice approach would help the school counseling field become better integrated by basing training, knowledge generation, and practice in the evolving knowledge base of the profession. They pointed out that use of the existing *outcome research* to guide both training and practice can help ensure that professional activities reflect best practices and are consistent with each other. We believe that an explicit model for evidence-based school counseling is needed to accomplish the promise for the approach noted by Sexton, Schofield, and Whiston (1997).

outcome research

research that evaluates whether an intervention causes changes in behavior, affect, and/or cognition

A Model for Evidence-Based School Counseling Practice

We have developed the following model (see Figure 1.1) from Shlonsky and Gibbs's (2004) general model for helping professions.

Our model of evidence-based school counseling practice suggests that school counselors need to use evidence to determine what needs to be addressed (*problem description*), which interventions or practices should be implemented (*outcome research use*), and whether the implemented interventions or practices were effective (*intervention evaluation*).

Figure 1.1   A Model of Evidence-Based School Practice (EBP) in Counseling Practice

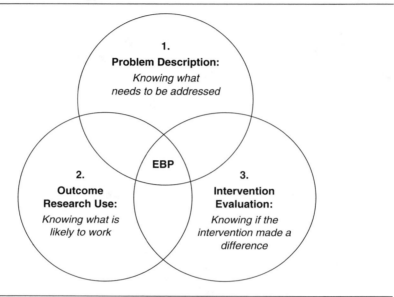

Knowing what needs to be addressed is accomplished through the integration of institutional data on student performance with data from sources such as school climate surveys and needs assessments. School counselors need to be able to access institutional data, collect essential supplemental data, and "mine" the data to come up with a description of problems that need to be addressed. In essence, to be operating in an evidence-based practice mode, school counselors need to have the evidence that a specific problem needs to be attended to. The best evidence is a quantitative description of the problem. A school counselor, for example, would want to collect data on the frequency and nature of disciplinary referrals before deciding that an intervention was necessary. Chapters 2 and 3 provide detailed explanations of how to know what needs to be addressed.

Knowing what is likely to work is accomplished through a survey of outcome research literature and an integration of this information with an analysis of what can be implemented with fidelity in the counselor's particular setting. School counselors need to understand the characteristics of good outcome research, be able to access evaluations of research-based practices, team with colleagues to identify effective interventions, and evaluate the feasibility of implementing these interventions with reasonable similarity to the way they were implemented in the outcome research studies. A school counselor, for example, would need to be able to determine both that a given bullying prevention program has been shown to reduce bullying behavior and that the format and time requirements of the program were compatible with the school's schedules and routines. Chapter 4 is an in-depth discussion of how to know what is likely to work.

Knowing if the intervention made a difference is accomplished through local evaluation. Knowing that a particular intervention is supported by sound outcome research does not assure that it will have the desired impact in all settings. It is still necessary to evaluate the impact of the intervention in the counselor's particular setting. This evaluation is for both program improvement and accountability purposes. It is important to know whether a given program should be continued. It is also pragmatically important to be able to document the positive impact of school counseling interventions for local educational decision makers who need to know whether the personnel and material investments in the program yielded benefits for students. Chapters 5, 6, 7, and 8 identify ways to know if interventions and program components are making a difference.

It would be helpful if integrative approaches to evidence-based practice existed to support effective school counselor practice. Current approaches to using data in school counseling tend to focus on either problem description or intervention evaluation. Several data-based decision-making models have been developed for school counseling (Dahir & Stone, 2003; Isaacs, 2003; Reynolds & Hines, 2001). These models connect with the larger movement to use data-based decision making in standards-based school reform. These models are very strong in supporting effective use of school data to define problems, but have less to say about the use of outcome research or program evaluation (Poynton & Carey, 2006). Other models show strength in terms of supporting the evaluation of school counselor–implemented interventions (Lapan, 2001; Rowell, 2006), but do not provide information to help school counselors to use data to define problems or to apply outcome research literature in determining what approaches would be likely to be successful. We believe that effective practice requires competence in all three domains of the model. All of these competencies are systematically covered in this book. Table 1.1 contains a brief self-assessment that will help you determine where you currently stand in relation to these skills. We suggest that you complete this survey now, save your answers, and take the test again after you have completed the book.

Table 1.1   Brief Self-Assessment of Essential Competencies Required for Evidence-Based School Counseling Practice

Please rate your present confidence in demonstrating each of the following competencies. Do not spend a lot of time analyzing the items; your first impression is usually the best. If you do not understand the terminology, chances are you do not yet know the content area. Use the following scale:

1 = I am unable to do it right now.

2 = I can do it with effort or support.

3 = I am proficient.

Problem Description.
School counselors can use existing school data and collect and use additional needs assessment data to plan and direct school counseling program activities and interventions and determine measurable outcomes for these activities and interventions.

1	2	3	I can describe the role of data-based decision making in school improvement and reform.
1	2	3	I can access data on school information systems.
1	2	3	I can collect needs assessment data to help plan interventions.
1	2	3	I can use data-mining tools (disaggregation and comparison) to generate useful planning information.
1	2	3	I can set measurable goals and benchmarks to guide practice.
1	2	3	I can lead a data-based decision-making team.

Outcome Research Use.
School counselors can access and evaluate outcome research in order to identify research-based activities and interventions and determine the feasibility of implementing these activities and interventions at their site.

1	2	3	I can describe the criteria for strong outcome research studies.
1	2	3	I can determine the quality of evidence that results from different types of outcome research studies.
1	2	3	I can access and search the outcome research literature.
1	2	3	I can describe the results of the major outcome studies of school counseling practice.

1	2	3	I can use meta-analytic and analytic reviews to help evaluate the outcome research literature.
1	2	3	I can use the work of expert panels to help evaluate the outcome research literature.
1	2	3	I can lead school teams to identify research-based approaches and interventions and assess the feasibility of implementing these practices in my setting.

Intervention Evaluation.
School counselors can assess the impact of school counseling activities and interventions, use evaluation results to improve practice, and communicate evaluation results accurately and effectively to stakeholders.

1	2	3	I can use data to evaluate school counseling interventions and activities.
1	2	3	I can evaluate the extent to which activities and interventions accomplish immediate learning objectives.
1	2	3	I can evaluate the extent to which student competency attainment results in changes in achievement-related data.
1	2	3	I can evaluate the extent to which changes in student behavior following school counseling interventions impacts achievement.
1	2	3	I can analyze evaluation data.
1	2	3	I can design a comprehensive evaluation for the overall counseling program.
1	2	3	I can accurately convey evaluation results to a wide audience.
1	2	3	I can create a survey to meet program needs.
1	2	3	I can create a PowerPoint presentation to share my results.

Evidence-Based School Counseling in the Context of the Reform Movement

Public education in the United States—and therefore the practice of school counseling—is in the midst of dramatic transformations reflecting a move to a standards-based model of education. Understanding this shift is critical to understanding the importance of adopting an evidence-based approach to school counseling practice. The origins of the standards-based education movement have been traced to the famous report, *A Nation at Risk* (National Commission on Excellence in Education, 1983). With passionate rhetoric, this report highlighted perceived problems with public education in the United States. The most frequently quoted passage of the report reflects the Commission's sentiment about the magnitude of the problems and the urgency for change:

> If an unfriendly power had attempted to impose on America the mediocre educational performance that exists today, we might well have viewed it as an act of war. As it stands, we have allowed this to happen to ourselves. We have squandered the gains in achievement made in the wake of the Sputnik challenge. Moreover, we have dismantled essential support systems which helped make those gains possible. We have, in effect, been committing an act of unthinking, unilateral educational disarmament. (p. 5)

The report was effective in focusing public interest on the reform of public education and in motivating governors and state legislators to view public education improvement as a high priority. Educational reform became a consistent theme of the National Governors' Association (1991) and state leaders became more aware of and interested in ways that state government can influence public education. Energized by *A Nation at Risk,* state leaders began looking for ways that state government could effectively catalyze reform in public schools. In the 1990s, many states were passing comprehensive education reform legislation (e.g., Kentucky Education Reform Act of 1990, Massachusetts Educational Reform Act of 1993) requiring the development of state curricula and testing systems referenced to the state curricula. A variety of other reforms were also designed to increase the funding level of low-income schools, strengthen building-based management, and increase high school completion rates by creating state-supported alternatives to traditional public schools. At the core of these approaches is a commitment to what has come to be called "standards-based education." In the present, the vast majority of states are pursuing standards-based approaches to educational reform.

standards-based education

formal curricula that specify scope, sequence, and student performance expectations

On January 8, 2002, President George W. Bush signed the No Child Left Behind Act (NCLB, 2001) initiating an unprecedented level of federal control of public education. NCLB includes many of the features of standards-based education reform employed by comprehensive state legislation. NCLB requires frequent testing, the regular public reporting of quantitative indicators of schools' performance (related to standardized test scores, attendance, and high school graduation rates), and strengthened sanctions against schools that fail to meet adequate yearly progress expectations. NCLB requires the documentation of yearly gains in both improving general academic achievement and reducing the achievement gap between white students and students of color. Both individual schools and districts are accountable under NCLB.

> **empirical research**
>
> research that bases its findings on observation or measurement

In addition, NCLB has established the necessity for public education practices to be based on empirical research. The federal government now is committed to investing in evidence-based education—that is, to supporting educational practices that can be proven effective through rigorous, controlled, scientific research. Under NCLB, public school educators are expected to consider the results of relevant, scientifically based research before making decisions about implementing interventions.

School Counseling and Standards

The emergence of standards-based education as the predominant reform strategy in public education has presented a few particularly dramatic challenges to the school counseling profession:

1. *The government has higher expectations for the public schools and has focused the mission of public schools on academic outcomes.* School counseling evolved in the context of the vocational and humanistic education traditions. The former tradition emphasized that preparation for work is an important outcome of K–12 education. The latter tradition emphasized the importance of developing self-knowledge, social interest, and interpersonal competence as part of a rich public school education. By holding public education accountable for standardized achievement test scores and applying high-stakes sanctions, standards-based educational reform narrowed and focused the mission of schools. Activities that are clearly connected to this narrower mission have taken on greater legitimacy. Activities that have a less obvious connection to basic education and achievement have lost legitimacy. School counselors' traditional focus on vocation, self-knowledge, and interpersonal development, although obviously valuable, is not always seen as immediately connected to enhanced test scores.

2. Academically oriented state curricula and testing systems have taken precedence over local curricula as the foundation for comprehensive developmental school counseling programs. In the 1990s, comprehensive developmental guidance (CDG; Gysbers & Henderson, 2000) was the widely accepted standard for program organization. CDG emphasizes that school counseling should operate as an organized program designed to meet the developmental needs of all students. To provide organization and direction, CDG programs operated from a curriculum that was developed locally (as were all public school curricula before standards-based reform). The shift to state curricula with a focus on basic subjects rendered local school counseling curricula less relevant (however effective they may be). The school counseling profession also lacked its own national professional standards, seriously affecting its credibility as a participant in educational reform and improvement.

3. School counselors and guidance directors lacked the skills necessary to participate in data-based decision making and quantitative accountability reporting. These skills were not normally taught in school counselor education programs. Opportunities to develop these skills were not widely available through professional development mechanisms. The profession lacked standard ways of measuring its impact on students and of demonstrating effectiveness.

4. The school counseling profession has lacked a strong research base. Demonstrating that school counseling interventions are supported by empirical research has been difficult. Since the early 1970s, many authors have noted the dearth of good studies examining the effectiveness of school counseling interventions and have predicted dire consequences if the profession were to continue to function without a solid research base (Burch & Peterson, 1975; Gerler, 1985; Humes, 1972; Robie, Gansneder, & Van Hoose, 1979; Whiston & Sexton, 1998; Wilson, 1986). Whiston and Sexton (1998) conducted the most comprehensive review of the school counseling literature in recent years, focusing on studies published between 1988 and 1995. They located 12 outcome studies related to guidance curriculum, 10 studies related to individual planning, 25 studies related to responsive services, and 3 studies related to system support activities. Their study indicates that the school counseling profession is suffering from an evidence gap that limits practitioners' abilities to identify evidence-based best practices, which limits the credibility of the field. Unless the profession can demonstrate that its interventions are supported by empirical evidence, school counseling will be less legitimate in the emerging evidence-based education environment.

To operate in the current standards-based public school environment, school counselors need to be able to (a) demonstrate that their practice is guided by sound evidence, (b) use quantitative data in program planning and management, (c) use quantitative evaluation approaches to evaluate student outcomes, and (d) present quantitative data effectively to demonstrate that they are operating responsibly and effectively in local settings. For the school counseling profession to respond effectively to the research, evaluation, and data-use challenges of standards-based education, changes in school counselor role and function related to data, in school counseling program management and accountability practices, and in school counselor education practices will be required. Several current initiatives have the potential to produce these changes.

School Counseling Reform

The Education Trust
Transforming School Counseling Initiative (TSCI)

In 1996, the Education Trust initiated a project to transform the role of school counselors by connecting school counseling to standards-based education reform and by focusing the profession of school counseling on the goal of eliminating the achievement gap. The Education Trust first established a new vision for the school counselor's role and function and then worked with six funded lead counselor education programs and a number of unfunded companion institutions to accomplish reform in the initial preparation of school counselors. Participating university-based preparation programs committed to revising their school counselor education curriculum, reviewing admission processes to create a more diverse student population, redesigning their practicum experiences, and strengthening their partnerships with school districts and state education agencies.

The Education Trust defines school counseling as "a profession that focuses on the relations and interactions between students and their school environment with the expressed purpose of reducing the effect of environmental and institutional barriers that impede student academic success" (Education Trust, 2005). This model calls attention to the importance of interventions at the systemic level to promote change in the capacity of educational systems to educate all students and an explicit connection between school counseling and school reform. Several new skills have been identified by the Education Trust as essential to this reformed role. These skills include leadership, advocacy, use of data, teamwork and collaboration, and effective use of technology (House & Martin, 1998). Both the explicit skills and methods for teaching them have been refined by the lead and companion institutions. Some specific processes for data-based decision making and using data to facilitate education reform emerged from this process (see Dahir & Stone, 2003; Hayes, Nelson, Tabin, Pearson, & Worthy, 2002; Reynolds & Hines, 2001).

The Education Trust's new vision considers quantitative data skills to be critically important for school counselors. These skills are seen as necessary for counselors to track all students' academic performance, to use student achievement data to plan interventions, and to advocate persuasively for systemic changes in school policies, procedures, and practices. School counselors need data skills to participate effectively in and contribute to school level, standards-based educational reform.

American School Counselor Association National Standards

The American School Counselor Association has developed two major initiatives that directly connect school counseling with standards-based reform. ASCA National Standards were published in 1997 (Dahir & Campbell, 1997). Nine standards relating to three broad domains of student development (academic, career, and personal/ social) were developed as a statement of the intended student outcomes of all school counseling programs. Examples of specific student competencies were published with each standard. The expectation was that the standards would be useful for the design and construction of school counseling programs and that their use would increase the legitimacy of school counseling, position school counseling as integral to the educational mission of public schools, and facilitate the development of measurable indicators of student learning.

While ASCA hailed the significance of the National Standards, a study performed five years after they were released revealed that the standards did not contribute to increased legitimacy, to improved role and function, or to a change in school counselors' beliefs or behaviors with regard to the continuing performance of nonschool counseling activities (Hatch, 2002). While school counselors believed that the standards professionally legitimized them, operationally very little changed. As will be discussed more fully in Chapter 9, the National Standards did not provide the operational efficiency, institutional legitimacy, and political social capital that were hoped for (Hatch, 2002).

One reason that the expected positive impact of the ASCA National Standards did not occur may be that the standards themselves are not as elaborate or compelling as the standards of many national professional associations. The ASCA National Standards consist of nine general statements (e.g., "Students will acquire the attitudes, knowledge and interpersonal skills to help them understand and respect self and others.") with examples of student competencies. In contrast, the standards created by the National Council of Teachers of Mathematics in 1989 (National Council of Teachers of Mathematics [NCTM], 2006) provided a comprehensive description of the scope and sequence of mathematics learning, including grade level performance expectations.

In order for curriculum standards to meet national standards, they need to be based on existing research about what teachable skills have known relationships to achievement and to provide measurable indicators of student performance in those domains (Association for Supervision and Curriculum Development [ASCD], 2006). In part because of these weaknesses, the ASCA National Standards did not resolve a major cause of the lack of school counseling program legitimacy within schools: educational leaders' perceptions that school counseling program outcomes (especially outcomes related to personal/social development) are relatively unimportant. National standards are not enough if there is still not general understanding of how the content of those standards supports learning. Currently, the profession still lacks a set of agreed upon, measurable, student learning outcomes that have established relationships to student achievement, a plan for scope and sequence, and psychometrically sound instruments that are able to measure these outcomes.

The ASCA National Model: A Framework for School Counseling Programs (American School Counselor Association [ASCA], 2003) was developed as an overarching programmatic, organizational, and systems tool to explicitly link school counseling programs to the academic mission of schools and to connect school counseling programs with standards-based educational reform. The National Model was built upon the comprehensive developmental guidance approach (Gysbers & Henderson, 2000; Myrick, 1993) of organizing services but calls for a standards- and results-based approach (Johnson & Johnson, 1991), program management, and accountability. The National Model also emphasizes that school counseling programs should recognize the critical importance of the goals of enhancing student achievement and eliminating achievement gaps.

Successful implementation of the management and accountability systems of the National Model requires that school counselors have a broad range of data skills including the following:

- Using student information systems to monitor student performance
- Analyzing student performance, school process, and perceptual data to plan, monitor, and evaluate interventions

- Analyzing disaggregated student performance, school process, and perceptual data to plan, monitor, and evaluate interventions designed to address achievement gap issues
- Developing and implementing data-based, decision-making systems in the school counseling program (Isaacs, 2003)
- Identifying research-based practices and interventions
- Developing ways to measure and evaluate student outcomes
- Evaluating interventions
- Presenting quantitative outcome results to a wide variety of constituencies
- Conducting effective program evaluation

The ASCA National Model and the Education Trust initiatives mentioned earlier require that school counselors develop facility in and comfort with data use at a level that has not traditionally been expected in school counselor education programs. They address two of the three components of our evidence-based practice model (Figure 1.1): *Knowing what needs to be addressed* by collecting and analyzing data and *Knowing if the intervention made a difference* by measuring the results of the intervention. This model includes the additional factor, *Knowing what is likely to work* by referring to the outcome research. These three skills combined constitute evidence-based practice in school counseling.

Summary

Evidence-based school counseling is a new approach to practice that requires that school counselors be able to use data-based evidence in program planning, evaluation, and accountability efforts. This approach calls for school counselors to have knowledge and skill sets that differ from those traditionally taught in counselor education programs. These skills sets can be organized into the domains of problem description, outcome research use, and intervention evaluation. We believe that adopting an evidence-based practice approach will lead to better alignment with the academic mission of schools, increased effectiveness of school counseling programs, and improved ability to communicate successfully about this enhanced effectiveness. Competence in an evidence-based practice approach to school counseling will enable school counselors to use evidence to determine: What needs to de done? (Chapters 2 and 3); What is likely to work? (Chapter 4); and What difference did the intervention make? (Chapters 5, 6, 7, and 8).

2

Data-Based Decision Making

Knowing What Needs to Be Addressed

Consider two scenarios:

Scenario 1: *Sheila is a middle school counselor in a low-income, urban school district that has a high number of detentions occurring in the eighth grade. She decides to develop and implement a social skills training intervention consisting of both peer-to-peer conflict resolution training and student-teacher communication skills training. Sheila develops the materials and trains personnel. The program is implemented in the advisory period. Her pretest-posttest evaluation indicates that most students learn the targeted concepts and can describe instances in which they employ the conflict resolution skills.*

Scenario 2: *Sheila is a middle school counselor in a low-income, urban district that has a high number of detentions occurring in the eighth grade. She does a quick analysis of the reasons for detention and finds that 70% of the students are sent to detention for chronically missing homework and 30% for inappropriate conduct. She recommends to her administration that detentions be for conduct problems only, and sets as her goal reducing the weekly detention referral rate by 50% by midyear. She organizes a school homework group and publicizes this group both to the general student population* *and specifically to students with chronic homework problems and to the parents of these students. Sheila also establishes a conflict resolution group, recruiting as members students who were sent to detention for inappropriate conduct. Sheila tracks participation in both interventions and tracks the weekly detention rate. By midyear it has dropped by 55%.*

In the first scenario, Sheila follows an intuitive path in her professional decision making. She knows that many students are being referred to detention and intuits that this is because they are misbehaving. Sheila read in a journal article that interpersonal skills training is an effective way to teach appropriate behavior and reduce inappropriate behavior. She believes such training will be helpful in addressing the detention problem in her school. Sheila gathers evidence that the social skills training intervention she adopts is being effectively implemented and that it is leading to changes in knowledge and skill. She believes that if students show these changes, a reduction in detentions will follow. Intuition, however, is sometimes wrong and can lead to a tremendous expenditure of time, energy, and resources that are not aligned with the problem as it actually exists. In the first scenario, Sheila took the "ready-fire-aim" approach. Unfortunately, when educators encounter a problem, sometimes they immediately jump to a solution (an intervention) without taking the time to clearly define the problem or goal. This can lead to wasted effort, inefficiency, and ineffectiveness.

A data-based decision-making approach instead relies on evidence to define problems and requires that we state goals in ways that will allow us to gather evidence to show that we have attained the stated goals. The second scenario is an example of data-based decision making. Instead of directly jumping in to try to solve the problem, the counselor first defines the problem by gathering data on why students are being sent to detention. She discovers that over 70% of students are in detention because of chronic homework problems. After further investigation, she concludes that they need in-school support. Sheila sets a measurable goal of cutting weekly detention rates in half and spends most of her energy on an intervention designed to help students complete their homework. By tracking the weekly detention rate, Sheila is able to provide evidence that her intervention and resources have addressed the problem. By using a data-based decision-making approach, Sheila aligned interventions with the problem and identified an attainable goal. Ready. Aim. Fire.

This chapter discusses how school counselors can use a data-based decision-making process to choose which interventions to implement for which students. Before we go further in our discussion of data-based decision making, it is important to define and give examples of a few key terms: achievement data, achievement-related data, and competency-related data. These terms will be developed further in Chapter 3.

Types of data	Definition	Examples
Achievement data	Reflect the academic learning and progress of students	Standardized test scores, grade point averages, SAT and ACT scores, graduation rates, AP test scores
Achievement-related data	Contribute to students' ability to achieve and directly impact student achievement data	Course enrollment patterns, discipline referrals, suspension rates, attendance, parent involvement, homework completion rates
Competency-related data	Reflect the student learning outcomes of the school counseling program	Six- or four-year academic plans, job shadowing participation rate, peer mediation sessions, knowledge of graduation requirements

Data-Based Decision Making and School Improvement

Data-based decision making (DBDM) is a school improvement approach that uses quantitative data analysis techniques to help describe problems and to direct activities and resource allocations. DBDM is a procedure for knowing what needs to be done. The rationale for implementing DBDM in schools is that "using information to help clarify issues, identify alternative solutions to problems, and target resources more effectively will lead to better decisions" (Protheroe, 2001, p. 4). While the importance of using data to plan school activities has been recognized for some time, formal models of DBDM have only recently emerged, concomitant with standards-based school reform approaches. DBDM was more formally incorporated into the school counseling field with the development of *The ASCA National Model: A Framework for School Counseling Programs* (ASCA, 2003). The ASCA National Model was developed to connect school counseling with current educational reform movements that emphasize student achievement and success (ASCA, 2003). Using data to plan and direct school counseling interventions is a critical feature of the ASCA National Model's management system, making DBDM an important management tool.

Data-Based Decision-Making Models

Several models of DBDM exist. Some are general whole-school models that address DBDM as a systemic change approach (Johnson, 2002; Love, 2002). Other models are specific to school counseling programs (Dahir & Stone, 2003; Isaacs, 2003). One model uses DBDM, initiated through the school counseling program, to address whole-school reform (Reynolds & Hines, 2001). In this whole-school model, a school counselor leads an interdisciplinary team through the DBDM process to define problems and decide on interventions. The types of leadership, collaboration, and teaming skills needed differ depending on whether the school counselor is participating in a whole-school DBDM initiative, leading a whole-school DBDM initiative through the school counseling program, or trying to establish a DBDM initiative in a school that is not invested in DBDM. All DBDM models primarily focus on the use of data to

- define problems,
- set goals, and
- target interventions.

Many models also include steps related to evaluation and accountability, and we will discuss these issues in later chapters.

The DBDM Team

Most DBDM models explicitly acknowledge that DBDM is a group process, conducted as a team. Poynton and Carey (2006) indicate that the composition of the DBDM team and the school counselor's role on the team will largely be determined by whether the DBDM process is a whole-school reform initiative or a component of the school counseling program's management and accountability systems. In whole-school reform teams, the school counselor may be the designated leader of the team if the counselor is perceived as possessing expertise and centrality to school reform initiatives. The rest of the DBDM team will include school personnel from a wide range of departments. If the DBDM process is confined to the school counseling program, a school counselor will typically lead the team, and the team will consist of advisory group members and other school counseling program stakeholders such as administrators, teachers, parents, and students. In assembling a DBDM team, Poynton and Carey (2006) suggest that the leader should consider the following questions:

- Does the team include all the needed perspectives to correctly identify problems and potential solutions?
- Does the team include all the needed perspectives to correctly identify strategies and barriers to intervention implementation?
- Do team members have the necessary data literacy skills?
- Do team members show the capacity for effective collaboration?

Once the team is assembled, has the requisite skills, and is ready to work together, the DBDM process can begin.

A General Model for Data-Based Decision Making

Figure 2.1 contains a general process model for data-based decision making. In this model, the DBDM team engages in seven sequential steps:

1. Describing the problem

2. Generating vision data

3. Committing to benchmarks

4. Identifying where and how to intervene

5. Selecting interventions

6. Evaluating interventions

7. Monitoring problem data

Describing the Problem

The DBDM team's first task is to describe the problem using school data, eventually establishing a quantitative definition of the situation. The DBDM team needs to have access to a wide range of institutional data and may need to collect additional data. The data must also be in a form that team members can work with and understand (we recommend Excel, which is commonly available and familiar to most people). Important data to use include the following:

- Achievement data (e.g., state test scores)
- Achievement-related data (e.g., attendance)
- Guidance curriculum competency data (e.g., percentage of students who demonstrate knowledge, attitudes, and skills referenced to program learning objectives)
- School climate survey data
- Relevant student health and well-being data (e.g., youth behavior rating scale, drug use survey data)
- Needs assessment data
- Demographic data (e.g., race, gender, SPED status, ELL status, free/reduced lunch status)

Figure 2.1   A General Process Model for Data-Based Decision Making

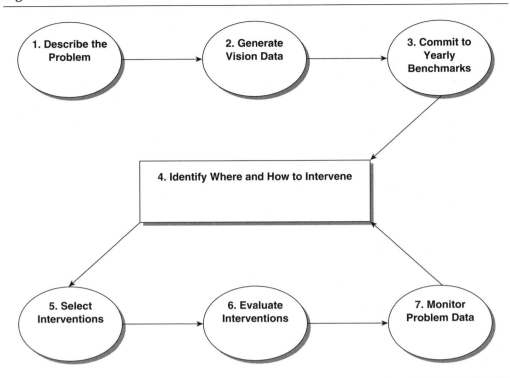

The next step in describing the problem is to disaggregate the data. Data can be disaggregated by gender, race/ethnicity, socioeconomic status, language, grade level, or numerous other factors that allow the school counselor to determine how certain subgroups of the student population are doing relative to the general population. When disaggregating data, no subgroup should be smaller than 10, as it is an unethical use of data to put it into a form that would allow identification of any person in the data set. Thus, if a school has only three Native American students, student race and ethnicity could not include this group. Analyzing disaggregated data allows the DBDM team to engage more effectively in a deliberate process to identify problems and certain subpopulations of students that may need interventions.

As an example, suppose a middle school team was initially concerned by data that suggested that their school was not scoring especially high on the state eighth

> **disaggregated data**
>
> data that has been broken down into smaller, more defined groupings
>   Disaggregation helps compare the data from different groups of students in order to get a better understanding of the meaning and implications of the data.

Table 2.1   Hypothetical DBDM Data: Percentage of Students in Eighth Grade Algebra

Student Group	Problem Data	Benchmark Year 1	Benchmark Year 2	Benchmark Year 3	Benchmark Year 4	Vision Data
High SES	50%	56%	62%	68%	74%	80%
Low SES	20%	32%	44%	56%	68%	80%

grade math achievement test. After disaggregation, the team noted that a higher percentage of low–socioeconomic status (SES) students (based on free and reduced lunch status) were performing below the state average. The team also observed that only 50% of students in the school were enrolled in eighth grade algebra and only 20% of the low-SES students were enrolled in this advanced math class (see Table 2.1). They also note that enrollment eligibility was determined solely by the recommendation of the seventh grade math teacher, although this recommendation could be overridden by parent request.

Generating Vision Data

The team's next step is to generate vision data. Vision data reflect the future goal toward which school effort and resources need to be directed, and the goal needs to be stated in concrete and measurable terms so that it can be determined whether the intervention(s) worked or not. Most tough problems take several years to solve. Vision data therefore reflect the team's vision for what the data should look like in three to five years' time. Vision data need to be both ambitious and attainable. An ambitious goal serves student interests and engages the passion of the adults in the school. An attainable goal is more likely to motivate efforts to change. Setting 100% or 0% as a goal is almost always problematic, as it all but guarantees that you won't be successful.

In our example, the DBDM team in consultation with the school community set a goal that in five years, 80% of students, regardless of SES, will score "advanced" or "proficient" on the state mathematics achievement test (see the vision data in Table 2.1). This vision reflects the school's goals of eliminating the achievement gap in mathematics in five years and increasing the school's overall passing rate on the state's math achievement tests.

> **vision data**
>
> the anticipated value that currently problematic data will have at some specified time in the future, after interventions have been implemented

Committing to Benchmarks

The next step involves breaking down the goal expressed as vision data into yearly goals. Typically, yearly benchmarks reflect equal increments of change needed each year to reach the vision. Sometimes, however, DBDM teams create unequal increments, figuring either that more progress will be made in the early years or that less progress will be made in the early years. In our example, the DBDM team chose to use equal intervals. To achieve the vision in five years, the percentage of high-SES students scoring "advanced" or "proficient" must increase by 6% each year, and the percentage of low-SES students scoring "advanced" or "proficient" must increase by 12% per year.

> **benchmarks**
>
> markers specified in intervals (e.g., yearly) against which progress toward the vision is measured

Identifying Where and How to Intervene

The DBDM team now needs to make recommendations about where and how to intervene to move the data. Intervention can occur at several hierarchically organized levels. Lee and Goodnough (2007) have identified seven levels for programmatic intervention: individual, group, classroom, grade level, schoolwide, home/family, and community/society. They point out that it is often necessary to intervene simultaneously at multiple levels to address complex problems. Some interventions will be within the scope of the school counseling program and others will not. It is important that the DBDM team identify problems that need to be solved at multiple levels.

In our middle school example, it may be clear that attention to mathematics curriculum, mathematics instructional approaches, teacher expectations, and teacher instructional competence is needed. Several issues more directly in the work domain of school counselors may also need to be addressed. All students would gain from school counseling curriculum-based interventions designed to improve academic self-efficacy, enhance achievement motivation, and improve study skills. In this example, parents may profit from outreach targeted at conveying the importance of rigorous math courses, the availability of academic supports, and the ways they can effectively advocate for their children. Finally, the school counselors can advocate for a change in the eighth grade algebra placement policy to include multiple indicators of placement decisions and for the development of additional academic supports for students who need them.

Selecting Interventions

Once specific targets for intervention are selected, a decision must be made about which interventions will be used to address the defined problem. Chapter 4 deals with this issue in detail. In general, every effort needs to be made to select interventions that are supported by strong research evidence rather than familiarity or packaging. In this example, the middle school counselors elected to implement the student-focused, curriculum-based intervention titled Student Success Skills (Brigman & Campbell, 2003) because of evidence that shows that this program can boost state achievement scores.

Evaluating Interventions

The process of collecting and analyzing outcome data to evaluate the effectiveness of interventions is covered in detail in Chapter 5. Here it just needs to be said that each intervention should be evaluated at three levels. First, it is important to know whether the participants learned the knowledge or skill the intervention intended to teach or whether their attitudes shifted. Second, it is important to know whether the participants changed their behavior in the problem data in ways that predict success. Finally, it is important to measure the actual change in problem data and to compare it with the benchmark targets. In our example, the school counselors would measure (a) the immediate learning after Student Success Skills lessons (attitudes, skills, and knowledge), (b) students' classroom behavior (completing homework), and (c) examination performance in math class after the conclusion of the intervention. The DBDM team would track state achievement test results to determine whether longer-term changes had occurred.

Monitoring Problem Data

Each year the DBDM team needs to review the problem data in comparison to the stated benchmarks, examine evaluation data, and decide whether the current strategies and approaches need be continued, modified, or abandoned. In our example, all groups of students made the first-year benchmarks. Evaluation data indicated that students learned Students Success Skills concepts and skills and improved in terms of classroom behavior and performance. The DBDM team decided to continue its multilevel approach, with Students Success Skills as the primary student-focused intervention. Figure 2.2 links the steps in our hypothetical situation in the text to the visual model presented in Figure 2.1.

Enabling Conditions for Data-Based Decision Making

Effective DBDM can only occur within a school context that facilitates the process. Therefore, school counselors need to be able to orchestrate and/or collaborate with other people in the school to establish the conditions necessary for engaging in DBDM. Once these enabling conditions are understood and addressed to the greatest extent possible, the actual process of DBDM can be engaged.

Love (2002) identified four conditions that she asserts are necessary for effective data-based decision making in schools:

- Collaborative culture
- Collaborative structures
- Widespread data literacy
- Access to useful data

For school personnel to have productive data-based conversations that are focused on improving student learning and development, a collaborative school culture must be established. Collaborative structures (e.g., teams and scheduled meetings) are necessary to create regular, officially sanctioned opportunities for school personnel to work together on DBDM activities. Love further contends that widespread data literacy is necessary so that school personnel have the requisite skills to collect and make sense of data and to develop measurable goals. Finally, Love suggests that school personnel need to have access to accurate data on both student learning and characteristics of the school system that impact student learning. In schools where DBDM is operating as a whole-school initiative, it is likely that these conditions are operating. School counselors trying to initiate DBDM within their own programs (in schools that are not practicing DBDM) need to attend both to establishing these conditions within the program and to coordinating the DBDM with traditional whole-school processes. In such settings, it will be more difficult to satisfy the enabling conditions, and gaining access to the needed data may be a problem. Even when counselors are able to create a collaborative culture, collaborative structures, and ensure widespread data literacy within the school counseling program, access to needed collaborators may be difficult, and colleagues may not speak, understand, or value the language of data.

Critical Questions

To be effective leaders and participants on DBDM teams, school counselors need to ask the following questions:

Figure 2.2   A General Process Model for Data-Based Decision Making: Example
From Text

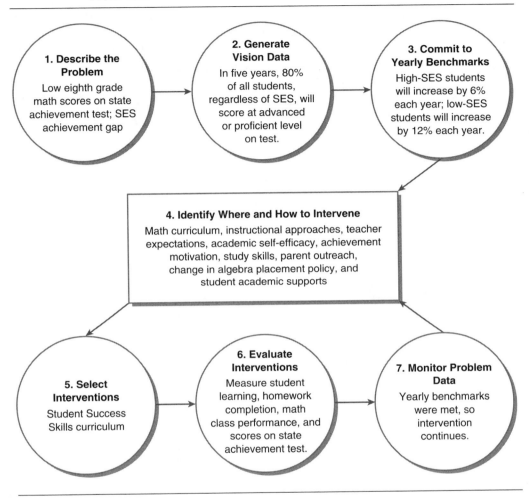

- Is DBDM a whole-school or a school counseling program component?
- Am I a leader of the process or a member of the team?
- Does the DBDM team have the range and diversity of perspectives needed to understand the problems and set goals?
- What process will the team follow to accomplish its work?
- Does the team have access to all the needed data?
- What additional data need to be collected?
- Do colleagues across the school have the data literacy skills necessary to understand and appreciate the work of the team?

Summary

Using data-based decision making to identify problems prior to implementing interventions provides the necessary proactive and mindful approach that successful school counseling practice requires. Using data to carefully define a problem—and following a series of planned steps to decide the best way to address that problem—creates a greater likelihood that any remediation efforts will be effective. Using data-based decision making creates more efficacious school counseling programs and ultimately helps us make the difference that we want to make for students.

3

Practical Considerations in Using Data

Consider two scenarios:

Scenario 1: *Yolanda, a school counselor in a diverse K–8 rural school, is justifiably proud of her comprehensive, competency-based school counseling program. She has developed a guidance curriculum with measurable learning objectives based on the ASCA National Standards. All students in the school have the benefit of guidance lessons that cover the essential competencies in the curriculum. Yolanda monitors competency attainment through assessments she built into her guidance lessons. She is able to document that an average of 85% of the students demonstrate competency on most of the major personal/social, career, and academic standards.*

Scenario 2: *Yolanda, a school counselor in a diverse K–8 rural school, is justifiably proud of her comprehensive, competency-based school counseling program. She has developed a guidance curriculum with measurable learning objectives based on the ASCA National Standards. All students in the school have the benefit of guidance lessons that cover the essential competencies in the curriculum. Yolanda monitors competency attainment through assessments that she built into her guidance lessons. She is able to document that an average of 85% of the students demonstrate competency on an important academic standard. Just to be certain that she is reaching all* *students, Yolanda disaggregates her competency data by grade level. She discovers some troubling disparities, including the fact that while 97% of the eighth grade students are using test-taking strategies, only 70% of seventh graders are. This disparity exists even though everyone received the same guidance lessons. She uses this information to design an intentional guidance presentation to reach the 30% of seventh grade students who need more.*

Using data to drive decisions ensures that every student receives the benefits of a school counseling program that is developmental in nature, preventive in design, and comprehensive in scope. School counselors use data for a variety of purposes:

- To ensure that every student receives the developmental instruction that is described in professional standards in the academic, career, and personal/social development domains (ASCA, 2003; Campbell & Dahir, 1997)
- To make decisions regarding which areas of need require additional support or intervention (Hatch, Holland, & Meyers, 2003; Hayes et al., 2002)
- To measure the effectiveness of their activities and interventions and to share their successes with the school community and other stakeholders (Hatch, 2004b)
- To evaluate the effectiveness of their programs and for program improvement (Curcio, Mathai, & Roberts, 2003; Hatch & Bowers, 2002)

This chapter discusses practical information and considerations in the use of data for effective school counseling programs. Specifically, it will help you develop the practical knowledge and skills to lead and participate in DBDM teams, use data-based decision-making models, identify essential competencies that all students need, and determine when intentional guidance activities should be implemented to close achievement gaps by addressing the particular needs of certain groups of students. This chapter focuses on the knowledge and skills needed to describe problems and determine what needs to be done.

Types of Data

Data have multiple intentional and diagnostic uses and are categorized differently. It is useful to distinguish among different types of data. School counseling data can be broken down into three different types: student achievement data, achievement-related data, and competency- and standards-related data.

Student Achievement Data

Student achievement data include the "big ticket items." These data reflect the academic learning and progress of students and have great urgency in school districts. These are the data that impact property values and that motivate newspaper reporters to call principals to ask why one school's data are better or worse than another's. Examples of student achievement data include the following:

- Passing rates for state achievement tests
- Standardized achievement test data (e.g., Iowa Test of Basic Skills)
- SAT and ACT scores (college entrance exams)
- Algebra passage rates
- Grade point averages
- Drop-out rates and graduation rates
- College acceptance rates
- Completion of college prep requirements
- College freshman remediation rates
- Advanced Placement test scores

A DBDM team needs to "mine" this data to determine where resources need to be invested to improve the educational outcomes of the school. School counselors sometimes find it hard to see the connections between what they do and specific student achievement elements since most of these elements appear to reflect the work of classroom teachers more than that of counselors. Certainly, efforts to improve achievement require a schoolwide initiative. While it would be impossible to improve student achievement with only school counseling interventions, it would be difficult to do so without them. School counselors cannot take all the credit for achievement-related improvements, but they certainly should not be denied recognition for their part of the success. A DBDM team should be able to analyze student achievement data and identify problems that need to be addressed by teachers, administrators, and counselors.

> **mining data**
>
> using data manipulation strategies (e.g., disaggregation) to obtain a more complex understanding of patterns in the data and their meaning

Achievement-Related Data

Educational and psychological research has identified several factors that contribute to students' ability to achieve and that directly impact student achievement data. The following are examples of achievement-related data:

- *Course enrollment patterns.* Students who take more rigorous course work do better on standardized tests (e.g., Smith & Niemi, 2001).
- *Discipline referrals.* Students who behave better achieve better (e.g., Van Horn, 2003).
- *Suspension rates.* Students who are suspended are less likely to be high academic achievers (e.g., Williams & McGee, 1994).
- *Alcohol, tobacco, and other drug use.* Students who use drugs or alcohol perform at a lower rate academically than those who do not (e.g., Jeynes, 2002).
- *Attendance rates.* Students who attend school perform better than those who do not (e.g., Easton & Engelhard, 1982).
- *Parent involvement.* Students whose parents are involved in meaningful ways in the school outperform those whose parents are not (e.g., Marchant, Paulson, & Rothlisberg, 2001).
- *Extracurricular activities.* Students who feel connected to school participate in extracurricular activities and perform better than those who do not (e.g., Mahoney, Cairns, & Farmer, 2003).
- *Homework completion rates.* Students who complete and turn in homework do better in school (e.g., Cooper, Lindsay, Nye, & Greathouse, 1998).

Better achievement-related data are linked to improvements in achievement data. Students who are enrolled in rigorous course work are more likely to complete college prep requirements; students who complete homework do better in school. The same is true for students who come to school more often or who have fewer disciplinary referrals: Achievement is likely to improve.

Achievement-related data can provide valuable information about how to improve achievement data. Achievement-related data may be more easily accessible to school counselors, may appear to align or correlate with their activities or services more directly, and may be more closely linked to specified outcomes of the school counseling program than student achievement data. Both are important components for a DBDM team to consider for identifying what problems need to be addressed and what approaches are needed. Focusing on achievement-related data in planning provides a way to identify how school counselors can contribute to the schoolwide effort to improve achievement results.

Standards- and Competency-Related Data

Standards- and competency-related data directly reflect the student learning outcomes of the school counseling program. These data indicate that as a result of the school counselor's activity or lesson, students were able to demonstrate through knowledge, skill, attitude shift, or completion of the task that they have achieved that specific competency. While the competencies measured may come from a variety of sources (e.g., the ASCA National Standards, the National Career Development Association guidelines, or state school counseling competencies), it is valuable for each school counseling program to have its own set of measurable competencies and student learning objectives that reflect the particular needs of the students in its school and the goals of its program. It is important to identify the most essential competencies to sharpen the focus of the curriculum and to simplify data collection. Careful attention should be given to identifying quantitative indicators of competency attainment, such as the percentage of students who

- know the credit requirements for graduation,
- demonstrate knowledge of study skills and how to use an academic planner,
- use test-taking strategies,
- can identify the steps in setting goals,
- demonstrate conflict resolution skills, and
- believe that it is important to come to school every day.

One area of weakness within the school counseling profession is the lack of research about how these three types of data are causally related. If we knew how attainment of specific competencies caused changes in achievement and achievement-related data, planning would be much easier. Imagine the power of research that showed increases in achievement-related data (attendance) and achievement data (test scores) when school counselors taught guidance curriculum about time management, goal setting, decision making, or competencies that align with the goal of attendance. While the research base for the school counseling profession is being established, our best course of action is to rely on what is known from outcome research, combine this knowledge with our best professional wisdom, and work to construct the causal linkages that explain the theory behind the practice. For example, a school counselor teaches competency-based curriculum on homework tips and study strategies (competency) with the goal of improving homework completion rates (achievement-related), which is intended to improve academic performance (achievement).

Data Relationships

The relationship between competency attainment, achievement-related data, and achievement data can be demonstrated in a linear model with movement occurring in either direction. As illustrated in Figure 3.1, you can think about guidance curriculum as moving in the direction of

Figure 3.1   Types of Data and the Relationship Between Competency Attainment and Achievement

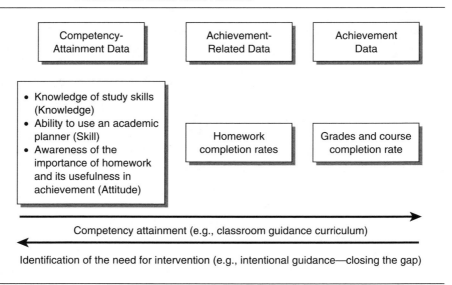

left to right: first competency attainment, then achievement-related data, and finally achievement data. Conversely, moving from right to left in this model provides a data-driven mechanism for determining when interventions are necessary to address certain competencies.

Once a DBDM team has identified an achievement data problem, we can ask, "What achievement-related data must we move to address the problem and what competencies must be developed to move the achievement-related data?" For example, data could show a decline in grade point averages (achievement data). After examining achievement-related data, the DBDM team discovers that while discipline and attendance data are in the acceptable range, homework completion rates have dropped significantly. Next, it is important to determine what standards and competencies students lack, such as the knowledge of study skills or the awareness of the importance of homework and its usefulness in achievement. By moving from right to left in our model, the DBDM team can create intentional interventions aimed at addressing the needs of individuals or larger groups of students. To evaluate the impact of the intervention, the DBDM team would reverse the direction and move from left to right.

Collecting, Analyzing, and Disaggregating Data

In order for counselors to use data well, they must be proficient in data collection, analysis, and disaggregation. The best way to dissipate fear, anxiety, or concern about the use of data is to have some concrete experiences doing this work. Teaming or collaborating with a colleague who enjoys data can ease the learning curve.

Collecting Data for Program Planning

Getting access to district data is a necessary first step. Some districts are fortunate enough to have central office personnel who collect, disaggregate, and disseminate data to schools, making data collection a less daunting task. Sometimes data are given to the principal or an administrator and not to the school counselor. When school counselors are included on the school's DBDM team, school counseling data-based program planning is intimately connected to school improvement. If a DBDM team does not exist, school counselors can gain access to the data by informing the principal or administrator who holds the data that school counselors are interested in using the data for planning within the school counseling program. Attending committee meetings where data are reviewed (such as accreditation teams or school leadership teams) can also save counselors a tremendous amount of time in data collection.

Existing Data

Departments of education in most states have school, district, and/or state data available on their Web sites. Using statewide data allows school counselors to analyze their school or district performance in relationship to other districts statewide. Most states also provide detailed information to schools on how students performed on state achievement tests. Often these data include classroom level data and contain information on why students may have performed poorly on a subset of the test. Companies that provide testing services (e.g., the College Board) also provide schools with individual student level data on performance.

Schools will often collect data on a regular basis or participate in statewide data collection for various purposes. Tapping into these ongoing surveys is usually a helpful and cost-effective way to get valuable data that can be very useful in planning. For example, many schools conduct yearly school climate surveys that typically capture data on students' and parents' perceptions of important achievement-related factors such as school safety, inclusiveness, and teacher expectations. Also, many schools carry out surveys that gather a range of data about students' levels of involvement in potentially dangerous behavior (e.g., drugs, alcohol, and violence).

New Data

School counselors may need to collect new data that are not available from archival sources. Data on successful college applications and scholarship support, for example, typically fall into this category.

As much as possible, data collection needs to be built into the normal routines of the school counseling program since collecting new data places a large demand on time. One high school, for example, has a "Wall of Stars" that recognizes every student who is accepted to a college by placing his or her name in a star and posting these on the wall. Students report acceptances to the program secretary, who tabulates the data for analysis.

Analyzing Data

Once collected, data must be analyzed to be useful. The basic approach to this analysis is to make appropriate comparisons. This requires that all data be put on a comparable metric. The conversion of raw data to percentages, ratios, and/or probabilities is the most common way to achieve comparability. Knowing that 150 students from BMG High School go on to two- or four-year colleges while 450 students from another high school also do so offers little informational value. The data are not comparable. But by converting the raw data to a comparable form, we could discover that

- 50% of BMG High School students go on to two- or four-year colleges, while 70% of students from the other high school do so;
- five out of every 10 BMG High School students go on to two- or four-year colleges, while seven out of 10 students from the other high school do so; and
- seniors at BMG High School have a 50% probability of going on to a two- or four-year college, while seniors at the other high school have a 70% probability of going on to a two- or four-year college.

Data-based decision-making efforts are most successful when they use appropriate comparison groups and comparisons across multiple measures. For example, in the previous scenario, it would be helpful to compare BMG High School to schools within the district or state with similar profiles on achievement tests and similar demographics. If there still is a big difference between college placement rates when comparisons are made among schools with similar achievement profiles and demographics, increasing college placement rates should emerge as a potentially important focus for school improvement.

It is also instructive to make comparisons within the same school at two or more periods in time to get a sense of whether data are improving, staying the same, or getting worse. Again, the data need to be put on a common metric. A school with a 50% college placement rate that sees improvement from a 30% rate two years ago probably wants to stay the course. Its strategies and interventions seem to be working.

A school with a 50% college placement rate that sees a decline from a 70% rate two years ago needs to focus efforts on understanding the potential causes of this decline and allocate resources to reverse it.

Disaggregation of Data

It is also useful to compare and contrast data from different groups of students within a school. This type of analysis helps to reveal inequities that exist in schools and often provides a necessary key to school improvement. Each of the types of data previously mentioned (competency-related, achievement-related, and achievement data) can also be disaggregated by a wide range of groupings including the following:

- Gender
- Race/ethnicity
- Socioeconomic status
- Language
- Special education placement
- English language learner (ELL) status
- Grade level
- Achievement quartile
- Teacher/classroom

Disaggregating data allows the DBDM team to focus attention where resources are most needed. For instance, a school could cite its high school graduation rate as 91%. However, when the data are disaggregated, they show that female students are graduating at a 97% rate, while male students are graduating at only an 85% rate, revealing that while some students are succeeding, others need additional intervention or support. Or perhaps a middle school shows a 92% attendance rate, but when disaggregated, the data indicate that eighth graders' attendance rate is 85%, while sixth graders have a 98% attendance rate. Rather than develop a schoolwide activity to improve attendance, the school counseling program should focus interventions on the eighth grade. To ensure that even more specific attention is given to those in need, the counselor could further disaggregate the data by gender, ethnicity, or other factors.

Developing Data-Based Action Plans

School counselors provide a variety of services and activities as part of their comprehensive school counseling program. In the delivery component of *The ASCA National Model: A Framework for School Counseling Programs* (ASCA, 2003), four are described: guidance curriculum,

action plans

According to The ASCA National Model, for every desired competency and result, there must be a plan outlining how the desired result will be achieved. Each plan contains (1) competencies addressed, (2) description of the activity, (3) data driving the decision to address the competency, (4) a time line in which the activity is to be completed, (5) who is responsible for delivery, (6) means of evaluating student success, and (7) expected results for students.

individual student planning, responsive services, and system support. The ASCA National Model presents in its management system section two types of action plans: the "guidance curriculum action plan" and the "closing the gap action plan." In this text, we will refer to "closing the gap" activities as *intentional guidance* because the activity is conducted on purpose and with a data-driven deliberateness to address a specific student or systems need (or gap).

Guidance Curriculum Action Plans

The first prong in a two-pronged approach to addressing the needs of all students is the guidance curriculum action plan. Developmental in design, educational and preventive in nature, and comprehensive in scope, the guidance curriculum ensures that every student in the school will receive services from the guidance program. Sample action plans are provided in Appendix A on pages 171–178. Typically guidance curriculum action plans are standards- and competency-driven and created using a developmental approach. The curriculum is identified, delivered, and evaluated by school counselors and usually addresses the standards and competencies of the ASCA National Standards (ASCA, 2003; Campbell & Dahir, 1997). With nine competencies and 122 indicators, however, how can school counselors decide which competencies to address first? In many districts, teams of experienced school counselors use their best professional judgment to make decisions regarding which competencies and indicators they believe their students need. This professional judgment should be supported by three types of information: national professional standards, DBDM team analyses, and needs assessment data (see Figure 3.2). National standards can be used to develop a comprehensive set of student competencies that are the responsibility of the school counseling program. DBDM team analyses can indicate which of these competencies are important to address to move achievement data and contribute to achieving school goals. Needs assessment data can indicate which of these competencies students, teachers, administrators, and parents perceive as most important.

Once the standards, competencies, indicators, and sequence are agreed upon, school counselors assemble standardized interventions or create curriculum to teach the knowledge and skills necessary for

Figure 3.2   Sources of Information Guiding Development and
Prioritization of a Competency-Based Guidance Curriculum

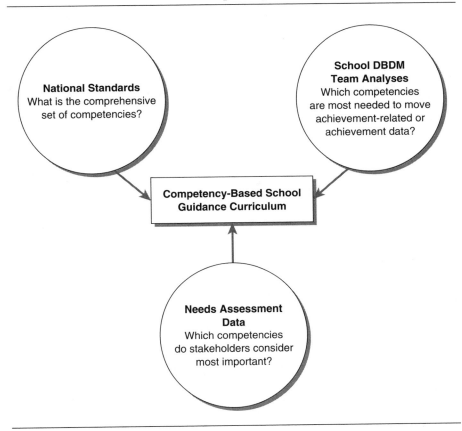

competency attainment. For example, all second graders might be taught a "Second Step" lesson (Committee for Children, 2006) or all fifth graders might participate in Student Success Skills (Brigman & Campbell, 2003).

While professional standards and professional judgment play an important role in this planning process, data should also be used to help ensure that the school counseling curriculum is aligned with student learning needs and schoolwide improvement initiatives. DBDM team analyses should be used to select school counseling curriculum that is aligned with identified school improvement goals and needs. If the DBDM team analysis indicates that attendance (and achievement) will be enhanced through creation of a safer school environment, the school counseling program should focus on developing student competencies related to violence reduction and consider implementing programs such as Bully Busters (2006) or PeaceBuilders (2006) that have demonstrated impact in this area.

Needs Assessment Data

It is also helpful to collect needs assessment data from students, parents, and teachers to supplement planning data. Needs assessment is a formal process of gathering information from a range of sources about their perceptions of the needs of the student population and the importance of particular curricular foci or specific interventions. In a typical needs assessment survey, various stakeholders would be asked how important it is for the school counseling program to ensure that students demonstrate competencies such as being able to

- maintain, review, and revise a four-year academic plan to successfully complete high school graduation requirements,
- develop and use study skills necessary to take, organize, and use notes effectively,
- identify appropriate choices during high school that will lead to marketable skills for entry level employment or for advanced education, and
- demonstrate appropriate anger management, self-control, and conflict resolution skills in a variety of settings.

Unfortunately, very few standards-based needs assessment instruments are available to school counselors. Thompson, Loesch, & Seraphine (2003) developed the Intermediate Elementary School Students Counseling Needs Survey (IESCNS) in response to the call for a more careful assessment of school counseling needs as a crucial component when implementing an effective elementary school counseling program. They report that the IESCNS has the potential to be used in many ways, including "administering it to all students in a school to achieve indication of the general (i.e., schoolwide and/or classroom) level of counseling needs among students" (p. 38).

In Appendix A, we've provided an example of a high school needs assessment survey (see page 179). The survey was designed to collect needs assessment data from students, parents, and teachers. A survey such as this can be helpful in curriculum planning because items are organized according to career, academic, and personal/social domains that fit well with the way that school counseling standards are typically organized.

Intentional Guidance (Closing the Gap Action Plans)

The second prong of the two-pronged approach to addressing student needs is called intentional guidance. *The ASCA National Model* (ASCA, 2003) refers to these activities as "closing the gap" activities because they are designed to close identified gaps in achievement between groups of students. While receiving standards-based guidance curriculum may be adequate for most students, the intentional guidance philosophy is that "some kids need *more*," and it is the responsibility of the school counseling program to address these needs. By disaggregating the data, we can focus on where additional help is needed.

Disaggregating data can uncover equity and access issues, and school counselors can design intentional activities to specifically address these concerns. Intentional guidance interventions can be targeted at one or multiple levels (individual, group, classroom, grade, schoolwide, home/family, and community/society) to reinforce students' competency development and to remove barriers to learning. With intentional guidance, the school counselor initiates an activity to ensure that all student groups receive what they need to thrive in school. Data analysis is essential for describing achievement problems that result from inequity and for identifying intentional guidance interventions to address these inequities.

Disaggregation of schoolwide data is vital to these analyses and enables school counselors to address questions such as the following:

- Are all groups of students attending college at the same rates?
- Are all groups of students taking the PSAT at the same rates?
- Are all groups of students completing a college preparatory curriculum at the same rates?
- Are all groups of students completing four-year plans at the same rates?
- Are all groups feeling safe at school?
- Are all groups aware of the dangers of substance abuse?

As mentioned earlier in this chapter, it is helpful to target identified needs by using data to determine what the actual needs are. For instance, not all students who are struggling academically require tutoring. Achievement data might lead the DBDM team to decide that issues with attendance, behavior, or homework completion might instead be contributing to the achievement gap. Thoughtful use of data allows school counselors to create interventions that address specific needs.

Below is a list of sample sources for designing intentional guidance activities for students:

- Lists of students who have received grades or D or F
- Lists of credit-deficient students
- K–5 report cards (that inform about homework completion and the ability to follow directions)
- Attendance data
- Discipline, suspension, and expulsion data
- High school exit examination results
- Referrals to the school counselor

Using Report Card Data

Many middle and high schools have student database systems that allow school counselors access to academic data that can be used to impel specific interventions. Elementary school counselors might find that student report cards are a better source of data for determining which students at this level are in need of intentional guidance. Report cards for elementary school children describe whether a child is able to follow directions, work cooperatively in a group, complete assignments successfully, demonstrate responsible behavior in the classroom, and much more. By reviewing the data found on report cards, school counselors can target identified needs for students who might not otherwise have been referred. Report card data can also be used to select students who might benefit from a group intervention specifically designed to address a data-driven need. Once an intervention is implemented, school counselors can review new report card data to assess change.

School Counselor Referral Forms

School counselor referral forms typically ask teachers to state a concern or reason for a referral. These forms rarely include important data elements. A school's DBDM team may want to review the referral form to ensure that a returned form will provide the data necessary for appropriate intervention. Using referral forms that identify attendance, behavior, or achievement concerns allows school counselors to create interventions that address specific needs. If a referral form also asks teachers to rate the severity of a problem on a 1–10 scale, school counselors can use a triage approach to assist those in greatest need.

Intentional Guidance for Systems Change

Intentional guidance efforts can be directed toward students and also toward systemic factors that affect students. When directed toward students, school counselors use data to determine which groups of students need additional support and then implement interventions that have the promise of providing that support. There are times, however, when the problem does not lie with the student but with the system. When students are registering for courses but are denied access due to prerequisites, when 90% of the students enrolled in a given class are failing the class but passing all others, or when a certain classroom is responsible for five times the behavior referrals of other rooms, systemic issues need to be addressed. When school counseling efforts are directed toward systems, changes in policy or practice that seem to be disadvantaging a subgroup of students in the school are the focus. Often both student-focused and systemic interventions are needed to adequately address equity issues and to close gaps in achievement.

While the guidance curriculum is influenced by standards, needs assessment data, and DBDM team analyses, the decision to implement an intentional guidance intervention is most strongly driven by problems described in the DBDM process. As we will see in later chapters, whenever possible it is critically important to select intentional guidance interventions that are research-based and to evaluate the impact of these interventions after implementation. Part of the evaluation will include a determination of whether the improvement in problem data is achieved and whether there is evidence that the intentional guidance intervention is contributing to that improvement. The decision to continue a particular intentional guidance intervention is driven by the evaluation of its effectiveness.

Creating an Action Plan With Evaluation in Mind: Using Process, Perception, and Results Data

As school counselors create action plans, it is helpful to consider how the activities will be evaluated for effectiveness. *The ASCA National Model* (2003) recommends collecting process, perception, and results data to measure the effectiveness of a school counseling program's activities and to gain information that can be used for program improvement. It is important to understand the differences among these three different types of data.

Process Data

Process data provide evidence that an event occurred. It tells us who received services, activities, or lessons; when they received it; and for how long. Process data give us the who, what, when, where, and how often information. For example, all 1,350 sixth through eighth grade students in a middle school received two one-hour violence-prevention guidance lessons in their classroom during the fall semester.

While some might be impressed with a counselor's process data, others might ask, "Did the students learn anything? Are they now more or less likely to be violent in school?" Process data cannot tell us whether students are different as a result of a counselor's actions.

Perception Data

While process data tell us what a counselor did, *perception data* tell us what a student learned. Perception data inform us what a student believes, knows, or can demonstrate as a result of a lesson or activity.

When school counselors teach a guidance lesson or hold group counseling sessions they are delivering (or aligning with delivery of) the ASCA National Standards and competencies (Campbell & Dahir, 1997). Standards-based education encourages educators to measure knowledge, attitudes, and skills (Darling-Hammond, 1998). The words *attitudes, skills,* and *knowledge* form the acronym ASK, which reminds us to assess what students gained or learned from a lesson or activity (Hatch, 2005). Perception data measure whether (a) students' a̲ttitudes or beliefs changed or shifted as a result of an activity or intervention, (b) students learned the s̲kill (attained the competency), or (c) students' k̲nowledge increased. School counselors can collect ASK data about an activity or intervention to determine if it benefited students.

"Attitudes" measures the beliefs or feelings a student possesses:

- Twenty-nine percent of fifth grade males feel safe at school, according to district or state health survey data.
- Fifty-three percent of African American females believe they can succeed in college.
- Before a guidance lesson, 30% of students believed taking college prep courses was important; after the lesson, this number climbed to 80%.

"Skills" (competency attainment) are measured through a variety of methods, such as having students conduct role plays, complete certain activities, take pre- or posttests, or engage in some other task:

- Every seventh grade student completed an interest inventory.
- Eighty-five percent of fifth graders accurately role-played the conflict resolution process.
- Ninety-seven percent of ninth through twelfth grade students completed a four-year plan.

"Knowledge" provides an indication that students learned the information as intended:

- Prior to guidance lessons, 15% of students in the seventh grade demonstrated knowledge of promotion/retention criteria; after the lesson, 89% of the students demonstrated knowledge of such criteria.
- Before a series of group counseling sessions, 56% of fifth grade males referred for anger management issues knew three ways to divert anger in a healthy way; after the sessions, 92% of the group's participants were able to do so.
- Before individual counseling sessions, 53% of eleventh grade, academically at-risk Latino students knew what their

postsecondary options were if they graduated from high school; after the session, the number jumped to 97%.

Putting Together Attitudes, Skills, and Knowledge

Attitudes, skills, and knowledge (ASK) work together to influence behavior change. When school counselors design activities and lessons that both address and measure all three of the ASK perception data areas, behavior change is more likely to follow. It is this behavior change that we hope will lead to improved student results (see Figure 3.3).

Figure 3.3   ASK Diagram

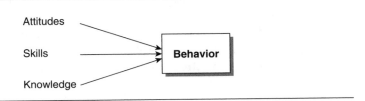

Many school counselors can tell a story about a group of students who seem to know that fighting is against school rules, know that there are consequences for fighting, even know alternative strategies for expressing angry feelings; and yet a great deal of fighting is still occurring in the building. A school counselor might collect information regarding how the issue of fighting is being addressed as part of the department's accountability data. Process data would show that the school counselor taught anger management or conflict resolution lessons in a classroom three times in a month or that a certain number of identified students received additional small-group intervention. Perception data might indicate that students know fighting is wrong. The students may know how to handle the situation differently and may even be able to demonstrate conflict-resolution skills. Yet the data might reveal that behavior has not changed. What might be the missing piece? Perhaps it is attitude. If students do not believe that fighting is against the rules, they are less likely to stop their fighting behavior. As a result, overall incidences of fighting might not decrease.

Stakeholders want to know that school counseling activities and interventions make a real difference. They want to see that the number of fighting incidences, referrals, detentions, or suspensions has decreased. If the data do not show improvement, the lessons may have been only partially effective. By assessing ASK, the school counselor can determine where additional motivation, skills development, or education is needed. When all three areas are improved, the likelihood of behavior change is much greater. And behavior change leads to the next level of program evaluation: results.

Results Data

Results data are the "hard" data, the application data. Results are the proof that the activity or intervention either has or has not positively influenced the students' ability to use attitudes, skills, and knowledge to change their behavior. Behavior changes and their results may be measured with two types of data: achievement or achievement-related. Earlier in this chapter, we discussed how competency attainment is intended to lead to positive changes in achievement-related data and that research tells us that achievement-related outcomes are linked to student achievement. When school counselors measure results and find improvement in student achievement-related data, it is good practice to see if academic achievement is improving also. Achievement-related results are often able to show that school counselors are contributing in a meaningful way to the overall academic achievement of students although such findings do not demonstrate a causal relationship.

When school counselors collect process data for the activities they conduct within the school counseling program, important questions about what is being done are answered. When school counselors measure competency-attainment data (perception data), they are collecting evidence that their objectives (improving student attitudes, skills, and knowledge) are being met; is intended to lead to behavior change that can be measured by achievement-related and achievement (results) data.

The Results Conceptual Diagram (Hatch, 2005), Figure 3.4, is a visual representation of how school counseling activities can contribute to student achievement. Competency attainment falls under the category of perception data, and achievement-related and achievement data are both under results data. The Results Conceptual Diagram explains how school counselors' activities are designed to contribute to students' achievement and how the various types of data relate to each other.

Data Over Time

Outcome data can also be reviewed using three different time categories: immediate, intermediate, and long-range (data over time).

Immediate data are data collected very soon after an activity, lesson, or group session is completed. They give the school counselor immediate feedback about whether an intervention had any impact on students' knowledge, attitudes, or skills. For instance, a school counselor might

Figure 3.4   Results Conceptual Diagram

PROCESS DATA	PERCEPTION DATA		RESULTS DATA	
	Competency-Attainment Data		Achievement-Related Data	Achievement Data
Guidance lessons, group counseling, etc. Who? What? When? Where? How long?	Attitudes Skills Knowledge	Behavior Change	Attendance Discipline referrals Parent involvement Homework completion Course enrollment patterns	State standardized tests SAT/ACT scores Graduation rates Grade point averages AP tests (passing) College prep course completion

GUIDANCE CURRICULUM ⟶

⟵ INTENTIONAL GUIDANCE (intervention)

GUIDANCE CURRICULUM: Move from left to right (e.g., teach lesson, measure ASK, and look for impact on achievement-related data and achievement data).

INTENTIONAL GUIDANCE (intervention): Move from right to left. First look at achievement data (GPAs, for instance). If they are not what is expected, move to the left to achievement-related data. Ask, "What is the concern here? Not attending school? Not behaving? Not doing homework? Once an answer (not doing homework, for example) is apparent, move to the left again and ask, "Is it that they don't have enough *knowledge* of the subject to do the homework? That they don't have the *skills* (reading, writing)? That they have the *attitude* that it is unimportant? (ASK). Once the answer is known, go back to process data and decide what to do to address the need.

Therefore, curriculum goes from left to right and intervention right to left—and then, of course, back again to measure impact of the intervention.

SOURCE: Hatch, 2005.

give a new PowerPoint presentation on the subject of promotion and retention. If a pre-test was used to determine what needs to be taught, then a post-test can immediately determine if the lesson was effective. Without this information, an end-of-the-year situation could develop in which retained students report that although they received the promotion/retention lesson, they did not understand its implications. With immediate feedback data, a counselor can know right after a lesson if students understand the material and if the intended objectives were achieved. If the data indicate that these goals were not met, the counselor has the opportunity to revise the lesson and deliver it again in a timely fashion.

Intermediate data can be collected after a quarter, trimester, or semester. School counselors can use database systems to make queries on students and create a data set of students with a particular focus, such as students with 10 or more absences or three or more failing grades. This process is ideally done at the end of the first grading period. After an intervention, the counselor can again query the data set to look for overall changes in the targeted group. An experienced counselor can further disaggregate the data by gender, ethnicity, or other variables to see if the intervention was more effective for a certain subset of the group.

Long-range data are important because patterns, trends, and discrepancies in data can be discovered by analyzing and reviewing them over time. Long-term data or year-to-year data are often collected by the school district and may be available disaggregated for school counselors' use. Disaggregating data can provide useful information. For example, the graduation rate at a high school rose 3% for each of the past five years. However, when disaggregated, the data showed that while the graduation rates among Latino males rose 8%, graduation rates among African American females dropped 6%. When counselors further disaggregate and analyze data by specific variables, they often uncover pressing concerns that might not have been apparent in the original data set. Long-range data are best presented in charts and graphs so that trends are easily identifiable.

Summary

School counseling practice must be influenced by both national standards and local data. National standards provide professional assessment of what students need to learn. Local data allow this learning to be tailored to specific students. Institutional data and needs assessments data can tell us which standards-based competencies are most needed by all students. Disaggregating data can also tell us what additional intentional guidance help is needed by which groups of students. The use of local data promotes responsible and equitable practice by helping to ensure that all students get what they need from the school counseling program.

4

Choosing Interventions

Reading and Weighing Outcome Research

Consider two scenarios:

Scenario 1: *Katie is a middle school counselor. The principal asks the school counseling department to help create a safer school climate. The school's annual school climate survey indicates that many students feel bullying and the threat of violence detract from their ability to focus on their studies. Katie's department head asks Katie to develop a plan to address the issue of school safety. At the next state association conference, Katie attends sessions on peer mediation programs. She is particularly impressed with a program in which 30 student mediators were trained and supervised by a school counselor and then available to mediate disputes between fellow students. The presentation's data showed that most students who used the services indicated that they were very useful and that they believed the program made the school safer. After the conference, Katie recommended that her school adopt the program.*

Scenario 2: *Katie is a middle school counselor. The principal asks the school counseling department to help create a safer school climate. The school's annual school climate survey indicates that many students feel that bullying and the threat of violence detract from their ability to focus on their* *studies. Katie's department head asks Katie to develop a plan to address the issue of school safety. She puts together a team composed of teachers, parents, and the school nurse who use Internet resources to identify possible empirically supported interventions. The team identifies six potential programs that have strong research support and then identifies the program that is most feasible given the available resources, school routines, school culture, student population, and community expectations. The team presents to the principal their recommendation of implementing the Olweus Bullying Prevention Program (a Substance Abuse and Mental Health Services Administration, or SAMHSA, model program) because it has individual, peer, family, and school components that have been shown to be effective in reducing school violence by changing interactions within the school community. The intervention's requirement that the whole school community participate in implementation was seen as a good fit with the school staff's high level of interest, capacity for collaboration, and desire for engagement in solving this problem. The team's recommendation also includes a plan for implementing and evaluating the program.*

In the first scenario, Katie followed common educational and school counseling practice. She looked at how colleagues addressed a similar problem and paid careful attention to their evaluation results, which were quite positive. She decided to adopt a program that a colleague believed was effective.

The problem with this approach is that while evaluation results are critically important in determining whether an intervention is working in a given school, evaluation results are not helpful in determining whether an intervention is likely to be effective in a new setting. Generalization across contexts is difficult. Had Katie looked at the outcome research, she would have learned that peer mediation programs of the type she recommended can improve the skills of those involved in the program but have little impact on overall school climate of safety.

In the second scenario, Katie follows a different path. She forms a team to identify potential interventions with evidence that they are generally effective. This team uses Internet resources to look at a wide range of programs. By focusing on programs that have strong research support and some assurance of generalizability of findings, Katie increases the chances that the program that is selected will work. Because the team can choose from several programs with proven effectiveness, they can identify the program that best fits with the idiosyncrasies of their particular school. The team also provides implementation and evaluation plans so that from the beginning there is a clear understanding of how the intervention will be implemented and how it will be determined if it is having the desired effects.

Why Are Research-Based School Counseling Interventions Important?

While the term "research-based interventions" has a range of meanings, we prefer to reserve the term to refer to interventions that have evidence of effectiveness from high-quality outcome research. This evidence indicates that the intervention is generally effective in changing some important aspect of students' affect, cognition, or behavior. We believe that there are particular advantages to using research-based interventions.

Using research-based interventions can generally ensure that school counseling resources are invested wisely. Every decision to use time and material resources one way precludes the use of those resources in other ways. School counselors must choose between alternative ways to accomplish the same outcomes. In the ideal, this decision would be made based on an assessment of the relative costs of the prospective interventions compared with the expected outcomes of these interventions. Rarely can this ideal be achieved.

Outcome research typically provides evidence that a particular intervention is effective and only very rarely provides evidence that a given intervention is ineffective. The Second Step Violence Prevention Curriculum (Committee for Children, 2006), for example, has strong research support for its effectiveness (Carey, Dimmitt, Hatch, Lapan, & Whiston, in press). Most other interventions currently lack this strong research support. If there is no evidence that an intervention is effective, it does not mean that it is ineffective; it just means it hasn't been researched. Most of the time, school counselors are choosing between interventions that are known to be effective and interventions that may be effective but don't have any research support.

Often factors other than research support seem more salient when choosing an intervention. Many school counselors prefer to use self-generated materials (e.g., lesson plans) rather than commercially available materials because of the perception that they are less expensive. This decision may not take into consideration the cost of their own time in developing materials. The real measure of comparison is the cost-benefit ratios between the two interventions. While both the cost and expected benefits of research-based interventions are known, counselor-made interventions generally cost much more than people realize and have unknown outcomes.

The choice of intervention is also greatly influenced by testimonial endorsement and packaging. Many sessions at professional meetings are devoted to practices "that work." Often these sessions consist of an engaging demonstration of the intervention without outcome research information. Most professional conferences also have exhibit halls where vendors promote and sell interventions, many with beautiful packaging. School counselors' use of a particular intervention may be influenced by the packaging or by the engaging nature of the demonstration when in fact the most important issue is whether there is actual evidence that the intervention is effective. Often, there is not.

Using research-based interventions sets a standard for professional practice. Professions are effective and credible to the extent that practice is based on a scientifically tested body of knowledge rather than on consensually validated opinions about what is effective (Heppner, Kivlighan, & Wampold, 1992; Whiston, 2002). School counseling (like other educational professions) has, to date, relied on a knowledge base that was driven more by theory and collective practitioner experience than by research on what works for students. The outcome research literature does not currently have a major influence on either the training or the practice of school counselors. Both school counselor education and school counseling practice need to be aligned with the evidence base of effectiveness. Using the research literature on effective practice in both domains will advance the profession by unifying training and practice (Sexton, Schofield, & Whiston, 1997). We believe that rooting practice in the evolving outcome research base will enhance the professional status of the school counseling profession by increasing confidence that school counselors take proper care to implement only those interventions that are effective.

Using research-based interventions is more likely to generate good accountability data. The need to use evaluation to document the impact and effectiveness of the school counseling program to local educational decision makers has long been accepted as a necessary and important professional activity (Keene & Stewart, 1989). School counselors are much more likely to be able to document impact when they are using interventions and practices that have already been found to be effective.

Becoming an Informed Consumer of Research

Not all research is equal. Understanding how to read research critically—or becoming an informed consumer of research information—is a necessary first step in the process of moving toward an evidence-based practice. Here is a list of questions to ask about any research study:

What is the source of the research; where did it come from?

What type of research is it?

What are the strengths/weaknesses of the research design?

Was there a control group?

What was the quality of the sampling process?

How large was the sample?

How representative was the sample?

How random was the sample?

How strong was the finding?

How big was the effect size?

What measures/instruments were used?

How well did instruments measure what they were supposed to?

How reliable and valid were the instruments?

How did the researcher's ideas influence the research outcome?

What statistical procedures were used?

What was the research context?

Sources

Researchers (often at universities) collect and analyze data and then present at conferences and write articles and books for publication in order to disseminate their findings. This is called *primary research*. Many conferences and scholarly journals are peer reviewed, which means that for research to be presented or published, it must be determined by peers (usually a professional review board) to be of high quality. *Professional School Counselor* is the peer-reviewed journal for the school counseling field. Research published in a newspaper or magazine that is not peer reviewed needs to be evaluated carefully. Unpublished research presented at a conference is not as trustworthy as research in a peer-reviewed journal, though quality varies widely depending on the field of study.

When there is much research about a topic, *secondary research* summarizes the primary research. Secondary research includes meta-analyses, narrative literature reviews, and systematic reviews. There are Web resources (see Table 4.1) that provide access to research journals and secondary research findings. School counseling and other professions also have expert panels (see the National Panel for Evidence-Based School Counseling Practice; Center for School

Counseling Outcome Research [CSCOR], 2004), research centers, and institutes that disseminate summaries of research findings. The last section of this chapter provides a general summary of school counseling research, and Appendix B contains research articles organized by domain and findings.

Type of Research

Different types of research provide different information, and claims that can be made about the findings depend on the type of research done. *Quantitative research* uses data in numerical form, while *qualitative research* uses data in narrative form. Because it is less dependent on subjective analysis, quantitative research is considered stronger evidence. Quantitative and qualitative research can be combined, which allows for both measurable outcomes and the richness of narrative information.

Stronger research studies use random sampling procedures and comparison groups. A comparison group creates better evidence that any group difference found can be attributed to the intervention and not to chance. The strongest research evidence is provided by quantitative research using an *experimental design,* in which those participating in the study are randomly assigned to two groups: a treatment group and a control group. The *treatment group* then receives an intervention of some kind—for example, an educational program or mental health intervention—and then is compared to the *control group,* which did not receive the intervention. With experimental design, if a difference between the groups is found, it can be stated with more confidence that the intervention produced the effect and that there may be a causal relationship between the intervention being studied and the outcome(s) found. In general, the stronger the research design, the more confidence one can have that the findings are replicable in another context, which is called *generalizability.*

Experimental design research is rare in education for several reasons (though it is the research of choice in fields such as medicine and psychology). Such research is very expensive to conduct, and education, including the school counseling field, has not historically received the necessary financial support to conduct such research. In education, it is also frequently difficult to do true random assignment of subjects, since students are grouped by classroom or grade in complex ways. It can be impractical or unethical to assign students to a control group in which they would not have access to the intervention. In schools,

experimental research design

a type of research design in which subjects are assigned randomly to groups and groups are treated differently, typically with one or more group serving as a control group

Table 4.1 Information Sources on Research-Based Practices

Source	Types of Interventions Evaluated	Web Address
What Works Clearing House	Wide range of interventions, including character education	http://www.whatworks.ed.gov
National Center for Chronic Disease Prevention and Health Promotion	Wide range of school-based, prevention/health-promotion interventions, including suicide prevention, HIV/AIDS prevention, etc.	http://www.cdc.gov/HealthyYouth/index.htm
U.S. Department of Education's Safe and Drug-Free Schools Program; Safe, Disciplined, and Drug-Free Schools Expert Panel	Programs that promote safe, disciplined, and drug-free schools	http://www.ed.gov/about/offices/list/osdfs/index.html
Substance Abuse and Mental Health Services Administration's National Registry of Evidence-Based Programs and Practices	Wide range of programs related to substance abuse prevention and mental health promotion	http://www.modelprograms.samhsa.gov
Collaborative for Academic, Social, and Emotional Learning	Programs that enhance academic achievement through personal/social interventions	http://www.casel.org/home/index.php

selection bias

a threat to the internal validity of a research study that results when preexisting differences between groups, which affect the outcome, are present

To eliminate selection bias we use random assignment of subjects to study groups whenever possible. Also, matching subjects across groups or statistical procedures (e.g., analysis of covariance) may minimize the impact of selection bias.

quasi-experimental research design

a type of research design in which subjects are not randomly assigned to groups

As with experimental designs, groups are treated differently, typically with one or more groups serving as a control group. However, since equivalence of the groups cannot be assured, the control and experimental groups must be equated (e.g., by matching subjects or by statistical procedures) to permit between-group comparisons.

it is often challenging to separate context effects from the intervention being studied, as well.

Quasi-experimental designs are often used in education since they use groups of subjects who are similar but not randomly assigned to compare the effect of an intervention. Such studies can demonstrate a relationship between an intervention and an outcome but cannot demonstrate causality because there is not random assignment. For example, if a tutoring program raises test scores, it may be the result of the tutoring or it may be that the group participating in the tutoring began with more academic knowledge. Quasi-experimental designs are frequently the design of choice when studying complex social systems with large numbers of people and broader topics.

Qualitative research provides descriptive information about people's beliefs and experiences. It is useful in early stages of research for identifying what the outcomes of interventions might be or for gathering data about subjects' ideas regarding how they are different as a result of an intervention. When reporting to stakeholders, the narrative qualitative components provide a subjective perspective that paints a broader picture of the quantitative findings.

Sampling

The *sample* in a research study is the group of people being researched. Both sample size and the way the sample was collected are important when evaluating research quality. Sample size is important as the larger the group of people in the study, the smaller the differences between the groups will need to be to find statistical significance in the findings. Research showing that an intervention works with 10 students is necessarily less impactful than research finding the same outcome for 100 students.

The way the sample is selected, or *sampling*, is important because it impacts the generalizability of a study. In educational research, depending on what is being studied, it is often important to use samples that include a broad range of student demographic variables (such as age/grade, gender, race/ethnicity, socioeconomic status, special needs, and academic achievement status). Sampling can apply to the setting (urban/rural/suburban, size of the school, size of the district, geographical context, or funding level) as well as to the participants. If the sample is not *representative* (an accurate representation of the larger population), then the likelihood diminishes that the intervention will be effective with another group. *Random sampling*, in which each member of the population has an equal chance of being selected to participate, is the strongest type of sampling, as it is the best way to ensure that those in the control and experimental groups are representative of the population in general and that they are similar to each other. If researchers are using an experimental design, they will often report

statistical significance

the degree to which we can conclude that an observed difference between groups is real and does not reflect chance variation

generalizability

the degree to which a result obtained in one situation is likely to be obtained in a different situation

sampling

selecting a representative sample of individuals from a large population, such that the characteristics of the sample accurately reflect the characteristics of the larger population

on the demographic variables of the treatment and control groups to demonstrate that there are no significant differences between the groups prior to the intervention. If differences are found between the groups after the intervention, there is a stronger likelihood that the intervention caused the change.

In research that involves surveys or other written responses, the response rate is an important component of sampling. If a survey is mailed to 1,000 parents and only 200 return their answers, the group that participated in the study may be different in some key ways from the whole sample. A 50% response rate is generally considered acceptable, and an 80% rate is considered very good (Heppner et al., 1992).

Measurement

The way things are measured impacts research findings, and there are ways to measure differences that lend greater credence to the outcomes. A research topic is called a *construct*, or *variable*, and it

construct

a hypothetical psychological structure that is used to explain or predict behavior
    "Achievement motivation" is an example of a common construct.

is important that any research article define its constructs and variables very carefully. For example, if a bullying intervention is being researched, what are the behaviors under consideration? How are they measured? Ideally, researchers use definitions of constructs that demonstrate historical consistency (how have others defined these constructs prior to this?) as well as common sense (would most people agree with their definitions?).

Another important evaluation of measurement is whether a study measures outcomes using reliable and valid instruments. An *instrument* is any survey, test, procedure, behavioral observation process, or questionnaire that is used to measure the construct under considera-

reliability

a property of a measure that reflects its stability
    A perfectly reliable measure provides the same score every time it is used.

test-retest reliability

a method for estimating a measure's reliability based on correlating its results on two different occasions

split-half reliability

a method for estimating a measure's reliability based on correlating the results of the two halves of the measure

validity

the property of a measure that reflects the extent to which it measures what it is intended to measure

tion. If the research variable being studied is bullying, the instruments could include student surveys, teacher questionnaires, and behavioral observations. Research studies often report which instruments they used and whether the instruments were developed for the study or were pre-existing. The best instruments have been evaluated for reliability and validity. An instrument has *reliability* when it consistently measures what it is supposed to. With a reliable measure, if the same group is given the instrument at a later date, the results are consistent (called "test-retest" reliability) or people answer consistently on related questions (called "split-half" reliability).

An instrument has *validity* when it accurately measures what it is supposed to measure. For example, it would be time-consuming, if not impossible, to observe every interaction between students to identify bullying behaviors. If an instrument identifies a sample of the behaviors, and one can say with some confidence that what was measured was an accurate sub-sample of possible behaviors, then the instrument may have validity.

An instrument is said to have *content validity* if experts in that area have determined that it is measuring the content, or constructs, that it purports to be measuring. In order to have validity, an instrument must also have reliability. Reliability is thus necessary but not sufficient for validity, as a measurement may be consistent, but consistently wrong. Validity and reliability together suggest that an instrument is consistent and accurate.

> **content validity**
>
> type of validity that reflects the extent to which a test covers a sufficient sample of the material so that it can be considered an accurate measure of the material

Another component of effective measurement is whether the instruments used were developed for the sample being studied. For example, a measure of social skills developed for middle school students would need to be modified in order to be useful for elementary students. If it is modified from its original form, the reliability and validity of the instrument are altered.

Statistical Procedures

Both quantitative and qualitative research use statistical procedures, though the standards for each vary. When using numerical data, as in quantitative research, there are multiple rules for analyzing data in appropriate ways. There must be a big enough sample size, the statistical procedures must match the data, there must be controls for errors, and the statistical significance must be numerically determined. If a quantitative study reports *statistical significance,* that means that the differences between the control and experimental groups are likely to be due to the intervention studied rather than other factors.

A study may demonstrate statistical significance, but that only has meaning if the measurement was valid and reliable, if the sample is representative and large enough (though the larger the sample the more likelihood of finding statistical significance), and if the constructs were adequately defined and measured. Similarly, the lack of a statistically significant finding can still be helpful, as there may be trends in the outcomes, or it may be that a lack of difference between the two groups is useful information.

The Research Context

Any individual study is most valuable when it is placed in context with related research. Most research articles provide that context with an initial literature review of the related research. Knowing what has been previously discovered about an intervention provides a broader picture of what is known. If there is little prior information, any individual study must be considered only a part of the picture, not definitive proof.

When Can We Say That an Intervention Has Strong Research Support?

Strong research on the outcomes of school counseling interventions is research that can establish a causal link between an intervention and significant cognitive, behavioral, and/or affective outcomes. While the simplest outcome studies include one treatment and one control group, strong outcome studies typically have multiple control groups to protect against other threats to internal validity. "The Hawthorne effect" takes its name from the famous case of the Western Electric Hawthorne plant, where increased worker productivity was found to result more from workers responding to the attention of the researchers than from the specific interventions (e.g., changes in lighting). A strong outcome research study may need to compare the effect of an intervention to both a "placebo" control and a "no-treatment" control to determine that it is the specific intervention and not the general attention that is producing the positive effects.

Shadish, Cook, and Campbell (2002) present much more detail on the various threats to internal/external validity and design and on research design features that minimize these threats. The National Panel for School Counseling Evidence-Based Practice has developed an outcome research evaluation protocol that incorporates Shadish and colleagues' (2002) work. In constructing this protocol, the Panel also reviewed and incorporated the work of several other professional panels. The resulting outcome research coding protocol presented in Table 4.2 was strongly influenced by the What Works Clearinghouse's *Study Design and Implementation Assessment Device* (Valentine & Cooper, 2003) and the Task Force on Evidence-Based Interventions in School Psychology's *Coding and Procedures Manual* (Task Force on Evidence-Based Interventions in School Psychology, 2003). The protocol's seven domains reflect important characteristics of strong outcome research. Within each domain, a distinction is made between evidence that is promising and evidence that is strong. The protocol is an accurate and efficient way to evaluate the strength of the research evidence that suggests that a given intervention is causally related to important student outcomes. The Panel is actively engaged in using this protocol to continuously evaluate the school counseling outcome research literature.

What Are the Relevant Research Findings?

School counselors are in the challenging position of needing to know both the counseling interventions that are most likely to be helpful and the research relevant to educational practices. The research content in mental health and education is different, although

Table 4.2   Outcome Research Coding Protocol: Coding Studies and Rating the Level of Evidence for the Causal Effect of an Intervention

School counseling interventions will be evaluated by the Evidence-Based Practice Panel to determine the level of evidence that exists in outcome studies to support the contention that the intervention causes a change in an important student outcome. Seven domains will be used in this evaluation, and each domain has threshold criteria for two levels of strength: "strong evidence" and "promising evidence." To be considered an *evidence-based practice,* an intervention must exceed the strong evidence threshold in all seven areas. To be considered *promising practice,* an intervention must exceed the promising evidence threshold in all seven areas.

Three panel members will independently review the outcome research related to a given intervention and independently rate each intervention on all seven criteria. Consensus in ratings will be achieved through consultation. The Panel will disseminate its overall rating, and in cases where interventions fail to achieve evidence-based practice or promising practice status, an analysis of deficiencies in the evidence base will be offered.

The seven domains and criteria are included below:

Domain 1. Measurement

Principle: Important academic, career, and/or personal/social outcomes are measured using reliable and valid instruments.

Strong evidence:

1. Outcome measures have established high reliability and validity characteristics.

2. Outcome measures are established to be appropriate for the population under study.

Promising evidence:

1. Reliability characteristics are evaluated in the study and show adequate reliability.

2. Logical argument supports the appropriateness of the measures for the population under study.

Domain 2. Comparison Groups

Principle: Comparison groups with adequate controls are included so that resulting group differences can be attributed to the intervention.

(Continued)

Table 4.2 (Continued)

Strong evidence:

1. Active comparison groups (alternative treatment) with adequate controls (attention, placebo) are included in an outcome study.

2. Initial group equivalence is assured through random assignment.

3. Group equivalence in mortality/attrition is established.

Promising evidence:

1. Groups equated through matching or statistical procedures (e.g., ANOVA) or strong pre-/posttest designs are used with adequate controls.

Domain 3. Statistical Analyses of Outcome Variables

Principle: Statistical analysis documents low probability of Type I error and potency of intervention.

Strong evidence:

1. Statistically significant finding using appropriate test.

2. Control for experiment-wise error rate.

3. Adequate N (number of participants in study).

4. At least a moderate effect size for critical outcome variables.

Promising evidence:

1. Statistically significant finding using appropriate test.

2. Control for experiment-wise error rate.

3. Adequate N.

4. At least a small effect size for critical outcome variables.

Domain 4. Implementation Fidelity

Principle: Intervention can be delivered with fidelity across contexts and is not contaminated by implementer.

Strong evidence:

1. Intervention is extensively documented (manual or protocol) so that it can be reliably replicated.

2. Intervention is delivered by multiple people with adequate training and checks for adherence to protocol.

Promising evidence:

1. Intervention is standardized and can be delivered across contexts.

2. Intervention is delivered by multiple people with adequate training.

Domain 5. Replication

Principle: The same intervention independently implemented with an equivalent population results in equivalent outcomes.

Strong evidence:

1. Independent evaluators find equivalent outcomes with a similar population.

Promising evidence:

1. Same evaluator finds equivalent outcomes with same population.

Domain 6. Ecological Validity

Principle: The intervention can be implemented effectively in a public school with consistent effects across all student subgroups or with known differences between student subgroups. Limitations of the generalizability of results are clearly explicated.

Strong evidence:

1. Study conducted in a diverse public school.

2. Outcomes are assessed across different subgroups of students or clearly specified as valid for a specific subgroup.

Promising evidence:

1. Study conducted in a private, laboratory, or charter school or in a public school with limited diversity.

Domain 7. Persistence of Effect

Principle: The intervention results in a lasting effect on an important outcome measure.

Strong evidence:

1. Treatment-comparison group differences are demonstrated to persist for a practically significant time period.

Promising evidence:

1. Treatment-comparison group differences are demonstrated to persist beyond the immediate implementation.

both are valuable contributors to understanding how best to develop every student's ability to be successful; and the process of using the research literature to determine which interventions and practices are most effective is the same in both domains. This combination of information creates an optimal opportunity for counselors to impact student outcomes, advocate for student achievement, and be leaders in the efforts to close achievement gaps (ASCA, 2003). Appendix B (see page 183) provides an overview of relevant outcome research findings, organized by domain and findings.

Research About the Impact of School Counseling Programs

There are few studies that look at the impact of school counseling programs in general, although such studies are critical for the field. Sink and Stroh (2003) completed a statewide study to determine whether the presence of a comprehensive developmental guidance (CDG) program impacted students' academic achievement test scores. They found that early elementary school students who attend the same school for three or more years do better academically when there is a CDG program, even if the program is not fully implemented. Additionally, students who remain in the same school for multiple years with a well-implemented CDG program obtain higher achievement test scores than students who attend schools without such programs.

Gysbers and Lapan and their colleagues in Missouri have completed two statewide studies of the effects of implementing CDG programs (Lapan, Gysbers, & Petroski, 2001; Lapan, Gysbers, & Sun, 1997). School data from the Missouri accreditation program were gathered to study the relationships between the level of CDG program implementation and a variety of student outcomes. These studies indicated that students in middle and high schools with more fully implemented CDG programs reported earning higher grades, having better relationships with teachers, and feeling greater satisfaction with school. Students in these schools were also more likely to report that education is relevant to later life, school is safe, and at the high school level, that career and college information was accessible.

Though these results are promising, the findings in these studies are correlational rather than causal. In other words, it is not clear that it was the implementation of the CDG program that was responsible for the positive outcomes found. It could just as well be, for example, that the schools that are fully implementing the CDG model were also implementing other educational programs that impact academic achievement. More complete guidance implementation and higher student achievement might both result from the schools' organizational structure, leadership, and/or personnel strengths rather than be causally related to each other. In all likelihood, given the complexity of both human behavior and educational outcomes, many interacting factors are responsible for the findings, including the school counseling programs.

Meta-Analytic and Comprehensive Reviews of Research Literature About School Counseling Interventions

Increasingly, meta-analytic reviews are being used to determine intervention effectiveness. Meta-analytic reviews combine a number of studies, which permits the computation of effect sizes for the intervention. The *effect size* (ES) reflects the distance between the experimental group's mean and the control group's mean, thus demonstrating the impact of an intervention (Sink & Stroh, 2006). An effect size of 0 (ES = 0.0) indicates that the mean of the average treatment group participant is the same as the mean of the average control group participant and thus that the intervention had no impact. If the ES = 0.7, the mean of the treatment group participants is at the 76th percentile of the control group, which suggests that the intervention is having an impact. In general, an ES of approximately 0.2 is considered a small effect size; ES = 0.5 is a medium effect size; and ES = 0.8 or larger is considered a large effect size (Cohen, 1988).

> ### meta-analysis
>
> a quantitative procedure for reviewing outcome research studies that estimates the potency of the effects of an intervention (effect size) and then compares and contrasts studies based on their characteristics

Once effect sizes are computed for all outcomes, studies can be compared and contrasted on a number of potentially interesting variables (such as counselor variables, student variables, types of outcomes, and settings). Reviewers can ask important questions such as, "Are older students more likely to benefit than younger students from a particular intervention?" The questions that can be answered by the meta-analytic review depend on the number, strength, and range of studies being reviewed. If there are a number of strong outcome studies related to different interventions, it is possible to compare the strength of effect across interventions to determine which intervention has the greatest impact.

School counseling does not yet have enough strong outcome studies to conduct meta-analytic reviews. However, school counselors may find meta-analytic reviews published in related professions to be very useful. For example, recent reviews of group counseling with children (Hoag & Burlingame, 1997), school-based career education (Evans & Burck, 1992), and school-based programs designed to reduce aggression (Wilson, Lipsey, & Derzon, 2003) would be helpful for identifying effective school counseling interventions. Meta-analytic reviews can be found through standard library researches and increasingly through online search engines such as Google Scholar (http://scholar.google.com/).

Meta-analytic reviews and summaries of research give us a broad picture of what research is being done and what the research findings in general are. Research reviews can be helpful in providing information about which practices have commonly been found to be effective.

Because a wide range of interventions is considered, it is easier to determine what seems to be the most effective use of time, as well as which kinds of interventions are most impactful. Whiston and Sexton (1998) completed the most comprehensive review of the K–12 school counseling outcome research literature to date. They summarized 50 outcome studies published between 1988 and 1995 and found modest research support for interventions in the areas of career planning, group counseling, social skill training, and peer counseling. Gerler (1985) completed a review of school counseling interventions at the elementary school level with a focus on teacher consultations, counseling, and classroom guidance interventions. In the studies he reviewed, classroom guidance was related to improvement in elementary school students' behaviors. St. Clair (1989) reviewed school counseling outcome research at the middle school level. The interventions reviewed were relaxation training, group counseling, and career programs. The outcomes that were measured included academic achievement and student behavior, self-concept, and attitudes. The results of this review indicated that school counseling interventions for students aged 12–14 can impact grades, shift occupational stereotypes, and reduce referral problems.

Wilson (1986) focused on interventions with low-achieving students and their parents to determine whether school counseling interventions are effective in boosting academic achievement as measured by grade point average. This review included 19 studies over a 25-year period. Summary information suggested that counseling interventions can have positive effects on academic achievement with this population. Prout and Prout (1998) completed a meta-analysis of research about counseling and psychotherapy in school settings and concluded that there was strong evidence that these interventions are effective in this context. A meta-analysis of primary prevention efforts in school (Baker, Swisher, Nadenichek, & Popowicz, 1984) found that, overall, these efforts have moderate success.

Research About Interventions for Academic Achievement

The links between school counseling interventions and academic achievement have not been well studied, but increasingly researchers are focusing on this concern. Family-based interventions are an effective way to support student learning, and there is considerable research indicating that family involvement in schools promotes student achievement (see Appendix B for a summary of relevant research). The group format is a useful way to provide specific students with more information about how to be successful academically and can provide important opportunities for underachieving students to address emotional concerns. The research evidence suggests that small groups can positively impact academic achievement, especially when combined with interventions at the classroom or individual level (Hoag & Burlingame, 1997). Findings about the impact of individual counseling on academic achievement have not been consistent, with some meta-analyses finding strong links and others finding only weak results. There is evidence that individual counseling can be a key component of multiapproach interventions for students who are academically at risk.

In sum, the research suggests that the most efficient and effective ways to impact student achievement are through whole-school, family-based, and classroom interventions. For students who need additional support, small groups can be beneficial. There are mixed research findings about the impact of individual interventions on academic functioning. Appendix B contains research references about these intervention areas.

Research About Interventions
for Career Development

School counselors can most effectively promote student career development at the school level by developing partnerships, teaming, and collaborating with other school personnel to integrate career education materials and opportunities into a variety of school activities and contexts and by ensuring that career education materials are available to all students. Working with families to support student career development is an effective way to promote positive student career outcomes, particularly when family interventions are integrated with other career development interventions.

Classroom interventions for career education are generally effective at impacting career outcomes (Evans & Burck, 1992). These activities are an important component of school counseling programs, as there may not be any other school person focusing on this aspect of student development. Most models of career education promote K–12 interventions, but there is little research about career interventions at the elementary level. Because some classroom-based career education curricula have been evaluated, it makes sense to use existing materials where possible rather than create new ones.

School counseling programs have historically delivered career development services through individual planning and advising rather than in small groups or classroom settings, and there is much stronger evidence that this way of providing information impacts student outcomes. School counselors have to become more efficient at delivering student services, however, so identifying ways to effectively convey career information in larger groups would benefit the profession.

Research Linking Career
Interventions to Academic Achievement

Evans and Burck (1992) did a meta-analysis of research about the impact of career education interventions on academic achievement. They found minimal effects for career education (mean ES = .16) on academic achievement as measured by grade point average. They found that research indicates that career education has slightly larger effects on academic achievement for younger students and when integrated into math and English classes.

Career education interventions seem to be relatively domain specific, in that they successfully impact knowledge about career decision making, career planning, career maturity, and career awareness but do not seem to significantly impact academic achievement in general. School counselors need to promote systemwide understanding of the critical value of career development as an end unto itself, not just as a means to academic achievement.

Research About Interventions
for Personal and Social Functioning[1]

In an early meta-analysis of 75 studies about individual counseling, Casey and Berman (1985) found an overall effect size of .71 on outcome measures such as social and global adjustment and cognitive skills. Prout and DeMartino (1986) only considered studies conducted in schools (n = 33), and found an overall effect size of .58 on outcomes such as behavior ratings, observed behaviors, problem-solving skills, grade point average, and cognitive abilities. In a meta-analysis of studies that analyzed individual interventions designed to decrease disruptive classroom behaviors (N = 99), Stage and Quiroz (1997) found an overall effect size of −0.78 (the negative number indicates that the behaviors decrease after the intervention, which is the intended direction).

Eder and Whiston (2006) provided suggestions for school counseling practice derived from meta-analytic research about child and adolescent counseling. They concluded that anxiety, fear, and phobias in children and adolescents are most effectively treated through systematic desensitization, modeling, reinforced practice, and cognitive behavioral interventions and that depressive symptoms are most effectively treated through cognitive behavioral interventions. Usually school counselors refer students with these kinds of symptoms to community service providers for ongoing counseling and therapy, but knowing what kinds of interventions are most likely to work supports effective consultation with families about what kinds of services to seek.

Classroom Interventions

Research has found that classroom interventions can positively impact aggressive behavior, anxiety, self-efficacy, and conflict-resolution skills. There has been mixed support for classroom interventions addressing self-esteem. Second Step (Grossman et al., 1997) has had the strongest research support of any social/emotional classroom intervention.

Group Counseling

Group counseling is the intervention of choice if the presenting problem is a more serious personal or social concern, as this mode of intervening is often an effective and efficient way to support student social and emotional development in schools. There has been considerable research, though much of it outside of school counseling, that found group counseling interventions can successfully impact these domains.

Individual Interventions

Individual interventions have been and will most likely continue to be an important school counselor service for students. Knowing what generally works with what kinds of social or emotional difficulties can help school counselors be more effective. Research about individual interventions in schools suggests that they can positively impact behaviors, learning, and overall functioning. In general, cognitive-behavioral interventions have consistently been found to be the most effective type of intervention, regardless of the presenting problem, the type of outcome being measured, and the clients' social context (Eder & Whiston, 2006).

Research Linking Social and Emotional Functioning With Academic Achievement

Historically, the research about the impact of counseling interventions has looked at social and emotional functioning alongside academic outcomes. Much of the research discussed above has found that many interventions impact both outcomes simultaneously (Casey & Berman, 1985; Eder & Whiston, 2006; Hoag & Burlingame, 1997; Hoagwood & Erwin, 1997; Shechtman, 2002). Relatedly, research in education about what factors impact learning has indicated that social and emotional functioning is a core variable in effective learning (Wang, Haertel, & Walberg, 1993). Students who are socially skilled are more successful academically, and those who have social, emotional, or behavioral difficulties are less likely to achieve in school (Wentzel & Caldwell, 1997).

One question as yet unanswered is whether social and emotional functioning can be removed from the overall construct of academic achievement or whether they are intrinsically connected in ways that preclude such a split. The Collaborative for the Academic, Social, and Emotional Learning (CASEL; Elias et al., 1997) is dedicated to promoting social and emotional learning for its own sake. They argue that promoting social and emotional functioning should be a crucial core goal for, and result of, the educational endeavor.

Interventions to improve students' social and emotional functioning, whether at the individual, group, class, school, or family level, are likely to impact academic functioning as well. Much of the research in these areas has not made distinctions between cognitive and emotional functioning because so many of the research findings have suggested that effective interventions almost always impact both. Information-processing research has suggested that the social/emotional and rational/analytical modes of processing are independent yet interactive (Howard, 2006) so that impacting one mode necessarily involves engaging the other, although the way that information gets encoded may differ.

How Can School Counselors Find Interventions That Will Work?

School counselors have very demanding professional lives and need efficient ways to find interventions that are related to the problem they need to solve, have proven effectiveness, and fit with the organization and culture of their schools and communities. Because school programs exist within the larger context of public schools, locating interventions that will work is best done as a team enterprise. In public schools, this typically involves the establishment of a research-based practice (RBP) team led by the counselor with members drawn from other school professionals who need to be involved in solving the problem at hand. Teams usually come into existence when a problem is identified, for example when bullying is recognized as a problem that needs to be addressed. While the initial identification of the problem may not come from school administration, administrative endorsement of and support for the work of the team needs to be in place and communicated broadly across the school. The charge of the RBP team should be to (a) identify where and how to intervene (done with the DBDM team if possible), (b) identify interventions and approaches that are both research-based and feasible, (c) recommend interventions to the administration and school community, and (d) develop an implementation evaluation plan to guide implementation and determine whether the selected interventions are working. Depending on the school, the DBDM (data-based decision making) team (described in Chapter 2) may become the RBP team, or the teams may involve different people.

Defining the Problem

It is often necessary for the RBP team to further define the problem they are charged to address because many problems stem from multiple causes. For example, in the scenario we discussed at the beginning of Chapter 2, a school counselor who was charged with finding out how to reduce detentions discovered that most detentions resulted from students' failure to do homework rather than from bad conduct. Moving directly to implementing interventions designed to improve student conduct would not have significantly addressed the problem. Teams should not begin identifying interventions until they have a clear idea of what is causing the problem, which hopefully has already been accomplished by the DBDM team. Depending on the work that has already been done, analysis of institutional data or gathering additional data may be necessary to achieve this end.

Identifying Interventions and Approaches

The two key requirements for the identification of appropriate interventions are that the interventions be research-based and feasible. A research-based intervention can only be expected to work if it can be implemented in the same way that it was in the study in which it was evaluated; this is referred to as *fidelity of treatment*. If fidelity cannot be accomplished because of local circumstances, there is no assurance that equivalent outcomes will be achieved. For example, in one school, the administration decided to adopt the Second Step violence prevention curriculum, although the teachers were unwilling to implement the curriculum themselves or surrender sufficient class time so that the school counselors could implement the curriculum as designed. The school counselors had to modify the curriculum to accommodate the allotted time, essentially eliminating the interactive activities designed to help students personalize and internalize learning. The deviation from the standard Second Step format was so severe that desired outcomes were not achieved. Thus, identifying an appropriate intervention needs to occur in two stages. Teams should first locate all the appropriate research-based interventions and then determine which can be implemented with fidelity in their setting.

There are several ways that RBP teams can locate research-based interventions:

1. Professional journals provide up-to-date research information. A number of professional panels and organizations evaluate

the outcome research base and distribute findings through Web sites and print media.

2. The National Panel for School Counseling Evidence-Based Practice has developed a set of criteria for assessing high-quality school counseling outcome research and is engaged in the continuous identification of research-based school counseling interventions (Carey & Dimmitt, 2006). The Panel disseminates its findings both online (www.cscor.org) and in print (see Carey et al., in press). Additional sources of information on research-based practices are contained in Table 4.1 on page 53.

3. Finally, RBP teams can consult research briefs prepared and distributed by the National Center for School Counseling Outcome Research.

Using the sources above, it is relatively easy for the RBP team to compile a descriptive list of research-based interventions that are appropriate for the given problem and student population. This list then needs to be evaluated for feasibility. Here the basic question is, "Can the intervention be implemented with fidelity in our school?" The team needs to take into account very pragmatic considerations such as cost, time required, compatibility with existing interventions and approaches, training requirements, compatibility with the school's mission and philosophy, and compatibility with parents' values and sensibilities. Ultimately, the intervention will need to be implemented within existing school structures and routines and will need the enthusiastic support of administrators, teachers, students, and parents. Based upon a feasibility analysis, the RBP team should narrow the list of possible research-based interventions to a very small number (three or fewer) that can be recommended to the administration and school community.

Recommending Interventions to the School Community

It is essential that the school principal and administration be actively involved in this phase of the process since they are entrusted with the responsibility of ensuring that school resources are invested in ways that yield returns in terms of enhanced student learning. Reviewing the final recommendations with the principal and school leadership team is typically a first priority. Next, it is important to present the analysis and recommendation of the RBP team to the school staff that will need to be involved and to collaborate with any relevant stakeholders to assure a successful implementation. The team will need to be prepared to communicate about the problem that is being addressed, the research support for each recommended intervention, the team analysis of feasibility issues for each intervention, and the general expectations of school staff regarding their responsibilities in preparing for, implementing, and evaluating the interventions. Feedback should be collected to determine school community buy-in. It is also wise to make a truncated presentation to a representative parent group to identify any potentially problematic issues. Finally, the team needs to summarize its findings and report its final recommendation to the principal and/or the school leadership team, who will ultimately be responsible for the decision about which intervention to implement.

Developing the Implementation and Evaluation Plan

After the decision is made about which research-based intervention will be implemented, the RBP team needs to develop an implementation action plan and an evaluation plan. The implementation plan needs to include specific task assignments with time lines and identify responsible parties for each task. The evaluation plan should include information on both the *formative evaluation* (how the team will know that the intervention is being implemented properly) and *summative evaluation* (how the team will know whether the intervention has the desired impact).

Summary

Outcome research provides evidence that an intervention is likely to be effective. Strong outcome studies provide better evidence because of the assurances they provide that an intervention really causes important changes in affect, behavior, and/or cognition and that the same positive results are likely to be seen across contexts. The field of school counseling does not (and cannot) generate all the necessary research that is needed in order to determine effective practice. School counselors may use much of the research to aid in effective consultation and referral, more than in direct service to students. While school counselors cannot read all the relevant research, with professional journals increasingly available online, access has never been easier. Summaries of research will continue to be disseminated by ASCA and by the National Center for School Counseling Outcome Research.

Counselor-led research-based practice teams are an efficient and effective way to (a) identify research-based interventions, (b) determine which research-based interventions are best for the particular school in which they will be implemented, and (c) organize successful implementation and evaluation of research-based intervention. While the ultimate beneficiaries of moving to an evidence-based practice approach will be the students who receive better services, working in an evidence-based practice mode will also enhance the professional standing of school counselors locally and nationally.

Note

1. School counseling uses the words personal/social, while education and psychology often use social/emotional. In this text, both terms will be used interchangeably.

5

Evaluating School Counseling Interventions and Programs

Consider two scenarios:

Scenario 1: *Derek is the head of a high school guidance program. A new principal requests that Derek conduct a program evaluation to determine whether the school counseling program is helping students. Money is tight and the principal needs to make some difficult staffing decisions. Derek contacts a professor from a local counselor education program. The professor designs program satisfaction surveys for students, teachers, and parents. The professor analyzes the surveys and prepares a lengthy report summarizing the findings. Derek is pleased that the majority of respondents are "Satisfied" or "Somewhat Satisfied" with most services. He shares the report with his principal.*

Scenario 2: *Derek is the head of a high school guidance program. As soon as a new principal is hired, Derek requests a meeting to (a) review the program's last periodic program evaluation, (b) review data that have been collected since that evaluation, and (c) begin planning for the next evaluation. He examines the 10 student competencies and five program goals that were* *identified as most important in the last program evaluation, and he analyzes the yearly results data gathered on these since that time. Derek summarizes the outcomes of the interventions that have been implemented since the last program evaluation and illustrates how the interventions have helped to solve important school problems. He then reviews the need for additional services and interventions that were identified in the last program evaluation and indicates how the program has used its resources to address these identified needs. Derek ends by suggesting what the program would do if additional resources could be made available and by outlining the important role he hopes the principal will play in the upcoming school counseling program evaluation.*

Scenario 1 reflects one of the typical ways evaluation is currently handled in school counseling practice. Rather than being integral to the program, evaluation is occasionally and episodically grafted onto the program to satisfy external demands for accountability. Low-quality evidence of effectiveness is produced in a pinch. Scenario 2 reflects an evidence-based practice approach to evaluation. Interventions are continuously evaluated, and program goals, priorities, and impact are periodically evaluated to improve the quality of services to students. High-quality evidence of effectiveness is available as a by-product of the evaluation-based program improvement process.

What Is Evaluation?

Confusion in both concept and terminology regarding evaluation is common. It is particularly important to distinguish clearly between evaluation and research. We define *evaluation* as the use of the scientific method (hypothesis testing) to improve local decision making by determining whether it was likely that implementing an intervention resulted in desired changes in behavior and performance. *Research,* on the other hand, we define as the use of the scientific method to determine whether an intervention brings about changes in affect, cognition, and/or behavior (see Chapter 1). While evaluation and research share a common method, they have very different purposes. Evaluation is used to improve decision making in a single setting or context, for instance in a particular school or district. Research is used to identify practices that are *theoretically* effective across settings and contexts; it is designed to be generalizable to other schools in other districts. If we can be confident that an intervention will have the same effects across different types of schools and student populations, we would say that the results are generalizable.

Researchers strive for strong designs that ensure internal and external validity. It is necessary to determine that the intervention under consideration, not other factors, causes the change in students' performance. It is also necessary to determine that the same effect observed in the outcome research is likely to occur in other settings. It is very serious and costly if researchers make a *false positive error*

> **evaluation**
>
> the use of the scientific method to improve local decision making by determining whether it was likely that implementing an intervention resulted in desired changes in behavior and performance

(saying that an intervention is effective when it actually is not). People all across the country would waste time, money, and effort implementing an intervention that would not help students. Therefore, research uses very conservative statistical criteria to determine whether treatment-control group differences can be said to be real and not due to chance.

In contrast, evaluation is used to determine whether it is likely that a given practice is effective in a specific setting. Generalizing results across settings is not necessary. The strong controls and design features that are required in research, while helpful, are not needed. Also, the cost of a false positive error is not as significant. Evaluation can legitimately use "weaker" designs and less conservative statistical criteria for determining significance because it does not seek to prove conclusively that the intervention and only the intervention caused the observed change in student performance. Evaluation helps to determine whether a practice should be continued, modified, or discontinued.

Programs and Interventions

Within the area of evaluation, it is important to distinguish between the evaluation of programs and the evaluation of specific school counselor activities (e.g., guidance curriculum) or interventions (e.g., group counseling, crisis counseling). Defining evaluation terminologies can be confusing, so we will begin by reviewing definitions. Consistent with *The ASCA National Model: A Framework for School Counseling Programs* (ASCA, 2003), we define the *school counseling program* as a program within the school that is responsible for the design, delivery, and evaluation of a set of school-based activities and interventions that facilitate all students' academic, career, and personal/social development; address problems that interfere with learning; and promote successful transitions.

The program consists of a number of components, some of which may be thought of as interventions and others as practices.

---

intervention

a deliberate, systematic process that develops desired behaviors, thoughts, and feelings or reduces undesired behaviors, thoughts, and feelings

---

practices

the mechanisms that guide the professional decisions that are made within the program and mechanisms that ensure effective connection of the program to other school subsystems and professional best practices

---

An *intervention* may be defined as a deliberate, systematic process that develops desired behaviors, thoughts, and feelings or reduces undesired behaviors, thoughts, and feelings. The program also includes components that may be thought of as *practices*, which we define as the mechanisms that guide the professional decisions that are made within the program and mechanisms that ensure effective connection of the program to other school subsystems and professional best practices. In *The ASCA National Model*, these mechanisms are described in the foundation, delivery system, management system, and accountability system sections.

Evaluation occurs at both the intervention level and the program level. At each level, different questions are answered and different procedures followed. In evaluating an intervention, it is necessary to determine whether it is likely that the desired changes occurred as a result of the implementation of the intervention. The following questions are answered:

- What was your desired student outcome?
- What data were you trying to impact?
- What did you do to develop desired behaviors, thoughts, and feelings or reduce undesired behaviors, thoughts, and feelings?
- Is there any evidence that your intervention contributed to improving students' knowledge, attitudes, or skills?
- Was there a shift in students' behavior in achievement or achievement-related data that might be correlated to this intervention?

In evaluating a program, it is necessary to determine whether the program's interventions are effective and then to ask several higher level questions, including the following:

- Is the program accomplishing its goals?
- Are all the programs' current interventions needed?
- Is the program delivering all the interventions that are needed?
- Does the program have sufficient resources?
- Is it using resources efficiently?
- Does the program have the necessary practices in place to make decisions related to directions, priorities, resource allocation, and personnel?

- Are the recipients of the program's services satisfied?
- Can the program demonstrate its impact and cost effectiveness?

In the rest of this chapter, we will explore the key concepts necessary to understand how to evaluate specific interventions, as well as the overall school counseling program. We will also identify the evaluation skills necessary to improve decision making at both the intervention and program levels.

Evaluating Interventions

Planning for Evaluation

Retrofitting an evaluation to an ongoing intervention is challenging. Therefore, it is valuable to plan an intervention evaluation before it is implemented. Planning involves choosing measures of outcomes, specifying a procedure for monitoring implementation, identifying an evaluation design, and selecting a data analysis approach. Planning also involves developing a schedule for data collection and identifying who will be responsible for which aspects of data collection. An intervention evaluation action plan, contains all of the above elements, which are explained in detail below (see pages 94–96 for a sample intervention evaluation action plan).

Outcome Measures

The first consideration in developing an intervention evaluation action plan is deciding what measures or instruments will be used to gather evidence that the intervention had its desired effects. This is more complicated than it sounds because it typically involves several layers of change that need to be measured. For example, an intervention that teaches study skills to enhance academic achievement assumes that

- students will learn the skills that are taught,
- students will apply the skills to their classroom learning after the training is over,
- enhanced application of these skills will result in more learning,
- students will perform better in classes over the school year, and
- students will perform better on the state achievement tests at the end of the school year.

For many school counseling interventions, there is not a direct link between the intervention and the ultimate desired change in behavior and performance (the achievement data we are trying to "move"). Therefore, different measures are appropriate at different points in the causal chain that links the intervention with the change in achievement data.

For simplicity's sake, it is helpful to conceptualize three levels of intervention outcomes: immediate outcomes, proximal outcomes, and distal outcomes (see Brown & Trusty, 2005). *Immediate outcomes* reflect the desired learning or behavior change that takes place as a consequence of the intervention and can be discerned from the learning objectives. *Proximal outcomes* reflect what happens when the students use what they learned to make the desired changes in school behavior. *Distal outcomes* reflect the ultimate desired changes in school performance. Another way to think of "proximal" and "distal" is to remember that the proximal outcome occurs first and is therefore closer in proximity to the intervention than is the distal, or more distant, outcome.

outcomes

immediate outcomes

the immediate effects of an intervention, usually measured by a posttest

proximal outcomes

the effects of an intervention on the specific outcomes the intervention is designed to address

distal outcomes

the effects of an intervention on more distant outcomes such as school behavior and/or achievement; the eventual change that is desired

"moving" the data

improving performance data by implementing an intervention that is expected to produce a change in the data

Figure 5.1 maps the links between (a) immediate, proximal, and distal outcomes; (b) process, perception, and results data; (c) competency attainment, achievement-related, and achievement data; and (d) immediate, intermediate, and long-range data.

If the need for an intervention has been determined by a data-based decision-making process, the distal outcome measure (the ultimate desired change) will typically be known. Most likely it will be student achievement or achievement-related results data that the intervention is intended to move. Interventions, for example, may be intended to enhance state test performance, increase graduation rates, reduce office referrals for fighting, or increase college applications. In order to consider an intervention effective, a measurable change in target data should follow the implementation. However, this is sometimes difficult to demonstrate because many school factors in addition to the intervention impact the distal outcome and related data.

Immediate Outcomes

The assessment of immediate outcomes reflects the specific learning objectives

Figure 5.1   The Relationships Among Levels of Outcomes and Categories of Data

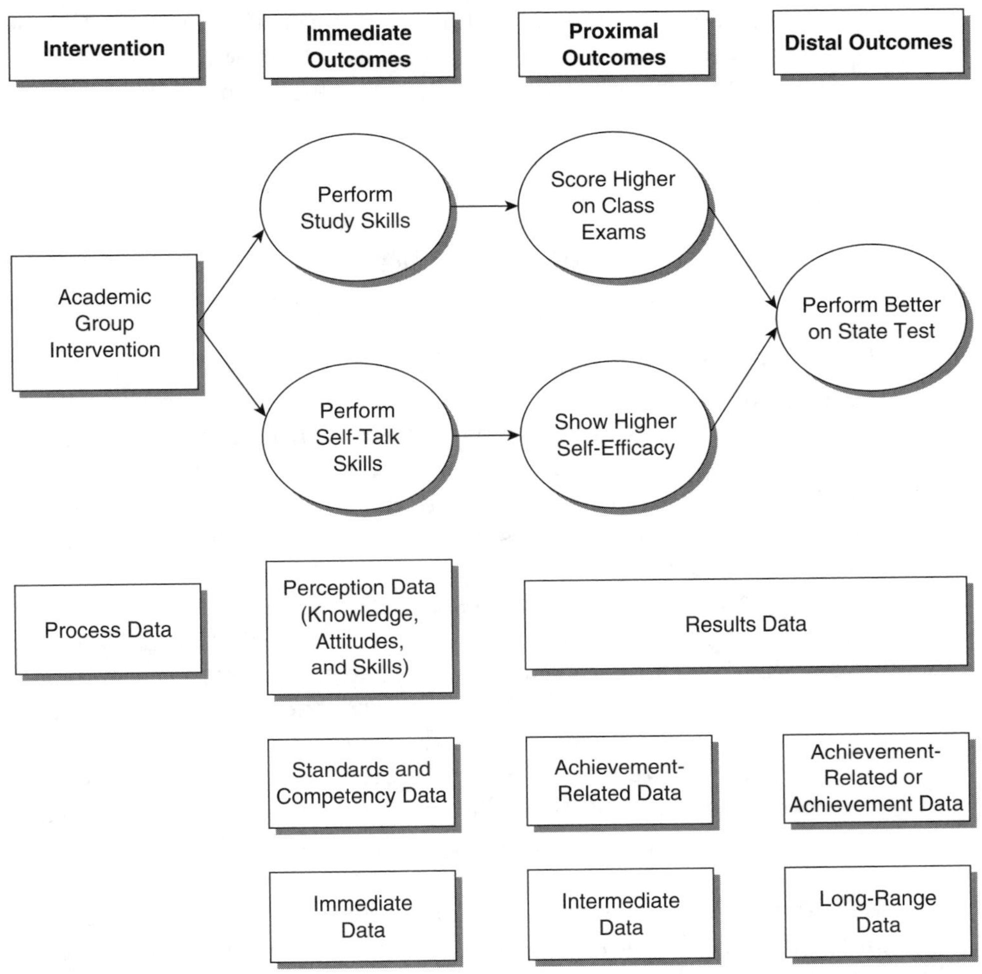

associated with a particular activity or intervention. Based on student scores on these measures, it should be possible to tell the extent to which they have changed in the ways intended by the intervention. Students may know things they did not know before, perform skills they did not have previously, or have changed beliefs or attitudes. Standardized interventions typically include evaluation instruments (e.g., tests, surveys, appraisals of performance) that measure the acquisition of knowledge and skills or changes in beliefs or attitudes that are directly related to the intervention. Often these instruments are given before and after the entire intervention or before and after specific components of the intervention. If an intervention does not come with evaluation instruments, it is necessary to develop ways to measure immediate outcomes using the instructional objectives of the intervention as a guide (see Chapter 7). With guidance curriculum interventions, the immediate outcomes correspond to the competencies (knowledge, attitudes, and skills) that the curriculum was designed to help students attain. At the end of the chapter (see page 94) is a sample evaluation of the Second Step guidance curriculum as implemented with fifth graders.

Proximal Outcomes

Measuring the proximal outcomes, or the specific outcomes or school behaviors an intervention was designed to address, is important and sometimes challenging. These outcomes are more multi-determined behaviors and outcomes such as using study skills, developing self-efficacy, making friends, managing anger, and increasing motivation for achievement. Difficulties arise because proximal outcomes are often not specified by the intervention and because even manualized interventions seldom include measures for these outcomes. Nevertheless, they are important to measure (when possible) because they are more responsive to the impact of the intervention than are distal measures and thus present a more sensitive test of the effectiveness of the intervention. Sometimes easily accessible proximal outcome measures are already available in schools, such as weekly conduct reports in elementary schools or scores on classroom tests. Often these proximal measures reflect achievement-related data that we identified in Chapter 3 and are readily available in school institutional data. Collaboration and teaming for this part of the work can be valuable. Colleagues in your building may be interested in gathering this data for other evaluation efforts. Sometimes the proximal outcomes that are of interest (e.g., student engagement, motivation, social skills, aggression) are not routinely measured by schools, in which case proximal outcome measures must be acquired. The time invested in searching both Internet and print resources for a measure that is reliable, valid, affordable, developmentally appropriate, and feasible (meaning that it does not require an inordinate amount of time to administer, complete, or score) is well worth the effort. The use of homemade measures is justified only when no other options exist.

In general, it will be easy to demonstrate a link between the intervention and its immediate outcomes, more difficult to demonstrate a link between an intervention and its proximal outcomes, and very difficult to demonstrate a link between an intervention and its distal outcomes. This increase in difficulty results because the farther you move down the causal chain, the more variables (other than

> **variable**
>
> In an experiment, the *independent variable* is manipulated by the experimenter and the *dependent variable* is measured.

the intervention) act and interact to influence the outcome measure. State achievement tests, for example, are influenced by so many factors that detecting the influence of a small-group intervention will be difficult. This does not mean that the group was not a valuable component of any improvement; it simply means it is a challenge to measure.

It is therefore much easier to evaluate an intervention that has already been thoroughly researched. Student Success Skills (Brigman & Webb, 2004), for example, has been shown to result in improvements in students' scores on Florida's state achievement test (Brigman & Campbell, 2003; Campbell & Brigman, 2005). If a school counselor implements Student Success Skills with fidelity, with a population similar to the one researched, and with a test similar to Florida's state achievement test, equivalent results can be expected. Evaluation can focus on the immediate outcomes to ensure that students are learning what Student Success Skills is designed to teach. Unfortunately, as noted in Chapter 4, few such empirically supported interventions exist.

It is important in the intervention evaluation action plan to include a fully developed map (see Figure 5.1) of the assumed relationships between the immediate, proximal, and distal outcomes. References to conceptual alignments with the other data terminologies we use in this book are presented as well. The links between outcome levels represent assumed causal relationships and may be based on known empirical relationships or logical relationships based on professional judgment and reasoning. As the school counseling outcome research base becomes better established, more of these links will be based on research.

Figure 5.1 contains a hypothetical map for an academic skills group intervention. This intervention was designed for students scoring in the lowest quartile on the state achievement test. It teaches specific study skills, and it also teaches students how to use "self-talk" to reduce self-defeating patterns of behavior and to keep themselves motivated and on task. At the immediate outcome level, it is important to know if students can perform the study skills and self-talk skills that they have been taught (perception data). At the proximal outcome level, it is important to know if students are applying these skills and if the application of these skills is resulting in more learning and higher self-efficacy (achievement-related data). Finally, at the distal outcome level, it is important to know that changes in classroom learning and self-efficacy are reflected in enhanced performance on the state achievement test (achievement data). Immediate outcome measures would be developed by the school counselors based upon the intervention's objectives. Proximal measures would be students' scores on class tests and on an academic self-efficacy instrument. The distal measure would be students' scores on the state achievement test.

It is extremely important to have a good sense of what outcomes an intervention can impact and to have ways to measure those outcomes collectively, even though finding good instruments to measure proximal outcomes is challenging. If you are measuring the wrong outcomes, or using an instrument that is not designed to measure the outcomes you are interested in looking at, the evaluation may fail to find results, even though the intervention itself may be effective. Your evaluation might just be measuring the wrong thing.

For example, an academic intervention could be expected to affect academic self-efficacy (beliefs in one's ability to impact one's learning and academic outcomes) but not general self-efficacy. Students' academic self-efficacy has been demonstrated by strong research to be related to high aspirations, productive school behavior, and academic achievement (Bandura, Barbaranelli, Caprara, & Pastorelli, 1996). In this example, one of the proximal outcomes you are hoping to impact is academic self-efficacy. Using an instrument designed to identify change in general self-efficacy may not find that the intervention had an effect because the intervention wasn't designed to impact efficacy in general in the first place. Precise identification of what proximal outcomes you think an intervention can impact, and an appropriate outcome measure, can assure greater alignment and better evaluation results.

Monitoring Implementation

Intervention evaluation plans ideally include a procedure for monitoring how well the intervention is being implemented. The quality of the evaluation results can only be as good as the quality of implementation. Two issues are of importance here: the dose of the intervention and the fidelity of the implementation. This aspect of evaluation is sometimes called *formative evaluation*. Implementation is monitored continuously so that if problems are detected, remedies can be immediately put in place.

The first aspect of formative evaluation is intended to ensure that all students are receiving an adequate exposure to the intervention (the "dose"). For simple interventions (e.g., a time-limited structured group), simple attendance data may suffice. For more complex interventions (e.g., career information systems), logs of student time spent on activities may be needed. Immediate outcome measures (e.g., pre- and postmeasures tied to weekly lessons) can also be analyzed to check whether students are learning what is intended. If all students are not getting the same exposure to the intervention, it is important to immediately determine what modifications need to be put in place to fix the problem. Continuing the implementation with unbalanced or unequal exposure will not result in the desired educational or evaluation outcomes.

Treatment fidelity refers to the level of match between the intervention as it is being implemented and the intervention as it was designed. Treatment fidelity also needs to be monitored as part of a formative evaluation. Unless the intervention is being implemented as designed, there is no

treatment fidelity
the level of match between the intervention as it is being implemented and the intervention as it was designed

reason to expect positive results. It is particularly important to closely monitor treatment fidelity when more than one person is responsible for implementing the intervention. A reasonable degree of standardization across implementers can be assured by adequate training, detailed implementation manuals, and periodic monitoring of actual sessions (audiotape, videotape, live peer supervision, or written logs).

Evaluation Design

Intervention evaluation uses the scientific method to generate evidence of effectiveness in order to improve local decision making. An evaluation design that compares the performance of a treatment group with an equivalent control group is desirable, though not always possible. Random assignment to treatment and control groups and the use of multiple groups (e.g., a nontreatment control and a placebo control) are rarely feasible in the public schools. Therefore, students in one classroom who experience the intervention can be compared with students in an equivalent classroom that do not. Or, students in one school who receive the intervention can be compared with students in another school who do not. Since we can't assume that the two groups are equivalent, it is important to gather data before the intervention (pretest) and after the intervention (posttest) whenever possible. In this way, we can know if the groups were different on the outcome measures before the intervention, and if so, we can compare the groups in terms of how much they change.

Often data cannot be gathered from a specific comparison group. If the district routinely collects distal outcome data on achievement, attendance, or discipline, comparisons can be made to district or school data. For example, students participating in an intervention can be compared with all students in the district in terms of their attendance rates. It is often feasible to use district data to generate an "artificial" comparison group. A group of students participating in an intervention can be compared on some performance measure with an equal-sized group of students determined to be equivalent on important demographic measures and selected from across the district. The most straightforward procedure would be to match each treatment group student with a control group student. Matching should be based on important factors that might affect the outcome of the intervention (e.g., sex, grade, English language learner status, special education status, racial/ethnic group, free/reduced lunch status, achievement test quartile). The two groups can then be compared on an outcome measure. If a college transition intervention is effective, for example, more students in the treatment group should transition to two- and four-year colleges than a matched group of students from across the district.

In many cases, a two-group design is not possible. If it is not, the best alternative is a one-group design that compares students' performance before and after an intervention. Ideally, outcome data will be gathered before and after the intervention or activity to determine whether change occurred.

Schedule for Data Collection

Often, the most difficult part of most school-based evaluations is collecting the evaluation data. An intervention evaluation plan should include detailed information on when each piece of data will be collected and who is responsible for its collection. Data collection needs to be monitored closely to make sure that it is indeed happening.

Evaluating Programs

Thus far we have been focusing on evaluation approaches for specific interventions. Now we turn to the issue of how to evaluate the school counseling program. Considerable variability in the nature of school counseling programs currently exists. Many school districts consider school counselors to be reactive service providers who "do whatever needs to be done." In such districts, the word "program" may not even be an accurate way to describe the situation. To say that there is a school counseling program present is to say (a) that there is a recognizable subsystem of the school that has both an organized set of interventions, curriculum activities, and services that are designed to accomplish specified goals and (b) that professional decision-making structures are in place to plan, manage, and evaluate its work. Programs require resources, and evaluation is necessary to determine if maximum benefits are accruing from resource investments and if resource levels are adequate for program functioning. While many program evaluation data-gathering practices occur continuously, a formal program evaluation is a periodic event, occurring every five to seven years.

It is also important to consider whether or not a school counseling program exists only at the level of the school or also at the level of the district. Most small districts and many large districts do not have district level school counseling leadership and coordination. In such districts, individual schools may have school counseling programs, but the district does not. Evaluation must therefore be conducted at the school level. In other districts, both building level and district level programs exist, and considerable effort and resources are invested in district level leadership and coordination of the school counseling activities. An evaluation in such a district would include evaluation of the program at both levels.

Presence of Best Practice Program Elements

Given the variability in the nature of school counseling programs, an important starting place for a program evaluation is an assessment of the extent to which the program elements that are considered to reflect "best practices" are present. The ASCA National Model for School Counseling Programs (ASCA, 2003) is the current standard for program best practices.

There are several approaches that can be used to assess whether a given program has implemented best practice elements. A self-study using the Recognized ASCA Model Program (RAMP) application (available online from ASCA at www.schoolcounselor.org) is very helpful. The RAMP application requires documentation of the critical elements of an ASCA National Model program (e.g., mission, competencies and indicators, school counseling program goals, results reports) and provides scoring rubrics to help raters determine the quality of implementation of each element. The process requires investment of effort and is probably most helpful where a program is fully elaborated and is striving for excellence.

The ASCA National Model also contains a program audit that helps school counselors determine the extent to which a program has implemented all of the components in the ASCA National Model. Each year, school counselors review the progress toward full implementation and revise program goals accordingly.

For programs that are less fully elaborated, the School Counseling Program Implementation Survey (SCPIS; on page 86) is probably more useful. The SCPIS is an 18-item self-assessment tool developed by the National Center for School Counseling Outcome Research (CSCOR) that is keyed to important ASCA National Model elements and associated professional standards. Raters are asked to determine whether each element (e.g., "The program has a set of clear, measurable student learning objectives and goals established for academic, personal/social skills, and career development") is best characterized as *Not Present, Development in Progress, Partly Implemented,* or *Fully Implemented.* The SCPIS should be completed by several raters to gather a range of perceptions and then combined and contrasted. In a rather short time, an accurate picture can be obtained of the extent to which school counseling best practice elements are present. The SCPIS can tell much about the extent to which your program practices are consistent with professional wisdom, but it cannot say anything meaningful about the effectiveness or impact of the program.

Program Impact

Two areas of impact can be documented in an evaluation: (a) the extent to which the program has provided general and targeted interventions and services to students, parents, and teachers; and (b) the extent to which these interventions and services produced positive cognitive, affective, or behavioral change in students. Accurate documentation of the provision of services to various constituencies requires that careful records of contact be kept (as should be the case with any program that is continuously monitoring its impact). For evaluation, these data just need to be compiled. If such records are not available, estimates can be obtained by surveying students, parents, and teachers about their participation in the various aspects of the school counseling program (a sample parent survey is on page 88). In the ASCA National Model, this type of data is called "process data." Disaggregating participation rates by important demographic variables (e.g., student sex, race/ethnicity, free/reduced lunch status, English language learner status) can yield very important information about which groups of students, parents, and teachers are being served well and where targeted outreach may be necessary.

School Counseling Program Implementation Survey
Please rate each statement below in terms of the degree to which it is currently implemented in your school's counseling program. Circle your response using the following rating scale: 1 = Not Present; 2 = Development in Progress; 3 = Partly Implemented; 4 = Fully Implemented
1. A written mission statement exists and is used as a foundation by all counselors.   1   2   3   4
2. Services are organized so that all students are well served and have access to them.   1   2   3   4
3. The program operates from a plan for closing the achievement gap for minority and lower income students.   1   2   3   4
4. The program has a set of clear measurable student learning goals and objectives established for academic, personal/social skills, and career development.   1   2   3   4

5. Needs assessments are completed regularly and
   guide program planning.   1   2   3   4

6. All students receive classroom guidance lessons
   designed to promote academic, social/personal,
   and career development.   1   2   3   4

7. The program ensures that all students have
   academic plans that include testing, individual
   advisement, long-term planning, and placement.   1   2   3   4

8. The program has an effective referral and
   follow-up system for handling student crises.   1   2   3   4

9. School counselors use student performance data
   to decide how to meet student needs.   1   2   3   4

10. School counselors analyze student data by
    ethnicity, gender, and socioeconomic level to
    identify interventions to close achievement gaps. 1   2   3   4

11. School counselor job descriptions match
    actual duties.   1   2   3   4

12. School counselors spend at least 80% of their
    time in activities that directly benefit students. 1   2   3   4

13. The school counseling program includes
    interventions designed to improve the school's
    ability to educate all students to high standards. 1   2   3   4

14. An annual review is conducted to get
    information for improving next year's programs.   1   2   3   4

15. School counselors use computer software to

    a. access student data,   1   2   3   4
    b. analyze student data, and   1   2   3   4
    c. use data for school improvement.   1   2   3   4

16. The school counseling program has the resources
    to allow counselors to complete appropriate
    professional development activities.   1   2   3   4

17. School counseling priorities are represented on
    curriculum and education committees.   1   2   3   4

18. School counselors communicate with parents to
    coordinate student achievement and gain
    feedback for program improvement.   1   2   3   4

High School Parent Survey

School Counseling Program Review

Thank you for taking the time to answer the questions in this survey. Your honest response to all questions will assist in the review of the school counseling program. All responses will be kept confidential.

What is the name of the school your child attends?

_____

Please circle the response that best answers each question:

| How many years has your child attended this school? | | | 1   2   3   4   5 |

What is your ethnicity?

African   Asian   Hispanic   Native   White   Other
American   American
                                                         _____
                                                         (please specify)

Do you know who your child's current
school counselor is?   Yes   No

Approximately how many times has your
child reported meeting with the school
counselor while at this school?   Never   1–2   3–4   5–6   7+

Approximately how many times have you
spoken with your child's school counselor? Never   1–2   3–4   5–6   7+

Please circle the number that best reflects your opinion:

1 = strongly   2 = disagree   3 = neither agree   4 = agree   5 = strongly
disagree   nor disagree   agree

---

1. I believe my child feels comfortable meeting
   with the school counselor.   1   2   3   4   5

2. The school counselor has helped my child to
   select appropriate courses.   1   2   3   4   5

3. The school counselor has not been helpful to
   my child during the process of scheduling
   or changing courses.   1   2   3   4   5

4. The school counselor has helped my child
   with personal and/or school problems.   1   2   3   4   5

5. The school counselor has helped my child to
   think about his or her goals after graduation
   from high school.   1   2   3   4   5

6. The school counselor provided information
   to my child about careers and the
   world of work.   1   2   3   4   5

7. The school counselor has not helped my child with future educational planning, college selection, and placement.   1   2   3   4   5

8. My child has participated in classroom or small-group programs covering topics such as study skills, violence prevention, and peer pressure.   1   2   3   4   5

9. The school counselor has provided services that have been helpful to my child.   1   2   3   4   5

10. The school counselor is not available to me when I have questions.   1   2   3   4   5

11. I feel satisfied with the work school counselors are doing.   1   2   3   4   5

12. I believe the school counselors work cooperatively with administrators, teachers, and other staff.   1   2   3   4   5

13. The school counselor is knowledgeable about services outside of the school system.   1   2   3   4   5

14. The school counselor has helped my child to develop socially, emotionally, and academically.   1   2   3   4   5

15. The school counselor believes my child can succeed.   1   2   3   4   5

16. The school counselor has been an effective advocate for my child.   1   2   3   4   5

Please list what you believe to be the most important activities of the school counselors.

_____

_____

_____

Please list the most significant strengths that currently exist within the school counseling program.

_____

_____

_____

Please list the most significant weaknesses that currently exist within the school counseling program. What would you change?

_____

_____

_____

Thank you again for taking the time to complete this survey.

Ultimately the strongest evidence of the impact of a school counseling program is the documentation of student outcomes (called "results data" in the ASCA National Model). Combining individual intervention evaluations is one valuable way to gain information about school counseling program impact on student outcomes. If the program's major interventions have been evaluated, immediate, proximal, and distal student outcome results will be available. If the need for the intervention was established using a data-based decision-making process, the distal outcome results should speak to the contribution of the school counseling program to school goals and priorities. For example, in a highly functioning school, a school data team might determine that bullying needs to be addressed in order to facilitate student learning and development. A team led by the school counselor would then identify a research-based approach to solve this problem. An intervention evaluation would document that this approach decreased bullying behavior, reduced office referrals for fighting, and increased students' perceptions that the school has a safe climate. These evaluation results, aggregated with other intervention evaluations, document both the impact of the intervention on students and the contribution of the program to the effectiveness of the school.

In addition to using information from intervention evaluations, evaluation of a program should include outcome data linked to the attainment of the most important student competencies and program goals. One of the major advantages of operating from a competency-based set of student learning objectives and/or setting specific program goals is that it is possible to know if the program is effective. A competency is a measurable statement about what students should know or be able to do. A program goal is a measurable statement about a desirable state toward which the program is willing to devote resources. "All students will be able to identify effective study skills and accurately describe the condition under which they learn best" is an example of a competency. "The number of credit-deficient students in the freshman class will decrease by 10%" is a goal. Both competencies and goals are established in order to guide program decision making and typically reflect program outcomes related to the learning of, or benefits for, all (or most) students. School counseling programs typically have too many competencies and goals to evaluate effectively. Remember, data related to these will need to be collected and analyzed continuously. It is necessary to prioritize the most important competencies or goals to be measured.

Each year a decision needs to be made about how many program components will be measured and how many new goals will be set. Setting attainable goals regarding measurement creates success and maintains motivation for the process. This will be unique for each person and setting, depending on your skills and what is happening in your building. For some school counselors, starting by measuring one outcome or intervention is enough. Ask yourself, "What are the most important measurable student competencies and the most important measurable goals for the school counseling program for the next five years?" Then rank these, starting with the most important. Important stakeholders (parents, teachers, administrators, and students) should be included in the process that answers this question. Structured surveys, focus groups, and/or interviews can be used to generate initial ideas, and a process that gets feedback on draft competencies and goals from the whole school community is advisable. If taken seriously, this process will ensure that the competencies and goals that are used to guide the program and document its effectiveness are connected to the values of the school community and needs of the school. An effective program evaluation will both prioritize student competencies and program goals for the next five-year cycle and document the attainment of competencies and goals from the last five-year cycle.

"Customer" Satisfaction

In addition to assessing impact, it is also useful to systematically gather information about the degree to which the program's various constituencies are satisfied with existing interventions and services and their level of desire for additional interventions and services. It is generally better to have separate "satisfaction" and "needs assessment" surveys rather than combine the two into one long survey. People are more likely to complete a shorter survey, and it may be more appropriate to gather satisfaction and needs assessment data from different groups. For example, senior high school parents may be the best group to survey regarding satisfaction with an existing program because they have had the opportunity to experience the full range of services and interventions. Freshman and sophomore high school parents may be the best group to complete a needs assessment because they have the most vested interest in seeing new interventions and services in place. An example of a high school parent satisfaction survey that was developed by CSCOR is located on page 88 of this chapter.

Unfortunately, there are very few needs assessment instruments linked to standards available to school counselors. The Intermediate Elementary School Students Counseling Needs Survey (IESCNS; Thompson, Leosch, & Seraphine, 2003) was developed as a way to measure students' beliefs (grades 4–6) about the school counseling program in their school. Many schools do brief exit surveys with graduating seniors to get a sense of what program components students found most helpful. A formal check with teachers and administrators in the building about what they believe to be the most effective or useful program components is a good way to both get their ideas and to unobtrusively disseminate information about the work of the school counseling program.

In addition, Appendix A contains an example of a high school needs assessment survey that was designed to collect needs assessment data from students, parents, and teachers. This survey is particularly useful because items are organized according to career, academic, and personal/social domains and because the items reflect measurable competencies. It can serve as a model for the development of a satisfaction survey as well.

Again, disaggregating satisfaction and needs assessment data by important demographic variables (e.g., student sex, race/ethnicity, free/reduced lunch status, English language learner status, special education status) can yield very important information about which groups of students, parents, and teachers feel they are being served well and where new targeted interventions and services may need to be developed and implemented.

Using External Experts in School Counseling Reviews

As is evident, a good program evaluation requires a major investment of time and energy. It also requires skill sets that many school counselors have not yet fully developed. Many programs use external evaluators to conduct or assist with program evaluations. Schmidt (1996) has presented several advantages for relying on external experts, including his beliefs that external experts may add broader perspectives that could benefit progress and that external experts may bring more objectivity to the evaluation process so that collected data is more reliable and valid. External evaluators can also be engaged to help answer specific evaluation questions (Schmidt, 2003), such as whether hiring an additional counselor would improve program outcomes.

There is an important role for external consultants in school counseling program evaluation, and we agree with Schmidt (2003) that it is helpful to have external experts who can often conduct objective evaluations with an outsider's perspective. We strongly believe that it is a mistake, however, to use an external evaluator to conduct the program's regular five- to seven-year evaluation. As noted above, a good program evaluation is a tool that allows school counselors to look at the evidence they have for their program's effectiveness and to modify the program accordingly. As is also obvious, while a thorough program evaluation only occurs every five to seven years, it relies on data that are collected continuously by the school counselors throughout that period.

An evaluation expert's time is best used to help design and implement a program evaluation system that is itself an integral part of the school counseling program. Despite the fact that evaluation is a critical program improvement function, few school counselors are actively engaged in evaluation activities (Fairchild, 1993; Fairchild & Zins, 1986). All of the authors have been regularly asked by districts and schools to conduct program evaluations of school counseling programs. Typically this request has resulted from a district leader (superintendent or school board member) wanting evidence that school counselors are doing something beneficial for students. Sometimes this request has come from school counselors who feel under fire and want to produce evidence that their program is effective. In almost every instance, these programs have not collected any intervention evaluation data or developed the structures (e.g., prioritized measurable student competencies and program goals) that would permit the collection of program evaluation data. At such times, we feel the same way a tax accountant must feel when someone shows up on April 14 with a shoe box full of cancelled checks and receipts. The accountant must want to say, "We can produce a tax return in a day, but what you really need are the financial skills to keep track of your money and make sure that it is invested wisely and is working for you 365 days a year!" Similarly, the best use of an external program evaluator's expertise is the expansion of local school counselor evaluation skills and the development of a systematic approach to evaluation that includes both the continuous evaluation of interventions and services and the periodic evaluation of the program as a whole.

Summary

A thoughtful, planned approach to evaluation of interventions and programs creates valuable evidence that school counselors are making a difference for students. It allows us to know with greater certainty that we are doing what works, spending our time and resources effectively, and truly supporting student achievement and success. Effective ongoing evaluation inherently generates data that can be used for several purposes, both within and outside of the school counseling program.

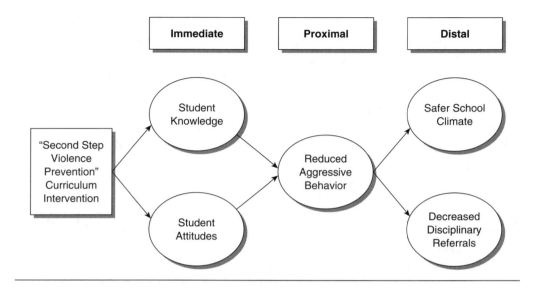

Sample Intervention Evaluation Action Plan: Evaluation of Second Step Violence Prevention Curriculum (Fifth Grade)

Outcome Map

Second Step is expected to increase student knowledge and change student attitudes. This change in knowledge and attitude is expected to result in a reduction in students' aggressive behavior. The cumulative effect of reducing aggressive behavior will be an increase in students' perceptions that the school climate is safe and a related decrease in office referrals for violent and aggressive behavior. Second Step will be implemented in the fall in two of the school's four fifth grade teams.

Outcome Measures

A. Immediate outcome measures:
    1. Second Step Grade 5 Knowledge Assessment (first session and last session)
    2. Second Step Elementary School Attitude Survey (first session and last session)

B. Proximal outcome measures:
    1. Teacher Checklist (6 items—measures proactive and reactive aggression; Dodge & Coie, 1987)

C. Distal outcome measures:
    1. School discipline referral forms, number of referrals for aggressive or violent behavior
    2. Annual School Climate Survey (school safety items)

3. Planning involves methods for monitoring implementation, evaluation design, and data analysis approach. Planning also involves the development of a schedule for data collection and an identification of who is responsible for which aspects of data collection.

Monitoring Implementation

The social studies teachers will administer Second Step in two fifth grade teams. The school counselor will train teachers, monitor the implementation, and evaluate the outcomes. After training, the counselor will consult with the teachers each week to review progress and daily logs summarizing sessions. Teachers will document Second Step lesson completion and track student attendance. Implementation problems will be addressed in these weekly meetings.

Evaluation Design

A two-group evaluation design will be used. Students from two teams (treatment group) will participate in Second Step. Students from the other two teams (control group) will not.

Data Collection

A. Baseline distal outcome data:
Fourth grade disciplinary referral forms and student School Climate Surveys, gathered by the school counselor from institutional data the spring of the year prior to implementation

B. Immediate outcome data:
The Second Step Grade 5 Knowledge Assessment and Second Step Elementary School Attitude Survey, gathered by a teacher from each treatment and control group team from students the days of the first and last lessons

C. Proximal outcome data:
The Aggressive Behavior Teacher Checklist, gathered by the school counselor from a teacher from each treatment and control group team two weeks prior to the start of Second Step implementation and four weeks after cessation of the implementation.

t tests

dependent *t* test

a statistical test that indicates whether the means, taken from the same group at two different times or under two different conditions (e.g., a group of students measured before and after an intervention) are so different that it is unlikely to result from random variation in group means

independent *t* test

a statistical test that indicates whether the means of two distinct groups (e.g., a group of students who have experienced an intervention versus a group who have not) are so different that it is unlikely to result from random variation in group means

D. Posttest distal outcome data:
   Fifth grade disciplinary referral forms and student School Climate Surveys, gathered by the school counselor from institutional data the spring after intervention implementation

Statistical Analysis

Changes in scores will be computed for both immediate and proximal measures (posttest minus pretest), using t tests to contrast scores. For distal outcome measures, School Climate Scale safety items from the spring prior to the intervention evaluation will be contrasted with both treatment and control group scores from the following year using a t test. Numbers of disciplinary referrals for violence and aggression from the spring prior to the intervention evaluation will be contrasted with equivalent data from after the intervention.

Expected Results

When compared with control group students, treatment group students will show greater gains in knowledge and change in attitude (immediate outcome) and a larger decrease in aggressive behavior in the classroom (proximal outcome). Compared with baseline outcome data from the prior year, fewer disciplinary referrals for violent or aggressive behavior will occur for fifth graders after the intervention, and both treatment group and control group students will rate the school climate higher in safety than they did the previous year.

6

Action Research and Collaborative Partnerships

Consider two scenarios:

Scenario 1: *Susie, a high school counselor, is implementing a new program for incoming ninth graders to support them during the transition to high school. Her department head has asked Susie to evaluate the first year of the program to see if it has an impact on the ninth grade dropout rate. At the end of the year, Susie uses her school data system to gather existing data about the dropout rate for the current ninth graders and compares it with the previous year's rate when she wasn't doing her program. The data show that more ninth graders did move on to tenth grade and fewer students dropped out. Susie reports this information to her department head and principal.*

Scenario 2: *Susie, a high school counselor, is implementing a new program for incoming ninth graders to support them during the transition to high school. She wants to know whether the interventions are having the impact she intends. Susie calls her nearest counselor education program and asks if they have a graduate student who could assist with an action research study. She asks several ninth grade teachers, an assistant principal, and some seniors in the school to work with her to develop an assessment plan for her transition program. The graduate student helps Susie and her colleagues find a good assessment instrument about school involvement. Susie and the assistant principal use the school data system to gather existing data about the* *dropout rate for the current ninth graders, and they compare it with the rate of the previous year when Susie wasn't doing her program. The action research team develops a survey for teachers to determine whether they saw a difference in student knowledge, motivation, and study skills. The school data show that more ninth graders did move on to tenth grade and that fewer students dropped out during ninth grade. An assessment of student learning and the teacher survey find that both students and teachers believed that the intervention helped to create better school connection and success. The student assessment indicates that the ninth graders did not retain the information presented about graduation requirements, so Susie meets with the action research team to identify ways to improve this part of the content. Susie reports all of this information to her department head and principal.*

Action research is a valuable and powerful way to use data to improve practice. Systematically collecting information about what is happening, evaluating the effectiveness of interventions and procedures, and disseminating the results helps school professionals become more intentional and hence more successful in supporting children's learning. At the school level, working collaboratively to improve practice builds community, develops understanding of the work of the school counseling program, and improves skills. At the national level, action research adds to the research base that the school counseling profession desperately needs (Dimmitt, Carey, McGannon, & Henningson, 2005; Rowell, 2006; Whiston, 2002). Action research is an opportunity to develop best practices and to demonstrate that the work we do makes a difference.

What Is Action Research?

Action research is a self-appraisal of current practice in which the practitioner asks questions, gathers data relevant to that question, reflects on the process and evidence, and determines a course of future action based on the findings (Ferrance, 2000). Some assumptions of action research (Watts, 1985) are that

- we work best on problems that are self-identified;
- we are more effective when encouraged to examine and assess our own work and to consider ways of working differently;
- we do our best work when we collaborate; and
- working with colleagues aids us in our professional development.

Like all research, action research follows the scientific method, which consists of identifying a question that needs answering, developing hypotheses about the answers to the question, gathering relevant data, and then analyzing and interpreting the data to see whether they support the hypotheses and answer the initiating question (Kerlinger, 1972). Action research adds a valuable additional step to the process, which is *taking action or making changes based on the research findings.* The purpose of action research is to learn more about what people are doing in a specific setting and then use the research results to improve practice in the context where the research occurred (Mills, 2000). Ideally, action research is a cyclical process whereby the answers found generate new questions and ideas that are then also evaluated, creating an ongoing engagement in generating information about what we are doing.

Action research is usually a study of one's own work, with a focus on practical issues (Creswell, 2002). Because it is conducted by school personnel who are not academic researchers, action research is less formal and more subjective than other types of research. The action research process encourages school counselors and educators to reflect on, evaluate, and improve their own understanding, skills, values, and knowledge. Ideally, it helps to bridge the gap between what people are doing and their vision of what school counseling and education in general can be (Mills, 2000; Rowell, 2005).

A key component of action research is collaboration, which helps to create an inclusive environment wherein the participation of many people (counselors, teachers, administrators, parents, and students) enriches and expands the potential for positive and empowering change (Rowell, 2006). Involving many stakeholders in a research process helps them become aware of both the challenges and the opportunities that exist in a given context. Creating an environment that encourages questioning and active engagement in intentional educational practice reduces blame and creates greater acceptance of new ideas.

The data collected in an action research project may be about any number of factors: how a particular school system or program operates, what students are learning, what behaviors impact on the learning process, or how an intervention impacts students (Creswell, 2002). Additionally, in some action research, the explicit goal is to empower and emancipate people from inequitable or unproductive educational processes (Kemmis & Wilkinson, 1998; Stringer, 1996). School counseling action research in particular can help counselors build connections in their schools and communities, meet the increasing demand for demonstration of accountability, and evaluate practices to ensure effective programs (Rowell, 2005, 2006).

Sometimes it can be challenging to understand what the differences are between a program or intervention evaluation and action research. In many ways, they are quite similar, especially if the evaluation is done well. Action research by definition is about at least one particular question, which is usually linked to research that has been done already. Evaluation efforts may link to existing research and may have a particular question, but they are mostly concerned with how something is working in a specific setting. Action research projects are usually larger than evaluation projects, often involve more people, and may use more methods and instruments for gathering data. Historically action research has a strong political orientation, involving the empowerment of those involved in the process of generating knowledge about practice and taking action based on findings. This can happen with evaluation, but it is not the explicit goal.

Action Research Partnerships

By definition, action research is conducted in collaboration with school colleagues, universities, community partners, parents, and students. Some school counselors do action research projects with science or social studies teachers and their students as part of the academic curriculum. The project then meets multiple needs for student learning, for meeting state curriculum standards regarding research knowledge, for building connections through the school, and for evaluating educational and counseling interventions. Collaborative research partnerships are one way that school counselors, educators, and school counselor education programs can more effectively and efficiently help all students to be successful, move toward evidence-based practice, and become proactive rather than reactive regarding program development (Rowell, 2005, 2006).

Equally importantly, collaborative research partnerships link theory and practice in ways that enhance the educational process (Hursh, 1995). When practice informs theory and theory shapes practice, the educational experiences of students at every level are improved and the potential for ongoing learning and understanding is increased. The educational practices and goals, organizational structures, and curriculum content that have now become common practice are the outcomes of continuing political and philosophical dialogue. Conversations about and evaluation of such practices and structures need to be ongoing (Hursh, 1995). All too often practices happen in schools because "that's how it's always been done." Action research allows for thoughtful reflection of institutionalized practice, with support for continuing what is working and a challenge to discontinue what is no longer effective. As our culture changes and students' needs shift in response to those changes, schools need to adjust accordingly. A culture of inquiry, wherein questions are encouraged and self-reflection is expected, enhances the experiences of all school community members. Action research partnerships are an effective way to proactively and thoughtfully engage in that change process.

Hursh (1995) also points out that connecting theory and practice reduces the school-university split. Collaborative research partnerships are an effective method of examining both school counseling theory and practice because school counselor education programs and school counselors can work together to make sure that theoretical understanding and actual practice are linked and mutually informative. When counselor education faculty do research with school counselors, they gain information about what is actually working and what is getting in the way of enacting best practices in specific school settings. Understanding the practical application of theory helps counselor educators become more effective in their training processes and, in turn, enriches the training experiences of school counseling graduate students. In research partnerships, school counselors gain knowledge about research, evidence-based practices, and resources, as well as support in the research process in their own buildings. With the increasing focus in education on documenting student achievement and the use of evidence-based practice, research partnerships can meet several needs simultaneously (Rowell, 2005; Thomas, 2005).

Another benefit of research partnerships is the increase in mutual value and respect for colleagues' work. All too often school counselors and counselor educators work in relative isolation. When we find out what others are doing, everyone's knowledge and range of potential action increases. Sharing ideas, resources, and evidence of best practices benefits all.

Why Conduct Action Research?

Action research allows school counselors, teachers, and administrators to evaluate programs and interventions in their own contexts. Practices can change immediately and in a continuous manner as the data are collected and analyzed. For this reason, it is particularly suitable for educational settings.

In school counseling in particular, the critical need for research (Dimmitt et al., 2005; Rowell, 2006; Whiston, 2002), and especially for research which demonstrates counselor efficacy (Whiston, 2002), points to the need for methods such as action research that can provide information as quickly as possible about effective practices. Greater collaboration between practitioners and university-based researchers would allow the field of school counseling to generate more relevant research for practice and greater awareness of the potential of research to improve school counseling programs (Rowell, 2006).

Educators are increasingly held accountable for conducting evidence-based practices. Action research ensures that decisions about change are based on actual data about student needs and that changes made are helping to attain stated goals. School counselors can use action research to show the many ways that their programs are making a difference in students' skills, understanding, and knowledge. For example, research could demonstrate if a particular curriculum sequence about career options actually increases student knowledge of career opportunities. If the curriculum is not making a difference, then counselors should not spend time on it. If the curriculum does make a difference, documenting that fact supports the school counselor's efforts and justifies the student time spent on that topic. Specific evaluation of what components of the curriculum are most informative and useful allows for more productive use of time and energy. Research showing that a school counselor's work makes a difference in student outcomes helps the educational community understand the value of the work of school counselors.

How to Conduct Action Research

As with other types of research, action research follows seven basic steps:

1. Identify the issue or problem and determine the purpose of the research.

2. Review what is known about the problem.

3. Develop your research question about the problem and plan the research process.

4. Gather data.

5. Analyze the data.

6. Interpret results, disseminate findings, and develop an action plan for use of the findings.

7. Evaluate the research process.

With action research, an important additional final step is taking action to rectify the problem using the information provided by the study.

1. *Identify the problem and determine the purpose of the research.* In order to begin the research process, it is necessary to identify and define the problem to be addressed or the question to be answered in

clear, specific language. Reflecting on and analyzing your current practice is a helpful place to start (Macintyre, 2000). If focusing on problems seems too negative, thinking about an area that needs improvement is another way to start the process (Kemmis & McTaggert, 2000). Questions to ask include the following:

- What do I do and what do I want to know about what I'm doing?
- What is the problem I want to solve?
- What is the question I want to answer?
- What do I wish was different in my school or school counseling program, curriculum, or counseling interventions?
- What kinds of information do I want and need?
- What information is already available to me?
- What do I want or need to know from these data?
- What are my limitations?
- Who will be seeing these data?

Once you have identified some questions or problems, ask yourself which one you want to focus on and why you want to solve this particular problem. Is it the most important one to solve or to gain information about? In this phase, it is important to get input from colleagues and to work with a team. Gillies (1993) recommends also considering what will happen if the problem remains unsolved. Research questions about problems can be general or specific:

- Why are so few girls and students of color taking AP math and science classes in our school?
- Is my group impacting students in ways that were intended?
- How can we improve our violence prevention curriculum?
- Why do some students who are accepted into college choose not to go?
- How can we deal with teacher burnout at our school?
- What is the most effective way of dealing with students who wear inappropriate clothing to school?

Research questions about nonproblematic issues can cover a variety of topics:

- Does the new math lab increase math grades or math test scores?
- Do identity development groups affect student attendance or achievement?
- Which elementary guidance curricula are having the greatest positive impact on student behavior?

- Does a study skills intervention impact seventh grade failure rates?
- Does the career exploration guidance curriculum unit improve student motivation?

Once a research question is identified, you must then consider what you will do with the solutions and/or answers to your question. What educational practices would you like to impact? What student outcomes are you hoping to influence? What decisions will the study help you make?

The research question will help you determine the purpose of the research. Some common purposes of school counseling action research include improving student academic or behavior outcomes, creating a safer school community, helping all students learn to the best of their abilities, demonstrating to stakeholders that the school counseling program is impacting on student outcomes, determining where limited resources should be spent, and choosing curriculum materials and class plans that most powerfully support student learning.

2. *Review what is known about the problem.* Before conducting any research or evaluation project, it is critically important to find out what others already know. In action research, resources often include colleagues and school records, as well as research literature. It is useful to find out whether anyone in the school has asked this question before. Brainstorming with colleagues to gain ideas about possible solutions or answers to the question can also facilitate the research process.

Relevant research in professional journals is another key source of information, as are Internet searches. Chapter 4 provides information about reading and evaluating research to support evidence-based practice.

Once you have discovered what others know through questioning colleagues, gathering relevant school documents, and reading research journals and online sources, summarizing this information will help you to develop ideas for your study.

3. *Develop research hypotheses or questions about the problem and plan the research process accordingly.* The next step in the research process is to develop a research question or hypothesis. A hypothesis is a tentative idea that identifies your central focus and helps guide the investigation of a problem. Ask yourself, "What is my hypothesis? What do I think are the answers to my questions or outcomes of the research?" Working collegially to narrow the focus and revise the research question helps to generate the best possible outcome.

This part of the process helps you identify your biases, which will necessarily influence the questions you ask and the answers you look for. It is important to be open to new information that doesn't fit your ideas because it is possible that the findings might be different from those you imagined.

Research questions or hypotheses need to be stated in testable form and in clear, concrete language. The use of vague terms that are not clearly definable makes it harder to show that the results have meaning. Operationalizing your research question and plan is important at this point. Ask yourself the following:

- *Why* do you want to study this topic?
- *Who* is your group?
- *What* is your intervention?
- *When* will you do the intervention (time of day, time of year, etc.)?
- *Where* will you do the intervention (class, group, individual, etc.)?
- *How* will the intervention be implemented and how will you measure the outcome?

Also consider the opposite of your hypothesis, which is called the "null hypothesis," as this can help you think about what the data would look like if you were wrong. For example, if you would like to evaluate a curriculum intervention, your hypothesis would be that there is a difference in student knowledge and/or behavior as a result of your intervention. The null hypothesis would be that there is no identifiable difference in students as a result of the intervention.

After determining the hypothesis, it is necessary to select a research design that will effectively answer the question you are asking. The research design includes plans for data gathering and data analysis.

4. *Gather the data.* What information do you need to look at to answer your question or solve your problem? Choose data sources that can accurately and thoroughly answer your research question. You may want to use one source of data or several, and you may want to consider a variety of kinds of data (see Chapter 3).

Once the type and source of the data are determined, you must decide how data will be gathered. Action researchers often generate their own sources of data through surveys, interviews, or observations, in addition to using existing data sources in the school. One benefit of using multiple data sources is that you are more likely to get at the complexity of the situation, whereas one measure or data source will only give you a partial view of the whole picture. When considering data sources for research, the accuracy of the data is important. As you are gathering data, it is important to ask yourself the following questions:

- Who will collect the information and interpret the data?
- If using existing data, how was it generated and who gathered it?
- What is not measured in the data?

In some situations, it will be necessary to select the instruments you will use to collect or organize your data. Possible instruments include surveys, tests (of achievement, aptitude, affect, attitudes, opinions, values), questionnaires, interviews, performance assessments, interest inventories, behavioral checklists, rating scales, behavioral observations, public documents, and school records (Creswell, 2002). Chapter 8 provides information about generating surveys and assessments of student learning. Ideally, an existing instrument that has been shown to have good reliability and validity should be used, but measurements specific to the context may need to be developed.

It is useful to think about how you want to organize the data for analysis prior to collecting it, because the way you gather data can make analysis easier or more difficult. For example, do you want data organized by grade, classroom, or school? Setting up data-gathering mechanisms so that data are collected with anticipated use in mind can save valuable time. Likewise, the data that you need will influence the decisions you make about the design of your project. Will you use single-subject design, case study, pre- and posttests, or comparison and control groups to get the information you need?

Identifying and following legal and ethical standards is a critical component of research. Prior to gathering data, researchers must determine the risks and benefits of conducting research. No research participant should be exposed to physical or psychological harm. If the use of confidential data is necessary, permission must be obtained. Informed consent from all participants is needed, with participation in a study always being strictly voluntary. Anyone who agrees to participate also has the right to withdraw from the study at any time.

Ethical guidelines regarding the right to privacy and confidentiality must also be followed. Research reports should be presented in such a way that others cannot tell how a particular participant responded or behaved (unless the participant has specifically granted permission, in writing; Creswell, 2002).

The next step in the process is selecting an appropriate sample of suitable size. The sample needs to be the biggest group possible and also the best group to measure if looking for changes. Ideally, either the entire sample is involved in the study (the whole class, grade, or school), or the sample is a random sample of the population. To be considered a *random sample*, each member of the population must have had an equal chance of being selected to participate. If a group is quite large, *stratified sampling*, in which the proportions of the sample are the same proportions as the whole population, can be used. For instance, if a high school grade has 200 boys and 300 girls, a stratified sample of 20 boys and 30 girls from that grade matches the full sample. Systematic sampling obtains a random sample from a larger group by selecting subjects by interval (every third, fourth, fifth, etc.). If a random sample of 100 is desired in a student group of 500, every fifth person on a list of students would be chosen, representing a systematically derived random sample of the population. Gender or race bias in sampling needs to be avoided.

Context constraints in action research often limit the size of the sample. If a curriculum or intervention is occurring with a small group of students, then the research will necessarily be limited to that group. Using volunteers means that there will be a biased sample that is not representative of the population in general. Also, if an intervention is occurring with students referred because of a need for that intervention, the sample is not random. If there is a small sample size, one relatively easy way to strengthen the find-ings is to compare one group with a comparable group who didn't receive the curriculum or intervention (a control group).

> **stratified sampling**
>
> method for selecting a representative sample by selecting sample members based on known frequencies of different subgroups in the population
>
> Stratified sampling might be used to ensure that different racial or ethnic groups are represented in a sample in the same proportions as in the general population.

With data sources, measures, and instruments chosen, ethical standards adhered to, and sample identified, it is time to gather data! Mills (2000) identifies the multiple ways to collect data in action research: experiencing (observation using field notes, performances), participant observation, active observer, passive observer, enquiring (researcher asks questions), informal interview, structured formal interview, questionnaires, attitude scales, standardized tests, examin-ing (using and making records), homework or test samples, demo-graphic information, grades, attendance records, archival documents, journals, maps, audio- and videotapes, and artifacts.

When using observation to gather data, researchers usually use field notes, which are a written chronological account of what occurred during each observation session. Field notes include an objective part, which contains a comprehensive and detailed description of what has taken place, and a subjective part, which contains the researcher's reflections about what occurred during that particular observation session.

Whenever possible, collecting more than one kind of data adds depth and validity to the findings. This is also called using multiple outcome measures. Linking mandatory No Child Left Behind data to any study adds usefulness to the study as well.

5. *Analyze the data.* Before data can be used, they are usually edited, coded, and organized for analysis. If a computing software program such as Excel or SPSS is being used, the data are transferred from the instrument or responses to a computer file to run the analysis (*inputting* or *coding* the data). Sometimes a set of data is missing information. An error may have occurred in the data collection process, or a participant may not have completed the entire instrument. That piece of the data must be considered invalid and not inputted or used for analysis. Sometimes the missing data can be gathered and added so that the data set is complete. Additionally, there can be errors made inputting the data. If coding is used, it must be checked to ensure that it was done accurately.

The initial component of data analysis consists of describing the data. If your data set is qualitative (narratives, open-ended survey responses, observation, or interviews) look for themes and repetitive concepts that emerge. There may be easily observed patterns in school data, such as absences, disciplinary actions, and grades. With quantitative data (close-ended survey responses, school data in numerical form), you can generate statistics using software programs such as EZAnalyze (2006). The statistical procedures used to describe the common characteristics of a sample are called *descriptive statistics* and describe general trends or patterns in the data. Descriptive statistics include measures of central tendency (mean, median, and mode), measures of variability (variance, standard deviation, and range), and measures of relative standing (percentile rank and z score). The use of descriptive statistics is often enough to answer action research questions, although there may be a need for further statistical analysis.

More complex questions and hypothesis testing usually require additional data analysis beyond descriptive statistics. If you are using pre- and posttests or if you have a control and comparison group,

---

measures of variability

statistics used to convey information about the spread of scores in a sample

The variance, standard deviation, and range are common measures of variability.

variance

a measure of variability that reflects the average of the squared difference between each score and the mean of a group

standard deviation

a measure of variability that reflects the square root of the variance

range

a measure of variability that reflects the difference between the highest and lowest scores in a group

---

measures of central tendency

statistics used to convey information about the most representative value of a sample
The mean, median, and mode are common measures of central tendency.

you can make comparisons between them. Inferential statistics give people additional information about the group(s) being studied and how applicable the findings are to the general population.

Collaborating with university or community partners when analyzing data can be particularly useful. While it is certainly possible and useful to develop the skills necessary to input and analyze data (and it is a skill that is increasingly valued by administrators and employers), it can also be helpful to work with school colleagues, graduate students and faculty from local universities, business people, high school students, or parents in your community who already have these skills and would enjoy being part of the research process. University faculty and graduate students frequently need data for their own research projects and will often be happy to input and analyze data in exchange for access to the database. School counselors often view the prospect of analyzing data as the primary roadblock to conducting action research. But it is important to remember that there are graduate students and faculty who want to analyze data and just need the access.

6. *Interpret research results, disseminate the findings, and develop or recommend an action plan.* Once the data set is analyzed, the next question is what do your results mean? What did you find out? Were your hypotheses accurate? What will you do with these results? What actions do the results suggest?

Research is most valuable and useful when the outcomes are communicated to an audience in which behavior or understanding will be impacted. Who needs to know your results? The findings can be presented to several different audiences, with reports and presentations structured so that each group receives the information that is most relevant to them. However, it is not ethical research practice to present only findings that support your hypothesis or to exclude important information or findings just because they are not what you hoped to find. People might experience some discomfort in realizing that

measures of relative standing

percentile rank

a statistic that reflects how a person scored on a given measure by indicating the percentage of people who scored the same or lower

Saying that someone scored in the 95th percentile on a test is to say that they scored as well as or better than 95% of the group that took the test.

z score

a scaled score that reflects the difference between the original score and the group mean divided by the group standard deviation

descriptive statistics

the use of statistical procedures to describe the properties of a sample

inferential statistics

the use of statistical procedures to estimate unknown characteristics of a population practices don't seem to be working, but ultimately it is in everyone's best interest to discover ways to be effective educators and school counselors. Presenting research findings that challenge existing practice can be an intimidating prospect, but it is important to trust that colleagues would like to make a difference for students and want to put effort into practices that are effective.

When presenting research findings, it is helpful for researchers to relate the results to the purpose of the study, the hypotheses, and previous research. This informs others, not only specifically about your research but also about the benefits of research and evaluation of counseling and educational practice in general. Creating a culture of inquiry in a school allows people to ask questions and become invested in effective practice in a nonthreatening way (Hursh, 1995; McNiff, 1988).

One of the distinguishing features of action research is its concrete goal to make recommendations and decisions based on findings and ultimately to improve educational practices. There are different ways to take action based on the research findings (Mills, 2000):

1. Make recommendations that will resolve the problem.

2. Involve participants and others in carrying out the recommendations.

3. Make plans and decisions about interventions based on the findings.

4. Make program plans based on the findings.

5. Develop action plans based on the findings.

Ultimately, the questions are what will you do that is similar and what will you do that is different based on what you have learned?

7. *Evaluate the research process.* The final step in the research process is evaluation. Some questions to ask those involved in the research are the following (Kemmis & Wilkinson, 1998; Mills, 2000):

1. Does the project clearly address a problem or issue that needs to be solved?

2. What worked and did not work about the collaborative process?

3. Does the instrument need revising if we are going to use it again?

4. Did the research generate the information we wanted?

5. Was sufficient data collected?

6. Did the plan of action derived from the research build logically from the data?

7. Has the research enhanced the lives of participants by empowering them, changing them, or providing them with new understandings?

8. Was the action research reported to audiences who might use the information?

9. What would we do differently in an action research project next time?

10. What new questions did the research generate?

The evaluation process, particularly when it involves all who collaborated and participated in the study, creates additional changes in how people think about counseling and educational practice and research. Asking participants what they learned from their involvement empowers them to think of themselves as active learners in an environment where evaluation is something to be used supportively for growth rather than something to be feared. Self-evaluation, as well as the findings of an action research project, can provide useful information and opportunities for increased self-awareness in addition to more effective practice.

Summary

Action research, particularly when done collaboratively, has the potential to be a key tool for supporting evidence-based practice in school counseling. It can bridge the gap between research and practice (Rowell, 2006) and can generate needed information, both locally and for the field of school counseling in general (Whiston, 2002). When practitioners engage in collaborative action research projects, greater valuing of and knowledge about school counseling programs are developed at the site, practice is evaluated and improved, accountability demands are met (Whiston, 1996), and the professional knowledge base is furthered (Rowell, 2006). Action research provides the opportunity to impact our programs, our work, and even our identity as school counselors. As Rowell (2006) has written,

> Action research recognizes the relationship between knowledge and power and opens up possibilities for linking new knowledge with concrete changes in practice that are realizable and beneficial within the context of particular schools in particular communities. Collaborative action research brings

people together in the service of change, and it can be both an informative as well as empowering experience. (p. 380)

Action research is a powerful tool for promoting efficacious and equitable schools. For school counselors to be empowered change agents in school communities, action research (and research in general) must be in their repertoire. When we take our work seriously enough to evaluate it rigorously, to take a hard look at what we are doing well, and to act on our findings for what needs to change, we are providing role models for students, not just about how to be professionals but how to live their lives.

7

Measuring Student Learning and Behavior Change

Consider two scenarios:

Scenario 1: *Juan has just joined the school counseling team at BMG High School. The head school counselor is excited that Juan will be working with the school's growing Latino population and counseling students in their native language. The school counseling team shares with Juan school data that show Latinos are severely underenrolled in college prep classes. BMG High School is committed to promoting equity and access and has already revised its prerequisites policy to ensure open access to courses. Juan and the school counseling team decide that when Juan next delivers guidance lessons to the four ELL (English language learning) classes, he will explain college entrance requirements and the importance of taking college prep courses. Juan prepares a well thought out lesson to present the next month. The day after Juan delivers this lesson, several students see him before school and thank Juan for coming to their class. Juan is happy to receive such positive feedback and leaves for home at the end of the day feeling proud of the work he is doing at BMG High School.*

Scenario 2: *Juan has just joined the school counseling team at BMG High School. The head school counselor is excited that Juan will be working with the school's growing Latino population and counseling students in their native language. The school counseling team shares with Juan the school data that show Latinos are severely underenrolled in college prep classes. BMG High School is committed to promoting equity and access and has already revised its prerequisites policy to ensure open access to courses. Juan and the school counseling team decide that when Juan next delivers guidance lessons to the four ELL classes, he will explain college entrance requirements and the importance of taking college prep courses. Juan prepares a comprehensive lesson and pre- and posttests to measure students' knowledge of and attitudes about taking more rigorous courses. Juan delivers the lesson and the pre- and posttests to the first of his four ELL classes and is surprised to discover that the students learned little during his lesson. The next day, several students see Juan before school and thank him for coming to their class. Juan decides to ask the students for feedback on the lesson. The students tell him that while they appreciated the information, it was a lot to take in at one time. Before going to his next ELL class, Juan decides to revise his lesson and focus on only a few of his original objectives; the rest he will discuss in later guidance lessons. Subsequent pre- and posttest results are more positive, and the following semester school data indicate that ELL enrollment for college prep courses has increased.*

Measuring the outcomes of our efforts can be disconcerting if we discover that we are not having the impact we had hoped we would. At the same time, spending time on interventions that are not creating the results we want is not effective school counseling practice. When we assess the work we do, however, and discover that there are identifiable changes in student attitudes, skills, and behaviors, we can know with much more certainty that we really are making a difference for the students with whom we work.

In the first scenario, Juan feels justifiably happy about the positive feedback he receives from the students, but he cannot say for sure that more of the students he talked with will actually take college prep classes. In the second scenario, Juan has some evidence that what he is doing is working and that not only do students appreciate his efforts but their behaviors have shifted as well.

How to best use our time to impact student outcomes is an ongoing concern for all educators. Because school counseling is by definition a job that requires considerable multitasking and constant decisions about the most effective ways to use time, it is imperative for school counselors to know that our efforts are having an impact. While it is true that measuring student learning and change takes time away from direct delivery of services, it is critical that school counselors take this time to ensure that students are learning what they should and that interventions are impacting knowledge, skills, and behaviors. When school counselors can consistently demonstrate that our work is impacting key student outcomes, the value and importance of the work we do is clear.

The measurement or evaluation of student learning (Slavin, 2006) provides

- feedback to students about their learning process and progress,
- feedback to instructors about their effectiveness,
- feedback to parents about what their children are learning,
- information for course selection and placement,
- information for accountability, and
- information to increase student effort and motivation.

Types of Assessment

As described in the scenario above, to support the effective development of all students, educators need to ensure that they are providing information that students do not already have. For this reason, assessment of learning needs to start with the identification of what students already know, or *diagnostic assessment*. Diagnostic assessment can identify students'

- prior knowledge,
- misconceptions,
- interests, and
- learning style preferences.

School counselors can do an informal diagnostic assessment by asking students, "Why do you think this is important to know?" or "Why do you think we are studying this?" or "What do you already know about this?" Pretests, student surveys, and skills checks can more formally ascertain learning needs. These assessment techniques are useful with individual, small-group, and large-group interventions and ensure that we are teaching students what they need to know.

Formative assessment occurs during an intervention. These are ongoing, informal checks for understanding that provide information to guide the rest of the intervention and can be as simple as asking, "Tell me your understanding of . . ." or as complex as "Please summarize for me what you understand about this content so far." Formative assessment provides feedback for pacing and determining need for repetition of content, as well as information about how to improve student performance (McTighe & Wiggins, 2004).

formative assessment

evaluation processes that strive to track the quality of the implementation of an intervention in order to permit ongoing improvements

summative assessment

evaluation processes that measure the outcomes of an intervention

Summative assessment follows instruction and identifies student proficiency or mastery of the content; it is what most people think of when they hear the word "assessment." When the focus of an intervention is developing student competencies, the summative assessment of learning content ideally is a chance for all students to demonstrate effective learning. If diagnostic and formative assessments have been done and the teaching content has focused on increasing knowledge and skill development, then all students should have reached competency and at least some students will have reached mastery by the end of the intervention.

Measuring Student Learning Effectively

Effective summative assessment of student learning starts with the end in mind: What is it you want students to know and to be able to do at the end of the lesson (McTighe & Wiggins, 2004)? The answers to these questions become the learning objectives, and the assessment of learning is directly linked to them. The most effective lesson plans have learning objectives and assessment of learning clearly stated (Slavin, 2006). When students know the learning objectives and methods of assessment, they understand the reason for the lesson and how their learning will be evaluated, and they are consequently more engaged in the learning process (McTighe & Wiggins, 2004).

When we evaluate or measure student learning, several key questions must be asked:

1. What is the desired learning outcome?
   - Learning outcomes need to be directly related to learning objectives that have been stated in the lesson plan and written on the board.
   - Students need to know the desired learning outcomes so that the goals of the lesson are apparent to them.
   - Whenever possible, learning outcomes need to be linked to state curriculum standards for academic content areas and to the ASCA National Standards (Campbell & Dahir, 1997).

2. How will we know what students have learned?
   - What do students already know? What data about student knowledge exist elsewhere in the system? What does diagnostic assessment tell us?

- Are the performance goals and standards clear to all?
- What are the students' roles in determining whether they know the desired content?
- What method(s) of assessment will be used to identify learning?

3. What is acceptable evidence of learning?
   - What would you like students to know and be able to do?
   - Is there more than one type of summative assessment so that different ways of knowing can be identified?
   - Are assessment methods matched to achievement goals?
   - Can students demonstrate their understanding through real-world applications of the content?
   - What percentage of students need to demonstrate evidence of learning?
   - What percentage of students need to demonstrate competence?
   - What percentage of students need to demonstrate mastery?

If a school counselor has thoughtfully prepared a learning situation through the identification of learning goals, communication with students about outcomes sought, and presentation of effective materials and class content, then measuring student learning can be a fairly straightforward process. Communicating with students each step of the way creates empowered, self-motivated learners.

Assessment of learning usually is only a brief snapshot of what is learned, unless the content is very concrete, such as with the alphabet or number facts. There is no way to measure all of the learning that has occurred or the ways that any person's unique brain will integrate and make use of the content. Identifying the most important, broadly applicable learning content is easier if one frequently returns to the core question of what do we want students to know and be able to do? The ASCA National Standards (Campbell & Dahir, 1997) is essentially a list of potential student assessment outcomes, although some indicators are a challenge to measure effectively. Below are some basic areas of knowledge, behavior, and beliefs related to school counseling outcomes (revised from McGinnis & Goldstein, 1997).

What we want students to know:

- Vocabulary
- Definitions
- Key facts
- Concepts
- Information
- Steps
- Processes

- Rules
- Key personnel
- Where to get help

What we want students to be able to do:

- Communication skills—listening, speaking, writing
- Study skills—test taking, studying, organizing, managing materials
- Interpersonal skills—joining, playing with others, turn taking, offering help, giving and accepting compliments, beginning and ending conversations, sharing, apologizing, being honest
- Classroom skills—paying attention, asking for help, asking questions, asking permission, completing assignments, contributing to discussions, setting goals, time management, goal setting
- Emotional skills—knowing feelings, expressing feelings, recognizing others' feelings, expressing concern, dealing with anger, expressing affection, dealing with fear
- Conflict resolution skills—using self-control, responding to teasing, avoiding trouble, problem solving, accepting consequences, negotiating, avoiding fights
- Stress management skills—dealing with boredom, dealing with losing, reacting to failure, accepting no, saying no, relaxing, dealing with group pressure, making a decision
- Planning skills—Completing academic plans, making postsecondary plans
- Career development skills—Completing a career interest inventory, identifying possible careers, linking academic plans to career plans

What we want students to believe:

- Every person can learn to high standards.
- Every person is ultimately responsible for his or her own learning.
- Attending school and going to classes leads to increased learning and achievement.
- Every person in the building is responsible for the safety of the school.
- Adults in the school want students to succeed.
- Every person deserves respect.

Bloom, Englehart, Furst, Hill, and Krathwohl's (1956) widely used taxonomy of knowledge names six levels of understanding: knowledge, comprehension, application, analysis, synthesis, and evaluation.

Knowledge

identify, name, define, describe, state, label, recite, select, recognize, list

Comprehension

explain, match, illustrate, compare, relate, restate, express, defend, distinguish

Application

apply, solve, interpret, classify, discover, model, show, sketch, report

Analysis

analyze, examine, classify, contrast, infer, compare, research, construct

Synthesis

combine, hypothesize, design, develop, originate, formulate, invent, produce

Evaluation

assess, weigh, critique, consider, relate, recommend

Simple posttests can identify whether students gained knowledge, but it can be more challenging to measure whether students can then apply that knowledge, which is skill development. This information is of particular importance to school counselors who are likely to be implementing curriculum that is seeking application and integration of knowledge in the form of behavioral change, not just knowledge itself. Having students perform certain tasks can help school counselors assess whether the desired skills have been taught. The following are some examples of skill-based assessments:

- Fill out a four-year plan
- Calculate grade point average (GPA)
- Find college information online
- Complete a job application
- Fill out a financial aid form
- Identify the location of classes on a school map
- Locate a part of their assignment planner
- Complete a career inventory

There are many possible methods for evaluating student learning. Some get at more complex and integrated learning outcomes. It may not be possible (or necessary) for school counselors to assess all classroom curriculum interventions, although school counselors can work with teachers to integrate school counseling curriculum content and assessments into existing class materials to allow for this kind of learning evaluation. The following list, revised from Slavin (2006), details the possible ways of assessing learning.

1. Multiple-choice tests, true/false tests, and quizzes (called selected-response format)

2. Rubrics or rating scales (simple checklists, rating scales)

3. Short-answer format (written responses)

4. Essays, papers, reports (extended written responses)

5. PowerPoint presentations, murals (visual products)

6. Oral reports, debates (oral performance)

7. Role plays, music performance, skill demonstration

8. Exhibits (long-term authentic assessment project)

9. Portfolios (integrated assessment)

10. Journals or learning logs

11. Informal observation of student behavior

12. Formal observation of students using observable indicators

13. Student self-assessment

14. Peer reviews and peer response groups

15. Learning probes through questioning in class

Effective assessment is ongoing and timely, with students having several opportunities to demonstrate what they know, believe, and are learning. It provides learners with opportunities for trial and error, for learning from mistakes, and for reflection and revision. The chance to self-assess and identify what has been learned is also valuable since students are not always aware of what they have learned unless given the chance to reflect on and measure how they are different. This awareness of change can be as important as the change itself, for when students realize that they have new information and skills, they are more likely to use them in the future.

Using Existing Assessment Tools

Some curriculum materials include learning goals and learning assessment materials. Academic textbooks often contain these materials, but few school counseling materials do. Also, assessment tools and materials included in curriculum materials are not necessarily well developed and may need to be revised to meet the developmental level of students or to ensure the most effective measurement possible. Questions for evaluating an existing assessment instrument are as follows (revised from Slavin, 2006):

- Does the assessment instrument link to important learning outcomes?
- Is the assessment appropriate for the learning goals of the intervention?
- Is the assessment measure developmentally appropriate for this population?
- Is the evaluation method appropriately comprehensive?
- Are important learning outcomes evaluated by multiple means?
- Do questions elicit information that will be useful for making improvements?
- Are questions clear?
- Does everyone interpret the responses the same way?
- Do the results make sense?
- Does other evidence corroborate the results?
- Is evidence gathered over time and across situations?

Measuring Changes in Attitudes, Skills, and Knowledge

Changes in student attitudes, opinions, or beliefs are frequently measured by using a scaled question. Scaled questions often use Likert-type scales, which indicate agreement or disagreement on a multiple-point scale. It is a matter of debate whether a Likert-type scale should have an even number of choices, forcing respondents to make a choice in one direction or the other, or an odd number of choices with a choice like *Undecided, Neutral,* or *Neither Disagree nor Agree* as an option. Forced choice may provide inaccurate responses, as it makes people choose a direction when they may in fact feel neutral, but the *undecided* or *neutral* option may be overused when people don't want to make the effort to choose. Some examples of widely used scales are provided on page 122.

1	2	3	4	5
Strongly Agree	Agree	Neither Agree or Disagree	Disagree	Strongly Disagree

1	2	3	4	5	6
Strongly Agree	Agree	Slightly Agree	Slightly Disagree	Disagree	Strongly Disagree

1	2	3	4	5
Strongly Disagree	Disagree	Undecided	Agree	Strongly Agree

If a standard Likert-type scale is not used, the response choices must exhaust the possible range of answers, with the extremes at either end included. In addition, choices cannot overlap so that two answers can both be true. For example, if your question is about how much time, on average, a student spends on homework every day, the range must include *none* and *more than* . . . (whatever your highest number is). The following are two possible scales for a question like this:

A: How much time, on average, do you think you should spend on homework every day?

1	2	3	4	5
More than 2 hours	Between 1 and 2 hours	Between 30 minutes and 1 hour	Less than 30 minutes, more than none	None

B: How much time, on average, do you think you should spend on homework every day?

1	2	3	4	5
None	About 30 minutes	About an hour	About 2 hours	More than 2 hours

With the first illustration, if answer 4 were simply *less than 30 minutes* and a student spends no time on homework, then choices 4 and 5 would both be accurate. It is therefore important to pay attention to the specificity of time ranges. The second scale is less specific than the first but would be appropriate if all you need to measure are approximate times.

The numerical link to each answer allows you to easily calculate an average for a group, which can then be used for comparison with other groups or with the same group after an intervention or over time. The order of choices does matter. For some questions, you may want to start with the highest or largest option, and for others it may be best to start with the smallest or lowest option. In the case of the homework question above, respondents may answer differently if you start with the smaller end of the scale (*none*) rather than the higher end.

It is also important to be consistent in the *direction* of the scale. In the first scale above, a choice with a lower number actually indicates more time spent doing homework. If a smaller number on the Likert-type scale means *more* for some questions and *less* for others, it can be challenging to remember what a high or low score on any particular question means when summarizing the outcomes. Furthermore, it is easier for respondents if you go in the same direction throughout an assessment. Therefore, whenever possible, scales should have consistent directionality across the assessment.

If you are measuring skills, you can ask students what they would do in a particular situation, you can have them role-play behaviors, or you can have them do a skill demonstration. For pre- and posttest measures of skill, a scenario approach is often used. For example, if your learning objective is that students will be able to calculate their GPAs, a scenario pre- and posttest question would ask them to figure out the GPA for a person with a hypothetical set of grades.

If you want to measure changes in knowledge, it is useful to ask yourself the question, "What is it students need to know that they do not already know?" If they know the information already (you can determine this by pretesting, or by doing diagnostic assessment), it should not be part of your curriculum. True/false or multiple-choice formats are efficient ways of measuring student learning.

Developing Pre- and Posttests

If you need to develop your own pre- and posttests, the process is relatively straightforward. Good learning goals are easily turned into simple pre- and posttest questions since they have already cited the key ideas to be covered. Start by measuring what you want students to learn. It is important to remember if the lesson is teaching knowledge, attitudes, and skills, all these areas need to be assessed, not just the knowledge construct. Linking learning outcomes and assessment to state curriculum standards and the ASCA National Standards also provides a focus for assessment.

The general process for creating pre- and posttests is as follows:

1. Determine key ideas and concepts using learning goals (knowledge, attitudes, and skills) linked to state curriculum standards and the ASCA National Standards whenever possible.

2. Brainstorm 10 to 15 possible questions that would effectively assess students' knowledge, attitudes, and skills prior to the lesson and after the concepts have been presented. If students are able to answer all of the questions without having the lesson, the lesson is not necessary. Any question should have an answer readily apparent in the learning content or goals, and every question should be related to the content of the lesson.

3. Select 5 to 10 questions (out of your original brainstormed list) using multiple-choice, true/false, and fill-in-the-blank answer formats. Use scaled questions for measuring attitude changes. Fill-in-the-blank questions can assess specific information well, but they take more time to grade. Ideally these questions spark students' interest in the material as well as measure changes in knowledge, skills, and attitudes. Steps 2 and 3 are ideally done in collaboration with teachers or colleagues so that the best possible assessment choices are made.

4. Type the 5 to 10 questions on an 8.5" × 11" page, taking note of the spacing and organization of the page. The top of the page should include space for a student's name and the date and also for the student or school counselor to designate whether it is a pre- or posttest.

5. Photocopy the pre- and posttests—one of each for every student—on separate sheets of paper. If students have computer access, Scantron answer sheets or an online software system such as Survey Monkey (www.surveymonkey.com) or Zoomerang (www.zoomerang.com) can facilitate this process.

6. Administer the pretest before the lesson is taught. Use this data to influence your instruction. Administer the posttest after the lesson.

7. Grade the pre- and posttests and calculate the percentage increase in knowledge.

Samples of learning goals and related pre- and posttest questions from school counseling curriculum materials are included at the end of this chapter (see pages 126–128). Here is how to calculate the percentage of increase in knowledge with pre- and posttests:

1. Write an answer key.

2. Make sure that you have an equal number of pre- and posttests. Do not use tests that are unmatched or incomplete.

3. Grade all of the tests. Put the number correct at the top of each page.

4. Add the total number correct for all the pretests (e.g., 70 total correct).

5. Multiply the total number of students by the number of questions on the test (e.g., 20 students × 5 questions = 100 possible questions).

6. Divide the number correct by the total number possible (e.g., 70/100 = .70 or 70% correct on the pretest).

7. Repeat steps 5 and 6 for the posttests (e.g., 90 correct, 90/100 = .90 or 90% correct for the posttest).

8. Compute the increase in knowledge with the following formula:

(Post - Pre)/Pre = % increase in knowledge (e.g., [.90 − .70]/ .70 = .2857 or 29% increase in knowledge).

We have provided a sample of a standards-aligned curriculum and the pre- and posttests for the content at the end of this chapter (see pages 128–130). Samples of pre- and posttests are also available at the Center for Excellence in School Counseling and Leadership (www.cescal.org).

Summary

Effectively assessing student learning allows school counselors to show that interventions and program components are making a difference in concrete, demonstrable ways. Assessment allows students, parents, teachers, and school counselors to gather necessary information about what students already know and can do and what instruction or training is needed to move them closer to stated goals. When we link school counseling intervention goals and outcomes to state and district curriculum standards, as well as to the ASCA National Standards, we are demonstrating our relevance to the mission of our school and to the broader educational endeavor as well.

Sample Learning Goals and Related Pre- and Posttest Questions

Sample Pre- and Posttest Questions: Student Success Skills (Fifth Grade)

1. Learning goal: Students will know that life skills such as eating well, exercising, and having social support can greatly affect a person's energy level and mood.

Related pre- and posttest question measuring knowledge:

One way to get oxygen-rich blood to the brain and help improve concentration during studying is to

    a. Play music
    b. Use study skills
    c. Walk or dance during study breaks
    d. Eat healthy snack foods while doing school work

2. Learning goal: Students will know that study aids such as graphic organizers, index cards, body location pegs, and acronyms can help to boost memory.

Related pre- and posttest question measuring knowledge:

Which study aid helps break ideas into small chunks that are easier to remember?

    a. Graphic organizers
    b. Index cards
    c. Acronyms
    d. All of the above

Sample Pre- and Posttest Questions: College Preparatory Requirements (Tenth Grade)

1. Learning goal: Students will know how many credits they need in order to graduate.

Related pre- and posttest question measuring knowledge:

How many credits does it take to graduate from high school?

    a. 220
    b. 230
    c. 240
    d. 250
    e. None of the above

2. Learning goal: Students will know the difference between graduation and college preparatory requirements.

Sample pre- and posttest question measuring knowledge:

What are the "college prep" requirements?

a. The courses required to graduate from high school
b. The courses required for a community college
c. The courses required to qualify for four-year college
d. The courses required to qualify for four-year university
e. Both c and d

Sample Pre- and Posttest Questions: Promotion Criteria (Ninth Grade)

1. Learning goal: Students in the ninth grade will know the criteria for being promoted to tenth grade.

Sample pre- and posttest question measuring knowledge:

To be promoted to tenth grade, ninth graders must earn the following number of credits:

a. 40
b. 45
c. 50
d. 55
e. 60

2. Learning goal: Students will gain confidence in asking for help to get support to graduate.

Sample pre- and posttest question measuring attitude:

I feel comfortable asking for help from people I believe will support me to graduate from high school.

a. Strongly agree
b. Agree
c. Disagree
d. Strongly disagree

3. Learning goal: Students will recognize the importance of connecting school success to future academic potential.

Sample pre- and posttest question measuring attitude:

I believe that understanding the college preparation requirements will help me make good academic decisions.

a. Strongly agree
b. Agree
c. Disagree
d. Strongly disagree

4. Learning goal: Student will learn the skill of calculating a GPA.
Sample pre- and posttest question measuring skill:

If this is your report card, what is your GPA?
English A; Math B; Science C+; Physical Education B; History
B–; Spanish B+

a. 2.0
b. 2.5
c. 3.0
d. 3.5
e. None of the above

Sample Standards-Aligned Curriculum and Pre- and Posttests

BMG Elementary School: Fifth Grade Guidance Curriculum

Name of the lesson:
   Transition from Elementary School to Middle School

Materials:
   Date and speakers lined up
   Pre- and posttests
   Master locks for lockers
   PowerPoint presentation
   Transportation to the middle school
   Pictures, maps, etc.

Goals:
   a. Improve students' attitudes, skills, and knowledge with regard
      to transition to middle school.

   b. Reduce the number of student stress-related referrals to the
      nurse and school counselor the first week of school.

   c. Shorten student transition time so that instructional time is
      increased and achievement improves.

Objectives:
The students will:

- Identify and be able to find classrooms
- Identify and be able to find restrooms
- Identify locker location and be able to demonstrate opening locker
- Identify lunchroom locations and have knowledge of procedures
- Identify their teachers, principal, school counselor, nurse, and office staff
- Have knowledge of adult school personnel roles and be able to locate their offices on a map
- Indicate on a posttest that their questions have been answered about the transition to middle school

Associated ASCA National Standards: Personal/Social Domain
Standard A2: Acquire Self-Knowledge
Standard B1: Self-Knowledge Application
Standard C1: Acquire Personal Safety Skills

State school counseling standards (list)

State teaching and curriculum standards (list)

Lesson 1:
- Introduce the topic of the lesson and share the objectives with students.
- Give pretest (attitudes, skills, knowledge).
- Ask students to list all the questions they have about middle school.
- Pass around sample locks for students to open.
- Determine how many already know how to open the lock.
- Provide a map of the school for each student.
- Give PowerPoint presentation on information about the following:
    - Classroom, library, cafeteria, nurse, gym, and restroom locations
    - Locker locations and lock procedures
    - Lunchroom procedures
    - Schedules
    - Roles of principal, school counselor, nurse, office staff, and other adults in the building (provide pictures and explain)

- Take students to locker rooms and have them practice opening lockers, ensuring everyone achieves success if possible. If necessary, have them help each other.
- Visit lunch areas and review rules.
- Conduct a question-and-answer session.

Lesson 2:

- Pass out a mock schedule to every student.
- Give a tour of the school. Have students locate the classrooms on their mock schedule.
- Divide students into groups (with adult supervision for each group) and have the groups move through the building finding specific lockers, classrooms, people, and offices. This can be a type of scavenger hunt or timed activity with a prize to the winning group.
- Provide question-and-answer session.
- Give posttest.

Thank the students for attending and let them know where to go for future questions. Thank teachers and fellow school counselors for their support.

Fifth Grade–Middle School Transition Lesson

Pre- and Posttest

I. On the school map, please find the following locations by placing the number of the location on the map and circling it.

Number	Location
1.	School counseling office
2.	Principal's office
3.	Room 45
4.	PE boys' locker room
5.	PE girls' locker room
6.	Library
7.	Nurse's office
8.	Restrooms
9	Band
10.	Other _____

II. Please identify the following people: Who is this?

Create a matching activity by copying from the previous year-book pictures of the principal, the sixth grade counselors, the nurse, the librarian, and anyone else you would like them to know. Have students draw a line from picture to title or identify people's picture with the letter of the matching title.

III. How do you feel about going to the middle school?

Tell students that the following chart contains many feelings that students often have and that they might feel too. For each feeling, have them put an "X" in the box to indicate their agreement or disagreement.

	Strongly Disagree 1	Disagree 2	Agree 3	Strongly Agree 4
1. I feel excited to attend middle school.	☐	☐	☐	☐
2. I feel prepared for middle school.	☐	☐	☐	☐
3. When I think of middle school, I feel worried.	☐	☐	☐	☐
4. I believe I will do well in my schoolwork in middle school.	☐	☐	☐	☐
5. I think the schoolwork will be harder in middle school.	☐	☐	☐	☐
6. I think the schoolwork will be too hard for me.	☐	☐	☐	☐
7. I believe I will make new friends in middle school.	☐	☐	☐	☐
8. I understand the lunchroom rules.	☐	☐	☐	☐
9. I am looking forward to middle school.	☐	☐	☐	☐
10. I know who to ask for help if I need it when I go to middle school.	☐	☐	☐	☐

IV. Please tell us what you think about the lesson:

What I liked most about the lesson:

_____

What I learned that I really needed to know:

_____

The best part of the visit to the middle school:

_____

One thing I think should be changed:

_____

Thank you for doing your best! ☺

8

Using Surveys to Gather Information

Consider two scenarios:

Scenario 1: *Joan, an elementary school counselor, would like to know whether her fourth grade career exploration day is having an impact on students since the event takes about 50 hours to organize and requires many parent volunteers. Joan decides to ask her principal, the teachers, and the parents who come to talk about their work what they all think about Career Day. Most of the people Joan speaks with say they think Career Day is a good idea, so Joan decides to continue to spend her time in this way.*

Scenario 2: *Joan, an elementary school counselor, would like to know whether her fourth grade career exploration day is a good use of her time. She creates a brief survey with measurable student competencies that are developmentally appropriate for elementary students in the academic, career, and personal/social domains. Parents and teachers are asked what competencies they believe are most important for their students. The survey overwhelmingly indicates that students need skill development in the areas of decision making and goal setting. She decides to use the 50 hours she had been spending organizing Career Day to implement a research-based, in-class curriculum on these topics. Pre- and posttests on learning content of this* *curriculum indicate that students are learning new information and applying it to their work in school. Joan works with her principal and the teachers in her building to develop a list of parent volunteer opportunities including a request for a coordinator of the Career Day.*

Surveys are a systematic way of collecting information from a group of people by asking a series of questions. They can be a valuable way to gather data about a wide variety of information. Surveys are related to but different from pre- and posttests, which are designed to measure student behavior changes, learning, and skill development, usually in a classroom setting. Surveys are designed to measure attitudes, beliefs, behaviors, knowledge, and so on and can be used with any or all members of the educational community. Several uses for surveys are described in detail below.

Surveys can be used to describe or clarify problems. Gathering information from students, teachers, parents, and community members about specific situations provides school counselors with much needed perspectives about what people perceive as problems and how they understand the problems that exist. For example, if you survey teachers about what they believe gets in the way of student achievement, you have valuable information about teachers' beliefs regarding students and about school practices in your building. This data then can help you identify how and where to provide interventions to best support achievement for all students.

Surveys can be used to develop benchmarks or vision data. A shared vision for the school counseling program and for student outcomes in a school community helps to focus planning and decision making. Surveys are a useful way to identify what members of a group— whether the group consists of 3 people or 300—believe to be important outcomes. For example, surveying parents about what they think the school counseling program could do better to meet academic, career, and personal/social needs of their children provides useful understanding about the beliefs of some key stakeholders. Within programs, a brief survey can help a student services team identify priorities and set goals.

Surveys can be used to identify where interventions are needed and which interventions are most likely to be successful. Providing students with interventions that will not be used is a waste of time. For instance, offering tutoring services at a time or in a context when students won't use them is an example of an evidence-based intervention used ineffectively. Using a survey to identify when and where students are most likely to use tutoring services provides information that increases the likelihood of positive results. Similarly, if you survey students in your school about what kinds of afterschool academic programs they are most likely to attend (after identifying evidence-based programs), then you are more likely to have an effective outcome.

Surveys can be used to evaluate interventions that have occurred. While pre- and posttests are the most commonly used assessment of guidance lessons and interventions, surveys can also provide information about changes in beliefs, attitudes, knowledge, skills, opinions, and behaviors. It is important to remember that all survey data is self-reported data and so is necessarily a reflection of what any person completing the survey chooses to or is able to report. For example, a survey at the end of a small-group intervention can provide practitioners with valuable information about what students received from an intervention, how they believe it impacted them, what was effective, and what could be changed. There may well be things that changed for the participants that they are not aware of and that would be a challenge for a survey to identify. The process of constant evaluation, with nondefensive appreciation of feedback, not only helps us practice more effectively but models key processes for students. Demonstrating that we value students' opinions, are open to information, and are constantly challenging ourselves to be the best at what we do provides valuable role modeling for our students. In addition to providing assessments of knowledge or skill development, asking students what they think about and what they learned from a curriculum intervention helps us to see their perspective and helps us to make decisions about using materials and setting learning goals.

Surveys can help us obtain feedback, impressions, and perceptions about programs. Gathering information from key stakeholders about how a school counseling program is perceived helps us to know where we need to increase communication about our work. It is important that parents, teachers, and administration have accurate knowledge about how we as school counselors are impacting student outcomes. The era of working behind closed doors is over. To ensure that school colleagues and community members understand in what ways school counselors' work is essential to systemic efforts to promote student achievement, we have to know how we are perceived and what people know about the work we do. A survey can provide key information regarding misconceptions, outdated beliefs, and opinions about a school counseling program, giving us a picture of which program components stakeholders understand and where more knowledge is needed.

Surveys can help us meet accountability requirements and report about program outcomes to stakeholders. In order to successfully let colleagues, administrators, parents, and our communities know how we are being effective, we need survey data that provide information about the impact of our interventions and program. A survey of school colleagues, students, and parents about their perceptions of the ways that the school counseling program or specific interventions are affecting student outcomes such as achievement, attendance, discipline, school climate, safety, or peer relationships—particularly when the results are linked to strong results or outcome data—is an invaluable way to document accountability.

Using Existing Surveys

Decide what information is needed. Once you decide to use a survey to gather information or data, it is important to determine the goal of the survey. Ask yourself what you are trying to measure: Is it beliefs, behaviors, perceptions, knowledge, or opinions? Surveys are self-report data, which by definition means they are biased since the person filling out the survey is necessarily subjective. We can only report what we believe to be our behavior or our opinion. For example, a survey of bullying behavior depends on teachers and students identifying and reporting on their own and/or others' behavior; these observations may or may not be accurate or truthful. This subjectivity can create a problem in measuring the impact of an intervention. For example, a posttest may report higher levels of bullying when in fact the amount of the behavior has remained constant or diminished. What changed may not have been bullying behaviors but people's awareness of or attention to that behavior.

Linking survey use to program goals helps to prioritize the questions and determine the data needed. If one of your primary goals for the year is to increase the number of students applying to college, a survey for students about their knowledge and beliefs about postsecondary options is more relevant than a survey of teacher perceptions about the school counseling program. In order to ensure that results are taken seriously, surveys must be used judiciously and cautiously so that there is awareness that we are using surveys only to impact key goals or outcomes and not for self-serving or merely political ends.

Once you know what you want to measure and how it is linked to program goals, identifying the specific variables you want to measure is the next step. Key school counseling variables have been identified throughout this book and include outcomes such as academic achievement, attendance, discipline, safety, career development, social skills, and postsecondary choices. Narrowing your focus to one or two key variables keeps your survey to a reasonable length, helps prioritize your questions, and gives you manageable amounts of data.

Who do you want to survey? In addition to knowing what information you want, you need to know from whom you want information. All students? Some students? Will a random sampling of a group be sufficient, or do you need survey results from all members (see Chapter 4 for a discussion of random sampling)? It is impossible to survey entire student bodies efficiently and inexpensively, so a careful decision about which students to survey is crucial.

How do you want to administer the survey? Surveys can be given in classes, through the mail, by computer, and by phone. The method of administration will determine the length and nature of the survey. Surveys can also be self-administered or interviewer administered. In order to be self-administered, the participants must know how to read and the content must be at the appropriate developmental level. If students don't understand what is being asked, the results cannot give you an accurate measurement. Computerized and online surveys allow for much quicker and easier data input and analysis. Zoomerang (www.zoomerang.com) and Survey Monkey (www.surveymonkey.com) are two online computer-generated survey software systems that can help you to design, collect, and analyze data from surveys. Both offer a limited number of free services with more advanced features that are reasonably cost-efficient. Counselorsurvey.org has survey resources. All require that the respondents have access to computers, however.

Determine whether a relevant survey already exists. Using an existing survey is considerably simpler than creating a new one, and there are several excellent sources for surveys. The Buros Institute of Mental Measurements Web site summarizes a wide variety of measurement instruments and is organized by category (http://buros.unl.edu/buros/jsp/category.html). The Measurement Excellence and Training Resource Information Center (METRIC) Web site (http://www.measurementexperts.org) allows you to browse by construct or idea.

The Web site for the Collaborative for Academic, Social, and Emotional Learning (CASEL) has several climate and educational practice surveys (www.casel.org). The Center for School Counseling Outcome Research (CSCOR) offers school counseling–related measures such as stakeholder surveys, a survey to determine readiness for the ASCA National Model, and a survey to measure school counselor time use (the SCARS; www.cscor.org). The Center for Excellence in School Counseling and Leadership (www.cescal.org) also has surveys on school counseling programs and services for students, faculty, and parents. The U.S. Department of Education and state departments of education often have educational outcome and career development surveys available.

Evaluate what's already available. To provide you with useful data, an existing survey must relate directly to your identified questions and variables of interest. Furthermore, it must be appropriate for the group with which you plan to use it. Ideally, an existing survey has been tested for reliability and validity (see Chapter 4) so that you can determine that it consistently measures what it is supposed to measure. The mere existence of a survey is no assurance that it is valid and reliable. If you can't find an appropriate, good-quality survey to meet your needs, consider revising an existing one. Creating a new survey only makes sense if you can't find what you need elsewhere, as it is expensive in terms of time and effort.

Survey Development

Sometimes there are no relevant existing surveys, or the questions you want answered are specific to your context and/or intervention. In those cases, you must develop your own survey. Surveys can be one question or 100, but the same basic process of development applies. If pre- and posttests will tell you what you want to know (did students attain the learning goals?), then there is no need to develop a full-fledged survey. See Figure 8.1 for a model of survey development.

Define the constructs. Constructs are the important factors that you want to know more about (the data variables). Once you have identified what information you need, you can identify your key constructs or concepts. Many constructs are composed of a number of subconstructs. For example, if you want to measure an intervention for the prevention of violence, your key construct is violence prevention and your subconstructs could be identifying feelings, managing anger,

Figure 8.1   A Model for Developing Surveys

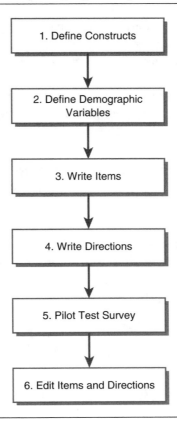

developing social skills, building empathy, standing up to peer pressure, and deciding when to ask for help.

For a different example, a survey with a primary construct of parental understanding of and satisfaction with a secondary level school counseling program could have subconstructs about academic advising, college and postsecondary planning, communication with families, support for students in need of services, referral to community resources, and so on.

In survey development, it is crucial to continually ask yourself what you mean by every word you use. What do you mean by *bullying*? What do you mean by *safety*? Every definition must be clear to you and to those taking the survey to ensure accurate interpretation of the findings.

Each of the constructs or concepts and subconstructs you identify as important needs to have at least one survey question devoted to it. It is critical to find a balance here: With too few constructs, you may not be getting all the information you need, but with too many constructs you will dilute your findings and overwhelm your survey takers. The shorter the survey, the fewer the constructs.

Research can be very useful in defining constructs because one function of research is to identify and define key constructs to be measured in a field. Even if you don't use an existing survey, seeing which constructs are used in other surveys can help you develop questions. The context and the population being surveyed also necessarily impact how constructs are defined and selected. For example, the behavior involved in anger management in the second grade is not the same as in the ninth grade, and measurement of that construct would need to reflect the developmental differences.

Define the demographic variables. Demographic variables provide important information about the people taking the survey. If the survey results are disaggregated, then demographic data can identify whether there are differences among the groups taking the survey. If you find that an intervention is working much more effectively for boys than for girls, for example, you now have valuable information that can be used to improve subsequent outcomes. Possible *demographic variables* are included below:

- Grade/age
- Male/female
- Race/ethnicity
- ELL (English language learner); LEP (limited English proficiency)
- SES (socioeconomic status: school lunch status, parent educational level)
- Special needs (individualized educational program [IEP], 504 plan)
- Mobility (years in current school)

As with defining constructs, it is important to determine how many demographic variables are necessary and appropriate. You may not need any demographic data if your survey is designed for a small-group intervention. If you are surveying a large and diverse population, several demographic variables may be warranted. Keep in mind that it is unethical to have disaggregated data for groups smaller than 10, as that would allow participants to be identified. If only three students in a surveyed group have special needs, then asking about and disaggregating by that demographic variable does not make sense. Additionally, students may not know the answer to some demographic questions, so providing the option, *Don't Know,* may be important. For example, some students may not know answers related to socioeconomic status, such as parental education level or eligibility for free or reduced-price lunch.

Write survey questions. There are two types of questions or "items" on surveys: open-ended and closed. *Open-ended items,* which don't limit the answer options, tend to be easier to write, though developing concise questions that elicit exactly the information you are looking for is more challenging than people think. Open-ended questions provide you with rich qualitative data but can be difficult to analyze and summarize. Closed questions on surveys often use Likert-type scales, which ask respondents to indicate agreement or disagreement on a multiple-point scale. Chapter 7 provides some examples of widely used Likert-type scales. *Closed questions,* which provide a limited number of answer options, are more challenging to write but provide quantitative data that is more specific and easier to analyze. When the respondent is likely not to know all of the possible answers to a question ("Why did you choose the college that you did?") or when there are many possible answers ("What careers are you interested in?"), use open-ended questions (Ary, Jacobs, & Razavieh, 2002). Many surveys use both kinds of items since each provides something unique. Below are examples of relevant open-ended items about a variety of school counseling–related content areas.

> Please list what you believe to be the most important activities of the school counselors. (for a stakeholder survey)
>
> Please list the most significant strengths that currently exist within the school counseling program. (for a stakeholder survey)
>
> Please list the most significant weaknesses that currently exist within the school counseling program. What would you change? (for a stakeholder survey)
>
> What did you get out of being in this group? (for a survey about a group intervention)
>
> What parts of the information we talked about in this group did you find most helpful? (for a survey of student beliefs about an intervention)
>
> How have you used the conflict resolution skills you learned last week? (for a survey of application of learning content)
>
> Is there anything else you would like us to know? (for the end of a survey)

As with good assessment questions, effective survey questions (items) have several identifiable characteristics, which are outlined below and then described in detail:

- Items are in clear and simple language.
- Items use precise words that don't have more than one meaning.
- Items are not dependent on specialized knowledge.
- Each item maps onto one construct or subconstruct.
- Each item contains only one idea.
- Items do not call for socially desirable or socially undesirable responses.
- Every item is there for a reason.
- Some items are reverse stated. (A negative answer actually reflects a positive opinion. An example of such an item might be, "The school counseling program does not help to enhance the academic achievement of all students.")
- Items do not contain double negatives.

Questions should be short and direct. All concepts, ideas, and language should be as simple as possible. It is recommended that surveys be written at the fifth grade reading level without any jargon or specialized language (Ary, Jacobs, & Razavieh, 2002; Fowler, 1995). For students younger than fifth grade, developmentally appropriate language is even more important, and you may want to consider using symbols or having the survey administered by an interviewer.

If word meaning is at all ambiguous, then definitions may be included as part of the survey. This practice is common in surveys of bullying behavior and drug use, for which common definitions are necessary to determine accurate information. Even simple words such as *often* and *sometimes* may have different meanings for people. For this reason, specific quantified answer choices are optimal.

Additionally, respondents should not need specific knowledge in order to respond to a statement. School counselors and educators sometimes talk about programs and processes in ways that students, parents, and community members may not understand. For example, in order to have an opinion about the item, "Since moving to the ASCA National Model, the school counseling program serves a wider range of students," respondents need to know what the "National Model" is. A more effective item is "My school counselor has been in my classroom on at least one occasion this semester," because it doesn't require specialized knowledge to answer and it asks about specific, observable behavior.

Each question needs to clearly measure one of the constructs or subconstructs initially identified as essential information. The item, "I feel safe at school," measures the construct of safety. The item, "I believe all ethnic and racial groups are safe at school," is measuring the constructs of both safety and race relations. An answer of disagree on the latter could mean that safety is of concern to the respondent or that he or she believes that there are discrepancies in how students of varying races and ethnicities are treated.

Each survey question or item should contain only one idea (Fowler, 1995). Otherwise, the level of agreement with any item cannot be accurately determined. Agreement with the item, "I have experienced bullying at school," is clearer than agreement with the item, "I have experienced bullying and violence at school." Bullying and violence are related constructs, but they may or may not be the same behaviors. An agreement with the latter statement could mean that the student has experienced bullying, violence, or both.

If an item or statement is clearly socially desirable or undesirable, it may be a challenge to obtain accurate answers. Because information on surveys is self-reported, people may choose to answer that they behave in socially acceptable or desirable ways, whether or not it is true. Conversely, adolescents may respond that they are engaging in more inappropriate behaviors than they actually are. Prioritize neutral language and avoid stereotyping, emotionally loaded, or superlative words (Ary, Jacobs, & Razavieh, 2002). The item, "I have met with my counselor," is a relatively neutral item, compared with the item, "Students should take the initiative to set up appointments with their school counselors." With the latter, students may believe that they should agree with this statement and answer accordingly, whether or not they actually do.

Questions that have answers that are available elsewhere and that respondents may not know ("What is your GPA?") or which ask about details people may not have committed to memory ("How many classes did your school counselor teach on conflict resolution?") should be avoided. When people taking surveys come across items that they find annoying or unanswerable, they are more likely to stop taking the survey (Fowler, 1995).

If you are asking questions that involve behavior and that have possible disciplinary consequences ("Did you cut classes this year?" "Have you ever stolen something from another student?" "Have you ever witnessed an incidence of physical violence in school?"), it is important that you ensure respondent confidentiality. If respondents are putting their names on surveys, these questions should not be asked, as they could create ethically problematic situations for school counselors who would come to know if specific students have either witnessed or engaged in this type of behavior.

To ensure that respondents are reading each statement carefully and answering thoughtfully, surveys use reverse-stated items. *Reverse-stated items* are those for which a negative response reflects a positive opinion. Such items help people pay attention to the specific questions being asked and are a valuable way to ensure that you are getting accurate responses. Examples of this would be, "I do not have a clear understanding of the school counselor's responsibilities," or "The school counselor has not played an important role in my child's educational experience." (Both examples are from the CSCOR stakeholder surveys, available online.) If a person turns in a survey with 1's or 5's circled for every answer and there are reverse-stated items, then you know that the survey is not valid. Caution should be taken to ensure that when a reverse item is created, it doesn't result in a question with double negatives, as this might confuse the respondent.

Any question that doesn't provide key data is irrelevant, no matter how interesting. When a survey is being constructed, many questions may be generated, but not all of them will provide answers to the questions that concern you. Clarity about the reasons for the survey and reviews of the information needed are thus essential.

Write the introduction and directions. A strong introduction that briefly communicates what the survey is about and the reasons for the survey can provide motivation and help ensure engagement. In order to get the information you want and need, respondents must understand why they should take the time to complete the survey, what you will be doing with their answers, and what you are looking for. Information about how to answer items is important, especially with younger students who may not have ever taken a survey. It is imperative to indicate whether or not answers will be anonymous and confidential.

In your directions, request that all participants respond honestly and answer all items. Particularly in a school setting, it is important to let students know whether their answers are an assessment of learning or solely for information gathering. It is helpful to state explicitly that there are no right or wrong answers and that they will not be graded on their answers, if that is true.

Put the survey together. Once you have your introduction, directions, demographic items, and survey statements or questions, you are ready to put the total package together. Several general guidelines apply. Introduction and directions about how to complete the survey are given first; more general survey items and questions then follow. Putting interesting and personally relevant questions at the beginning helps to build rapport (Fowler, 1995). The question order needs to make sense and should flow logically. Numbering questions consecutively without any repetitions or omissions aids in analysis. Questions or demographic items of a more sensitive or personal nature should be toward the end. Open-ended questions, if you are using them, also go near the end of the survey. Remember to provide respondents with enough room to answer questions completely. Last, thank the respondents for taking the time and effort to complete the questionnaire (Ary, Jacobs, & Razavieh, 2002).

Pilot test the survey. Pilot testing a new survey is the last step before implementation. Testing the survey can identify possible problems, ensure that items are clearly worded, discover problems with the directions, and provide information about how long it takes to complete. Surveys ideally are pilot tested with a group that is very similar to intended respondents. If this is not possible, choose readily available people (colleagues, friends, etc.) who will answer items as though they were part of the group you are interested in. Solicit as much feedback as possible about which questions were confusing, which were hard to answer, whether the instructions were clear, whether all testers interpreted items the same way, and how people felt after taking the survey. All of this information can then be used to revise the survey prior to actually using it. Finding out that a survey has mistakes after it has been given to the intended group can create headaches. An example of a stakeholder survey developed by the Center for School Counseling Outcome Research is located at the end of this chapter (see page 146).

Summary

School counselors can use surveys to support and evaluate their work in several areas, including student learning, stakeholder perceptions, needs assessments, and accountability efforts. Writing good surveys is more challenging than it first seems, and using existing surveys is always preferable. Every question asked of anyone under any circumstance should be important, worded clearly, and of value to all involved.

Sample Stakeholder Survey From the Center for School Counseling
Outcome Research

High School Teacher Survey

School Counseling Program Review

Thank you for taking the time to answer the questions in this survey. Your honest response to all questions will assist in the review of the school counseling program, including guidance and adjustment counseling. All responses will be kept confidential.

Name _____ School _____

What subject do you teach? _____

What grade do you teach? _____

Please circle the response that best answers each question.

1. How many years have you
   worked at this school?   < 1   1–5   6–10   11–20   21+

2. How much contact do you have
   with the school counselors?   Daily   Weekly   Monthly   Very Little

3. How many school counselors are
   working in your school?   1   2   3   4   5   6   Not Sure

Please circle the appropriate number after each statement that best reflects your opinion.

1 = strongly   2 = disagree   3 = neither agree   4 = agree   5 = strongly
   disagree   nor disagree   agree

4. I have a clear understanding of the school
   counselor's role in the school.   1   2   3   4   5

5. I meet with the school counselors when I
   have concerns about students in my classes.   1   2   3   4   5

The school counselors:

6. help students to develop socially and
   emotionally.   1   2   3   4   5

7. do not help to enhance the academic
   achievement of all students.   1   2   3   4   5

8. have the necessary resources to do their
   jobs effectively (i.e., clerical staff,
   computers, etc.).   1   2   3   4   5

9. are very helpful to students during course
   selection and scheduling.   1   2   3   4   5

10. are not available to students when they
    are needed.   1   2   3   4   5

11. do not help students with future
    educational planning, college selection,
    and placement.   1   2   3   4   5

12. are effective advocates for students.   1   2   3   4   5

13. provide important services to the students. 1   2   3   4   5

14. believe students can succeed.   1   2   3   4   5

15. do not work with teachers to provide
    classroom guidance curriculum.   1   2   3   4   5

16. provide important information to parents
    and students about services outside of
    the school setting.   1   2   3   4   5

17. work as a liaison between all parties
    involved in students' education.   1   2   3   4   5

18. are not viewed as an integral part of
    students' educational experience.   1   2   3   4   5

19. work cooperatively with administrators,
    teachers, and other staff.   1   2   3   4   5

---

20. I believe parents feel satisfied with the
    work school counselors are doing.   1   2   3   4   5

21. I believe students feel comfortable meeting
    with the school counselors.   1   2   3   4   5

22. Please list what you believe to be the most important activities of the
    school counselors.

    _____

    _____

    _____

23. Please list the most significant strengths that currently exist within
    the school counseling program.

    _____

    _____

24. Please list the most significant weaknesses that currently exist within
    the school counseling program. What would you change?

    _____

    _____

Thank you again for taking the time to complete this survey.

9

Moving to Evidence-Based School Counseling Practice

Consider two scenarios:

Scenario 1: *Kevin, a middle school counselor, had always felt that something was missing from his work. He was passionately committed to his students and felt a moral obligation to give them the highest quality help and services. It was important for him to think of himself as a responsible professional. He thought deeply about his work, attended conferences to keep sharp, and had excellent intuition about how to address problematic situations in his school. He knew that the professional literature talked about the importance of using data for planning, conducting needs assessments, reading research, doing evaluation, and demonstrating accountability. He was also painfully aware that he was devoting no time to these activities. In the hectic life of public school, something more urgent always seemed to need his attention. It bothered Kevin that his principal kept asking for information about what he was doing for students. It frustrated him that some of the teachers thought he had a cushy job. He wished that things were different, but it was so hard to figure out where to begin that he never did. Besides,* *why should he have to prove to anyone that he was effective? His students certainly knew that he helped them. Wasn't that enough?*

Scenario 2: *Kevin, a middle school counselor, had always felt that something was missing from his work. He was passionately committed to his students and felt a moral obligation to give them the highest quality help and services. It was important for him to think of himself as a responsible professional. He thought deeply about his work, attended conferences to keep sharp, and had excellent intuition about how to address problematic situations in his school. He knew that the professional literature talked about the importance of using data for planning, conducting needs assessments, reading research, conducting evaluation, and demonstrating accountability. He was also painfully aware that he was devoting no time to these activities. In the hectic life of public school, something more urgent always seemed to need his attention. He did not like the fact that neither his principal nor some influential teachers were sure about his value to the school, but he took this as a challenge. He attended a week-long summer professional development course on evidence-based practice and committed to implementing a five-year plan to change his practice. Over the next five years, he systematically added in activities—performing a baseline program evaluation, leading teams with the principal and teachers on data-based planning and selecting research-based interventions, organizing a collaborative action research project with a local university to improve attendance, and then conducting a follow-up program evaluation. To make the new work manageable, he negotiated a release from noncounseling duties, teamed with teachers and students to integrate data and research projects into relevant academic course content, and built his data collection activities into the regular routines of the program. He regularly shared results with the school, district, and community. As these changes occurred, Kevin became more confident that he was having an impact because he based what he was doing on evidence. Increasingly, the school and community realized that the school counseling program was an essential part of the educational process. The principal and teachers came to regard Kevin as an effective professional and a school leader who had much to offer the school community as it learned how to do its work better. Equally important, Kevin came to regard himself in the same way.*

The first scenario reflects the current status of the use of data and outcome research for planning and evaluation in many school counseling programs. While the professional literature is replete with calls for school counselors to embrace "accountability practices," this transition has been challenging. For the most part, the call for increased use of accountability practices has focused on the political aspects of data use—the need to demonstrate worth to the organization by proving that school counseling interventions produce important results. Perhaps because school counselors inherently believe that the work we do makes a difference, it is frustrating to have to prove this to others, and the need for political legitimacy has not proved motivating enough to change practice to any great extent. In the complex and demanding world of schools, it often seems that there are too many students who need services here and now to take the time to collect, analyze, and report on data. This changes when we realize that collecting, analyzing, and reporting data is an essential foundation for effective practice and a way to better meet the needs of the students with whom we work.

An evidence-based practice approach to school counseling places the generation and use of evidence to inform professional judgment at the center of school counseling practice. Data work is essential to effective practice. As Norm Gysbers has stated (personal correspondence, May 24, 2006), data needs to be used to improve what we do rather than just prove that what we currently do works.

When counselors engage in an evidence-based practice approach, they generate powerful information that can also be used for accountability and professional advocacy. This crucial information is produced as a by-product of the evidence-based approach. If we gather evidence for ourselves, we have more than enough evidence to share. Related to this, if this evidence is gathered through teaming (as this book suggests), the centrality of the school counseling program will be enhanced again as a by-product of the process itself.

Moving to an evidence-based practice approach is not easy; it requires some new skills and a concerted effort over several years. In the second scenario, we see an example of a successful shift that took five years to accomplish. This chapter deals with the transition to an evidence-based practice approach and with the very real and practical considerations in making a radical transformation in practice.

An Integrated Evidence-Based Proactive Approach

Moving to an evidence-based mode of school counseling is a subtle but profound shift that holds the promise of more effective practice and more powerful outcomes for students. The model that we discussed in Chapter 1 suggests that evidence-based practice consists of three basic domains: problem description, using outcome research, and intervention evaluation. Each of these domains includes activities that generate evidence that informs the school counselor's professional judgment. Problem description evidence helps us know what needs to be addressed. Outcome research evidence helps us know what has generally worked. Intervention evaluation evidence helps us know whether something we have done in our school was helpful or not.

Moving to an evidence-based practice approach requires a shift in the school counselor's professional orientation, a related shift in time use, and the development of a new skill set. It also requires a renegotiation of professional relationships among school counselors, teachers, and administrators. The work of school counseling is inherently collaborative. The work of school counselors cannot be restructured unless the working relationships among professions are also changed to include all stakeholders in the process. Over the past 10 years, we have trained thousands of school counselors and administrators, and our experience bears out that the most effective changes occurred in schools and districts where school counselors, administrators, and lead teachers worked as a team. In these cases, school counseling program improvement was collaborative and effective. Moving to an evidence-based practice approach means changing the ways you work with your colleagues.

School counselors need to be able to lead and participate in teams that use data to define problems, select research-based interventions, and manage implementation and evaluation projects. School counselors must to be able to involve the school and community in needs assessments and satisfaction surveys that generate evidence for the effectiveness of, and need for improvements in, the school counseling program. These results then have to be reported to leaders and decision makers. All of this takes time. In the next section, we will present a five-year process that will get you from where you are to where you need to be. Implementing this process will require you to redistribute your time. You will need to create time for data activities by negotiating a reduction in noncounseling responsibilities and by discontinuing things that you are now doing that you find to be ineffective or inefficient.

The Journey: Getting From Here to There

Knowing how to get someplace often depends on knowing where you are. School counselors are moving to evidence-based practice from a range of starting points, and there are a number of important factors that will influence how you generate change. The primary factor is whether or not your school is currently engaged in reform through data use. School reform through the establishment of professional learning communities is a growing movement (DuFour, 2004). Schools participating in these practices work to create a climate and collaborative structures (e.g., teams) that encourage school personnel to evaluate their results and look for better ways to educate children. Teams use data to inform professional judgment in both planning and evaluation. Where there is schoolwide data use, school counselors will need to be both (a) effective participants on an interdisciplinary data-based decision-making (DBDM) team (see Chapter 2) that identifies problems and (b) effective leaders of a school counseling research-based practice (RBP) team (see Chapter 4) that recognizes the empirically supported interventions within the scope of the school counseling program and oversees implementation and evaluation of these activities.

Figure 9.1 is a diagram representing the relationships of teams in a school that is fully committed to reform through effective data use. A schoolwide DBDM team describes the problem, generates vision data, and commits to yearly benchmarks. The DBDM team works with specialized RBP teams (including a school counseling RBP team) to identify where and how to intervene to address the identified problem. Multiple levels of and types of intervention (e.g., changes in school policy, curriculum modification, teacher-focused professional development, parent-focused outreach, and student-focused skill development) are likely to be needed to reach benchmarks and vision data. Some of these interventions will be within the scope of the school counseling programs. The school counseling RBP team would then select specific research-supported interventions, oversee implementation and evaluation of these interventions, monitor problem data, and report back to the school DBDM team, where a collaborative decision to continue, modify, or discontinue the intervention would be made. A schoolwide approach mobilizes the whole community to address common concerns and coordinates the expertise across the school that is needed to address problems at multiple levels.

If your school is not using a schoolwide data-based reform strategy, it is still possible to implement an evidence-based practice approach within the school counseling program. To move in this direction, the support of the administration is needed because it will require a modification in time use, a change in decision-making procedures, and alterations in the relationships between school counselors and other school staff. In this instance, the DBDM and RBP teams may actually be the same group. The team needs to be composed of people who have the needed perspectives to address school problems and the necessary knowledge and skills (or willingness to develop these) to engage in team functions. School

Figure 9.1   Integrating Team Functions in a School Implementing Schoolwide
Reform

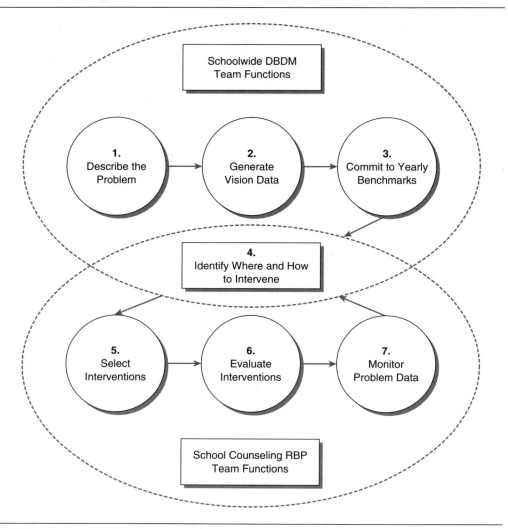

NOTE: DBDM = data-based decision making

RBP = research-based practice

counselors, key teachers, and an administrator should be included on these teams. Parental input is also helpful. When this approach is confined to the school counseling program, it will not be possible to address effectively many of the big issues that require a schoolwide response. For example, improving state achievement test scores is unlikely to result from school counseling program interventions alone unless these interventions can be connected to changes in school policy and instructional practices. It is best to tackle problems that can be significantly impacted by the interventions that are under your control.

A Five-Year Plan

Profound changes in school counseling practice require a multiyear approach. The five-year process we lay out assumes the starting point of a minimal use of data. To the extent that you are currently using data to generate evidence to guide your work, your starting place may be different. The following represents a recommended sequence:

Year 1

- Conduct a baseline program evaluation (the ASCA National Model program audit and the ASCA Readiness Survey are helpful tools at this step).
- Construct a set of measurable school counseling competencies/ student learning objectives using the ASCA National Standards and school and state curriculum standards.
- Join the schoolwide DBDM team or organize a school counseling DBDM team.
- Develop in team members the needed skills through professional development and collaboration.
- Create an action plan and collect results about at least one guidance activity or curriculum intervention.
- Share information with stakeholders about key activities and outcomes of Year 1.

Year 2

- DBDM team analyzes school data and identifies vision data and benchmarks.
- Define five key program goals.
- Identify important student competencies/student learning objectives for guidance curriculum.
- Identify research-based interventions, implementation, and evaluation plans that address program goals and student competencies.
- Select and implement intentional guidance interventions based on data-driven needs.
- Share information with stakeholders about key outcomes of Years 1–2.

Year 3

- Deliver and evaluate guidance curriculum.
- Deliver and evaluate intentional guidance interventions based on data-driven needs.
- Monitor problem data.
- Monitor school counseling program goal attainment.
- Share information with stakeholders about key outcomes of Years 1–3.

Year 4

- Deliver and evaluate guidance curriculum, making changes based on previous year's evaluation results.
- Deliver and evaluate intentional guidance interventions, making changes based on previous year's evaluation results.
- Monitor problem data.
- Monitor school counseling program goal attainment.
- Share information with key stakeholders about key outcomes of Years 1–4.

Year 5

- Continue to implement program components that have been found to make a difference for student outcomes and discontinue interventions or activities that have not.
- Continue to monitor student, school, and program data.
- Conduct full program evaluation (including program audit).
- Share comprehensive program evaluation information with key stakeholders, including school board.

Reporting About Results to Enhance Legitimacy

Throughout the history of the profession, school counselors have struggled to secure a legitimate position as integral to the educational mission of schools (Burtnett, 1993; Hayes, Dagley, & Horne, 1996). Many aspects of school counseling in public schools continue to be marginalized. School counselors often exist at the periphery of educational practice rather than at the center of resources, influence, and/or power. School counselors complain that they are not included in meaningful conversations that impact students, systems in schools, use of school resources, or their own work role within the organization (Hatch, 2002). During budget cuts, school counselors frequently bear a disproportionate burden in staff reductions. In many schools, counselors are assigned duties that are unrelated to school counseling and that detract from their professional work. This marginalization is in large part due to uncertainty about the value of school counseling, related to the lack of clear, compelling documentation of the impact of the school counseling program on student outcomes. Everyone knows that teachers are central to achieving quality educational outcomes. Opinion is less certain in the case of school counselors. Understanding the complexity of these issues requires a brief review through the lenses of three theoretical perspectives: organizational, institutional, and political theory (Hatch, 2002).

Organizational theory concerns itself with how effective an organization is in accomplishing its goals and achieving the results or outcomes the organization intends to produce. Organizational theory is also grounded in internal efficiency. Rowan and Miskel (1999) theorize that organizational performance is often the main determinant of organizational survival. If a program is perceived as inefficient, it is often eliminated or responsibilities of program personnel are shifted. Programs that are perceived as efficient survive and frequently grow. Often school counselors and principals are asked to produce proof that a school counseling program is working. School counseling programs have traditionally lacked data to prove that functioning in one way is more productive or produces better results than functioning in another. Since actual student outcomes can be relatively difficult to document, school counseling programs often use proxy measures to document productivity. School districts typically require that school counselors submit data about what they are doing, including, for example, the number of students served in guidance lessons or groups. These data express what school counselors do but not what students achieve.

At a state conference in 2004, a school superintendent stated the following:

> I love my school counselors; they are really *there* for students. They work so hard and are such nice people; but . . . (long pause) . . . I just don't know how to *justify* the expenditure of funds for hiring more and reducing their ratio because with all of the requirements of No Child Left Behind, I simply don't know how they are helping us to meet these vital goals.

From an organizational theory perspective, if administrators had evidence of how the work of the school counselors helps to support the capability of schools to attain important educational goals, they would be more reluctant to lose counselors during budget cutbacks and less likely to assign counselors duties that detract from their professional work.

According to an institutional theory perspective, organizations institutionalize program components and processes that establish rules, norms, and routines with the goal of securing social legitimacy (Ogawa, 1992, 1994). Schools are a social milieu where both actual results and the perception of value to the organization affect resource distribution. Many informal institutional rules are not challenged because they derive from public opinion and contain cultural and social pressures to conform to a given structural form. "We do it this way because we always have," might be one such prevailing belief that leads to school counselors performing noncounseling duties.

When school counselors share information about program results with opinion makers and decision makers within the school and community, the leaders come to understand that the school counselors' work contributes in crucial ways to student learning. The school counseling program thereby attains institutional legitimacy. By documenting their impact on student learning, school counselors demonstrate accountability for their contribution to the institution's mission, which leads to an enhanced position of the school counseling program within the school and to changes in related policies and processes.

Politics, as defined by Wirt and Kirst (2001), is a "form of social conflict rooted in group differences over values about the use of public resources to meet private needs" (p. 4). In political arenas, decisions are made based on two important weighted components: value versus resources. Schools are systems that use their authority to allocate resources that reflect their values. School counselors must operate within the system (much as a politician operates) by anticipating the "competing demands from school constituencies that have been organized to seek their share of values allocation from the school system" (Wirt & Kirst, 1997, p. 59). Schools must determine which demands they will meet and which they will not. These decisions are made with consideration of the belief in a concept or action as the "right thing to do." Those programs and people that are valued are said to have social capital.

The quest for political legitimacy within a school is an attempt to leverage the social capital necessary to obtain resources, authority, rights, and responsibilities. Schools are also political systems in which some individuals have more power and influence than others in determining how finite resources are distributed and in establishing the institution's policies, procedures, structures, and routines. School counseling programs earn political legitimacy and social capital when the program's value is believed to be worth the cost. When school counselors capitalize on institutional legitimacy and exert leadership and influence within schools, school counseling program functions are written into the formal structures (policies and procedures) of the school thereby institutionalizing these practices (Hatch, 2002; Militello, Carey, Dimmitt, & Schweid, 2006).

In sum, moving to an evidence-based practice mode of operation and communicating clearly about results will enhance the position of school counselors in three ways. First, the school counseling program will increase its own internal efficiency and will become more aligned with the school's educational missions and outcomes. Engaging in a continuous, self-reflective process will result in the adoption of effective interventions and practices and the discarding of ineffective interventions and practices. The school counseling program will then increasingly be respected for its accomplishments and efforts on behalf of students. If the results are communicated accurately and well, the program will gain institutional legitimacy. Increasingly, the school counseling program will be regarded as indispensable to the school, and the school counselors will be regarded as professionals who are capable of self-direction and self-correction. Finally, the increased value for the school counseling program leads to political legitimacy. School counselors will have more opportunities to participate in leadership activities that establish the school's policies, structure, and routines that define the role and work of school counselors. The program and its personnel will be regarded as essential to the work of the school and their value worth their cost (Hatch, 2002). The centrality of the program is dependent on school counselors' capacity to implement effective practices, document important results, use these results to improve practice, and effectively communicate these outcomes (and the processes used to obtain the results) to the school community.

Disseminating Results Effectively

Disseminating results effectively involves answering the following questions: What are your data about? Who is your target audience? What do you want the audience to know? Your focus will differ depending on your answers, although it is most efficient to develop materials that can be used in a variety of formats with a wide range of audiences. In general, results reporting needs to be concise, informative, logical, organized, interesting, honest, and clear (Heppner, Kivlighan, & Wampold, 1992). Holcomb (2004), Love (2002), and Johnson (2002) provide extensive guidelines for disseminating data findings effectively.

Disseminating Results Effectively

What is your data about?
- Interventions: (systemic, groups, individual)

Did it make a difference?
- Students: Current situation or changes over time
  Knowledge
  Behaviors
  Skills
  Attitudes

- Families: Demographics, school involvement
- Teachers: Survey results, collaborating
- Curriculum content:
  Scope and sequence
  Specific classes
- Program components
- Program as a whole

Who is your target audience?
- School counseling colleagues
- Principal/administrators
- Teachers
- Students
- Families
- School board
- Community, businesses

What do you want the audience to know?
- Sharing successes and challenges
  Interventions
  Curriculum
  Program components
  Program in general
- Proposals for changes that could better meet student needs
- Information about the school counseling program
- Need for services, numbers of students served

There are a variety of formats for the dissemination of data. There are various ways that information can be shared with stakeholders, and the next section of this chapter identifies general guidelines for creating effective materials. The following is a list of formats for disseminating data and program information:

- Verbal presentation
- PowerPoint presentation
- Inservice presentation
- Conversation/question and answer
- School Web site
- School counseling program Web site
- Handouts
- Pamphlets
- Memo
- E-mail
- Parent newsletter
- School counseling program newsletter
- Newspaper article
- School report such as a support personnel accountability report card (Tyra & Meyers, 2003)
- Bulletin boards/public spaces in schools
- Other

Sharing results about school counseling program outcomes requires communicating about data effectively. How data appear impacts whether or not people will look at and understand the data. If key stakeholders cannot access the information about your work, you will not have the impact you want and need. There are numerous online tutorials available through software manufacturers that can take you relatively painlessly through the steps involved in creating effective PowerPoint presentations, graphs, tables, charts, Web sites, and pamphlets. Collaborating with technology classes, district data technicians, and knowledgeable secretaries can be invaluable at this point in the process. Many high school students have relevant skills in these areas, and providing an opportunity for academic credit, internships, or work experience can be a win-win situation for all involved. Partnering with counselor education programs that have students needing practicum and internship experiences is another way to collaborate on data dissemination projects. Sample PowerPoint presentations are also available on the Web site of the Center for Excellence in School Counseling and Leadership (www.cescal.org). The following are some general guidelines about PowerPoint presentations:

- Keep font size at 28 or larger.
- Use headings to identify your focus.

- No more than 3–4 key points per slide.
- High contrast between background and text works best.
- White writing on a dark background is best for rooms where there is light.
- Dark writing on light backgrounds works only without background lighting.
- Avoid too much visual distraction—one animation at most.
- Visuals are available online by typing "image" or "clip art" into a search engine.

Before presenting, always do a run-through of the slide show and consider the following:

- In general, any piece of a data report should have three components: the introduction, the visual, and the summary, all of which need to fit onto one page for ease of distribution and communication (Holcomb, 2004). The introduction explains what was measured, who was measured, what specific instrument or test was used (provide the name, date, and reference, if available), and what any abbreviations, acronyms, or data terms stand for (SES, percentile, ELL, and so on).

- The visual component needs to be black and white with clearly differentiated patterns to distinguish between groups (avoid color, as it does not reproduce well and can lead to problems in later versions of a visual). The visual may be a graph, table, pie chart, and so on, depending on the data being shared. Holcomb (2004) also makes the following recommendations about the visual component: (a) label both axes of graphs clearly; (b) write percentile along the axis with numbers printed if scores are in percentiles (this prevents confusion about whether it is percentile correct versus percentile answering a question); (c) show the range from 0 to 100 if using percentiles; (d) use bar graphs for displaying data over time; (e) when displaying survey results, do not list all the items and all the responses—present a synopsis, the most relevant and important findings, or present a bar graph with the percentage of those who agreed with a statement.

- The summary component of a data report summarizes what you want people to get out of the information you have presented. What strengths, areas of concern, key outcomes, and so forth do you want to highlight? These points must be neutral statements of facts or observations, not interpretations or evaluative judgments (Holcomb, 2004).

As with any important public communication about your program, a data report element needs to be pilot tested with representative or available colleagues who can provide feedback about impact, clarity, and ease of use. Did they get your main points? Did you communicate what you intended? What are possible areas of confusion?

Once it is revised, the data report element can then be disseminated in several places—as a Web site page, as part of a report to administrators and school board members, as a PowerPoint slide in a presentation to colleagues, and as part of the school's or district's data materials. A few effective data components communicated widely are more effective than a confusing array of data elements and certainly much better than no communication or no data.

The ASCA National Model and Results Reporting

The ASCA National Model (ASCA, 2003) has several recommendations for reporting results, including annual reports and longer reports done every 5–7 years. The *ASCA National Model Workbook* (2004) contains templates and guides for creating annual results reports to key stakeholders. One suggestion is to start out by choosing to measure and report on one component of the school counseling program rather than try to measure the results of everything you do (Hatch, 2004a; Hatch, 2004b). Identify what data was used to make the decision to implement the intervention and specify the school counseling standards addressed in the activity. Indicate the process and perception data, the results/outcome data, and the implications for your findings. Then create your PowerPoint slides and share your successes with your school staff. Below is a sample order for this kind of presentation:

1. Introduction: What is the presentation about?

2. Data used to make the decision to implement the intervention

3. Standards addressed in the activity or intervention

4. Activity performed (process data—who, what, when, how often, etc.)

5. Perception data collected (knowledge, attitude, skill)

6. Behavior change measured

7. Results data (achievement-related and achievement)

8. What was learned from the results? What will be done differently and what will be done the same?

9. Reminder that correlation is not causation, but that school counselors are contributing in a meaningful way

10. Future plans for program improvement

11. Thank you for your support.

Focusing on one program component is less overwhelming than attempting to measure everything you are doing and allows you to tell a story that is manageable and memorable. When presenting about your intervention, you can engage in collegial conversation about what worked, what did not, and what you will do differently next time (if it was found to make a difference). This approach is a way to begin immediately to show the benefits of school counseling interventions using key concepts from this text or the ASCA National Model, even if you are just beginning to collect results. You do not need to have every component in place in order to report on your results. Professional school counselors simply cannot wait any longer to market the value of their resource.

When presenting about any educational outcomes, it is essential to remember that any change in student attitude, knowledge, skill, or behavior is the result of numerous factors. As Chapter 4 warned, correlation is not causation; and while any program or intervention may contribute to an outcome, it is never the sole cause. At the same time, it is important for school counselors to communicate about the meaningful ways they are contributing to the overall academic achievement of students through a variety of program components and interventions. We are in the picture but are not the whole picture, or out of the picture.

If your school counseling program is not yet a standing agenda item at staff meetings, reporting about data is a way to justify some time. Regular reporting on action plans and their related results in 5- to 10-minute presentations can inform the school community about the impact of the school counseling program in ways that build understanding, value, and respect for the work being done.

Once you have presented a few times about your program, it is important to move beyond reporting on one data element. Because there are so many potential factors that impact student success, it usually takes several related interventions to impact significant student outcomes. If in Year 1 the school counseling team reports on classroom guidance lessons about study skills and retention criteria, then in Year 2 they could add a report about the evaluation of a group component that was done with students who were still failing after the Year 1 intervention. Over time, especially if your PowerPoint presentations are put on a Web site, you have painted a picture that demonstrates the many ways you are supporting student success, and a more complete representation of the program emerges.

Planning Your Ongoing Professional Skill Development

Learning how to use data and research to identify, implement, and evaluate quality school counseling interventions and program components can show us that even when we do excellent work as school counselors, there is always more to be learned. It is a truism that the more we know the more we realize how much there is to learn. As new curriculum materials are developed and evaluated, as new evaluation tools are created, and as the ASCA National Model is evaluated as a program model, it will obviously be crucial to continue to learn more and to update skills and programs.

Traveling the country teaching school counselors how to implement the National Model, use data and research effectively, and become leaders in schools and in the profession, we have learned that ongoing professional development and a commitment to growth and new ideas are crucial to the future of school counseling. To have the desired impact on student skills and understanding, and to gain the legitimacy and institutional value that our efforts deserve, it is imperative that we do the best work possible. We can be role models in teaching our students the value of lifelong learning, the importance of setting worthwhile goals, and the rewards that come with hard work.

Reconstructing Professional Identity

The Moral Dimension of School Counseling Work

Throughout this book, we have identified ways to move to an evidence-based practice to better support the goal of helping all students achieve success in school (ASCA, 2003). School counseling is being transformed in order to truly serve all students, to address systemic barriers to achievement, and to advocate for effective educational practices. Implicit in these goals is the moral imperative to become an advocate and social change agent for the students and schools we work with in order to remediate existing inequities in educational access and outcomes and to provide the best possible services for all students (Education Trust, 1999, 2001; House & Martin, 1998; Paisley & Hayes, 2003; Stone & Dahir, 2006). The skills and procedures delineated in this book—data-based decision making, using existing research evidence to choose interventions, and evaluating interventions and programs—are all invaluable for addressing equity issues. Ultimately the goal of using evidence-based practice is helping all students reach their potential, and remembering this motivates us and gives meaning to our efforts.

Reconnecting to the Personal Meaning of Your Work

People go into the field of school counseling for a variety of reasons, but for most it has something to do with helping children and youth. It is crucial to find the links between your original reasons for becoming a counselor and the current situation in the field. Holcomb

(2004) has developed an activity to identify internal and external motivations for using data in schools. A version of this has been modified here for school counselors (derived from Holcomb, 2004, and ASCA, 2003):

- To do what is best for our students
- To satisfy our own need for excellence
- To reward and strengthen feelings of success and efficacy
- To be more proactive and less reactive
- To document student achievement and growth
- To test the assumptions we make about students and their capabilities
- To be more objective in decision making
- To prioritize efforts to support student success
- To promote equitable access to a quality school counseling program for all students
- To generate more opportunities for collaboration and teaming
- To be able to assess student learning in a variety of modalities more effectively
- To demonstrate the school counseling program's contributions to the school's mission
- To provide the community with information about the school counseling program
- To keep us from wasting time and money on things that do not work or do not matter
- To prove we are not afraid of feedback
- To report effectively to constituents
- To answer community questions about our effectiveness
- To show the connection of school counseling to school improvement
- To respond to public pressure for accountability
- To market ourselves
- To help advocate for reduction in ratios
- To improve legitimacy
- To improve political and social capital
- To improve operational efficiency

Which of these statements resonates with you? Are the reasons that you have identified for moving to evidence-based practice inner-driven or outer-driven or both? As we know from working with students who have been referred for counseling who do not see the need for change, it is a challenge to change behaviors based solely on external motivations or someone else's expectations. Without internal motivation, change may be dreaded and resisted.

The Risk of Change

Learning the skills and processes in this book is the first step in improving practice. Equally challenging is actually changing our behaviors. As with our students, knowing is different from doing. We know how to help people change; we know how challenging it is to do so; and we know how to address the fears and insecurities that change processes involve. It is imperative that we use the counseling skills we already have to support ourselves and our colleagues through this process.

What are the fears related to evidence-based practice and the use of data? The most commonly stated concern about any change in educational or school counseling programs is lack of time (Holcomb, 2004; Kuranz, 2003). Holcomb states, "When we are overwhelmed with all the things we know we *should* do, we resort to completing the things we know we *can* do. It is the only way we can maintain the illusion that we are in control of our professional lives" (p. 30). The most effective way to address time challenges is to evaluate current time use to find out where there are opportunities for more efficient practice (Holcomb, 2004; Johnson, 2002). Adding more to the plate when the plate is already full can feel untenable.

Under any circumstance, most people fear failure. When we learn a new skill, we risk failing to do it correctly. Sometimes the more successful we have been, or the longer we have been doing something, the less interested we are in taking on a new endeavor that may challenge our self-identity as successful and competent. With evaluation, we risk finding out that something we are doing is not working as well as we thought. With data, we risk discovering inequities in our schools that need immediate attention, and which people would rather hide.

While any of these possibilities may evoke concern or even anxiety, they are each actually also a potential opportunity for tremendous improvement in the outcomes we seek to address. In other professions, failure is seen as an opportunity for development and success, not as an end in itself (Manz, 2002). Like any skill, data use becomes easier with practice. Success does not derive from doing the same thing over and over again; it derives from challenging ourselves and those around us to grow and develop to our potential. If an intervention or program component is not working, then it needs to be changed. If there are inequities that need to be addressed, which are embarrassing or disheartening, we have increased motivation to improve the situation. The key is that we have some information about what we need to do—we are not operating out of assumptions, intuition, hunches, or hearsay. Presenting the results of an evaluation to our colleagues or to stakeholders—even if all the news is not good—demonstrates that we are professionals who are dedicated to improving our practices, that we are not afraid of challenging information, and that we want to do what is best for children, not just what is easiest for us or makes us look good.

Dialogue and Community

Fear of change or failure is one of the reasons that evidence-based practice is best done collaboratively and, in fact, why every single program component discussed in this book is best done in teams. Working with others means that we can share the challenge of learning new skills and support each other in the process. We can develop compassion for colleagues whose fear may come across as resistance or lack of commitment (Holcomb, 2004), and we can face our own fears through the support of our colleagues. Shared risk taking, as any group facilitator knows, promotes empathy and authentic connection for those involved.

In Chapter 1, we stated that evidence-based practice consists of using data and research to identify what needs to be addressed, what is likely to be effective, and what the results of the implementation were. All of these questions are best asked and best answered with a team of engaged colleagues who are invested in successful student outcomes. We know that one person can make a difference and that a small group of people can make an even bigger difference. School counselors know the tremendous power of modeling the behaviors we want to see, developing community, and creating success. Working together to create the schools we want to see is the best way to make a difference for the children we care about. This is what school counseling is about, and this is what evidence-based practice can help us achieve.

Courage and Conviction

Recall that in Chapter 1 you took the Brief Self-Assessment in Essential Competencies Required for Evidence-Based School Counseling Practice. Revisit that assessment and notice where you feel more confident and where your challenges still lie. When we work as a team, each person brings knowledge and skills to the table. As you begin to implement your evidence-based school counseling program, recognize how much you add to the conversation and remember that your challenges can become your personal and professional learning goals.

Once we have identified what our goals are, realized what fears are holding us back, and connected with our teams, we need the courage and conviction to follow through and do the necessary work.

Figuring out what is next is exciting for some people, a challenge for others. Likewise, some people are happy to get to the concrete work involved in actually accomplishing the outcome, while others are less interested in this part of the process. Identify what you love to do, find others who love to do other parts of the process, and work together to get where you want to go.

Appendix A

Guidance Curriculum Action Plans,
Intentional Guidance Action Plans,
and a Needs Assessment Survey

Authors' Note: The following action plans were designed by Trish Hatch.

XYZ Unified School District

XYZ Elementry School Guidance Curriculum Action Plan for School Year _____

Grade Level	Guidance Lesson Content (Topic Area)	ASCA National Standard	Curriculum and Materials	Projected Start/ Projected End	Projected Number of Students Impacted	Lesson Will Be Presented in Which Class/ Subject?	Evaluation Methods How Will the Results Be Measured?		Implementation Contact Person
							Perception Data: (ASK examples)	Results Data:	
4/5	Anti-bullying Violence prevention	*Personal/ Social* PS:A2 Acquire interpersonal skills PS:C1 Acquire personal safety skills	XYZ Violence prevention education prepackaged programs or anti-bullying programs	In January during National School Safety Week	All 4th and 5th graders in school @ 300 (All students; remember everyone receives guidance curriculum because it has been determined that this is a lesson all students should know.)	To be arranged with each teacher	*Attitude:* % who believe that calling people names hurts them % who believe it's okay to hit someone if he or she hits you first *Skills:* % who can role-play conflict-resolution skills % who can verbalize an "I statement" *Knowledge:* % who know the steps to conflict resolution % who know the consequences of bullying in schools % who know who to go to if help is needed	*Achievement Related (AR):* Number of students who are referred for discipline Number of students suspended Statewide youth survey (Title IV) data on bullying items *Achievement (A):* Achievement improvements in classes with improved climate	Elementary school counselor

Principal's signature   Date

Date of staff presentation   Prepared by

172

XYZ Unified School District
XYZ Middle School Guidance Curriculum Action Plan for School Year ____

Grade Level	Guidance Lesson Content (Topic Area)	ASCA National Standard	Curriculum and Materials	Projected Start/ Projected End	Projected Number of Students Impacted	Lesson Will Be Presented in Which Class/ Subject?	Evaluation Methods How Will the Results Be Measured?		Implementation Contact Person
							Perception Data: (ASK examples)	Results Data:	
6,7,8	Promotion/ retention guidelines Study skills Importance of homework	Academic A Competency A:A1 Improve self-concept A:A3 Achieve school success	Counselor- generated PowerPoint	10/03– 11/03	1,500 (All students; remember everyone receives guidance curriculum because it has been determined that this is a lesson all students should know.)	English (language arts)	*Attitude:* % of students who believe that doing homework matters % who believe that using study strategies will help them do better in school *Skills:* % who can accurately fill out an assignment planner % who can calculate a GPA *Knowledge:* % who demonstrate knowledge of best places, times, ways to study % with knowledge of promotion retention criteria % who know where to seek help (tutoring) % who can identify three study strategies	*Achievement Related (AR):* Homework completion rate *Achievement (A):* Compare academic improvement: GPA from Trimester 1 to Trimester 2 and/or Trimester 1 to Trimester 3	School counselors Team A (6) Team B (7) Team C (8)

Principal's signature _____ Date

Date of staff presentation _____ Prepared by

XYZ Unified School District
XYZ High School Guidance Curriculum Action Plan for School Year _____

Grade Level	Guidance Lesson Content (Topic Area)	ASCA National Standard	Curriculum and Materials	Projected Start/ Projected End	Projected Number of Students Impacted	Lesson Will Be Presented in Which Class/ Subject?	Evaluation Methods How Will the Results Be Measured?		Implementation Contact Person
							Perception Data: (ASK examples)	Results Data:	
9	Transcript review	*Academic Standard A3* Achieve school success *Standard B2* Plan to achieve goals	Counselor-generated PowerPoint using district graduation and state requirements Each student's own transcript Four-year plan	October (right after 1st quarter grades)	All in district @ 2,400 (All students; remember everyone receives guidance curriculum because it has been determined that this is a lesson all students should know.)	English or PE; Site-specific	*Attitude:* % who believe that grades earned in 9th grade matter % who believe taking college prep courses is important *Skills:* % who can accurately fill out a four-year academic plan % who can calculate a GPA *Knowledge:* % who know the graduation requirements % who can identify difference between types of GPA % who know college prep requirements	*Achievement Related (AR):* Homework completion rate Course enrollment patterns (college prep and advanced math and science coursework—honors, AP, etc.) *Achievement (A):* Course completion rates (9th grade credit deficiency rates) Completion of college prep requirements Graduation rates (data over time)	All high school counselors

Principal's signature _____ Date _____

Date of staff presentation _____ Prepared by _____

XYZ Unified School District
XYZ Elementary School Intentional Guidance Action Plan for School Year _____

Target group: all 3rd, 4th, and 5th graders; anger management issues.
Target group selection is based upon the following data: any student in 3rd, 4th, or 5th grade with three or more referrals.

School Counselor and Other Student Services Professional	ASCA National Standards	Type of Service to Be Delivered in What Manner?	Resources Needed	Projected Start/End	Projected Number of Students Impacted	Evaluation Method (How Will You Measure Results?) Perception Data (ASK Examples)	Results Data	Intended Effect on Academics, Behavior, or Attendance
Counselor A Counselor B	*Personal/ Social* PS:A2 Acquire interpersonal skills PS:C1 Acquire personal safety skills	Letter home to parents Group counseling for anger management and conflict resolution Contract with students Reward system	Purchase curriculum ($125.00) Time on staff agenda to explain program Disaggregated data from 1st quarter discipline referrals Group counseling facility (room) Clerical assistance for letters home to parents	November–March	60 students	*Attitude:* % who believe that it is okay to hit someone if he or she is hit first % who believe fighting is okay if someone calls you a bad name *Skills:* % who can accurately demonstrate conflict-resolution skills % who identify alternatives to fighting in a scenario *Knowledge:* % who demonstrate knowledge of conflict-resolution process % who have knowledge of what discipline occurs if you fight	*Achievement Related (AR):* % of improvement in discipline referrals *Achievement (A):* Compare academic improvement: GPA from Quarter 1 to Quarter 2	Students will improve behavior Students will improve academically (GPA)

_____ _____
Principal's signature   Date

_____ _____
Date of staff presentation   Prepared by

175

XYZ Unified School District
XYZ Elementary School Intentional Guidance Action Plan for School Year _____

Target group: all 3rd, 4th, and 5th graders with attendance problems.

Target group selection is based upon the following data: any student in 3rd, 4th, or 5th grade with five or more absences in 1st quarter.

School Counselor and Other Student Services Professional	ASCA National Standards	Type of Service to Be Delivered in What Manner?	Resources Needed	Projected Start/End	Projected Number of Students Impacted	Evaluation Method (How Will You Measure Results?)		Intended Effect on Academics, Behavior, or Attendance
						Perception Data (ASK Examples)	Results Data	
Counselor Smith	Academic A:A2 Acquire skills for improved learning	Letter home to parents	Purchase curriculum ($125.00)	November–March	40 students	Attitude: % who believe that coming to school every day is important	Achievement Related (AR): % of improvement in attendance and decrease in tardiness	Students will improve attendance
Nurse Jones	A:A3 Achieve school success	Group counseling on importance of attendance and time-management skills	Time on staff agenda to explain program			Skills: % who can accurately set an alarm clock		Students will improve academically (GPA)
	PS:B1 Self-knowledge application	Parents' meeting	Disaggregated data from 1st month's attendance data			% who can demonstrate time-management skills	Achievement (A): Compare academic improvement: GPA from Quarter 1 to Quarter 2	
		Contract with students	Group counseling facility (room)			Knowledge: % who demonstrate knowledge of time school starts		
		Reward system	Clerical assistance for letters home			% who have knowledge of what discipline might occur if student is truant from school		

Principal's signature _____ Date _____

Date of staff presentation _____ Prepared by _____

XYZ Unified School District
XYZ Middle School Intentional Guidance Action Plan for School Year _____

Target group: all 6th, 7th, and 8th graders in danger of failing.
Target group selection is based upon the following data: any student with a GPA below 1.3 at the end of first trimester (T1).

School Counselor and Other Student Services Professional	ASCA National Standards	Type of Service to Be Delivered in What Manner?	Resources Needed	Projected Start/End	Projected Number of Students Impacted	Evaluation Method (How Will You Measure Results?)		Intended Effect on Academics, Behavior, or Attendance
						Perception Data (ASK Examples)	Results Data	
School Counselors: Team A (6th) Team B (7th) Team C (8th) Social Worker	*Academic Standard A* Students will acquire the knowledge, skills, and attitudes that will contribute to effective learning in school and across the lifespan.	Multiple counseling groups 12 weeks of curriculum 45-minute sessions Alternating classes (so that students miss less class time)	Purchase curriculum ($125.00) Time on staff agenda to explain program Disaggregated data from 1st trimester report cards Group counseling facility (room)	November–March	100 students	*Attitude:* % of students who believe that doing homework matters *Skills:* % of students who can accurately fill out an assignment planner *Knowledge:* % of students who can demonstrate knowledge of best places, times, ways to study, or know where to seek help (tutoring)	*Achievement Related (AR):* Homework completion rate *Achievement (A):* Compare academic improvement: GPA from Trimester 1 to Trimester 2 and/or Trimester 1 to Trimester 3.	Students will improve rate and accuracy of homework completion Students will improve academically (GPA)

_____   _____
Principal's signature   Date

_____   _____
Date of staff presentation   Prepared by

XYZ Unified School District
XYZ High School Intentional Guidance Action Plan for School Year _____

Target Group: 9th grade students at risk of failure.
Target group selection is based upon the following data: all 9th graders who have two or more F's at 1st quarter grade reporting.

School Counselor and Other Student Services Professionals	ASCA Standards and Competency	Type of Service to Be Delivered in What Manner?	Resources Needed	Projected Start/End	Projected Number of Students Impacted	Evaluation Method (How Will You Measure Results?) Perception Data (ASK examples)	Results Data	Intended Effect on Academics, Behavior, or Attendance
Counselor A Counselor B Counselor C	*Academic Standard A* Students will acquire the knowledge, skills, and attitudes that will contribute to effective learning in school and across the lifespan.	Letter or phone call home to parent includes referral opportunities for tutoring and offer to place in student groups Referral to staff mentor Individual counseling session Group counseling for issues that are barriers to learning Alternating classes (so that student misses less class time)	Disaggregated data from 1st quarter report cards Purchase curriculum for groups Time on staff agenda to explain program Group counseling facility (room) Clerical help for letters home and scheduling of meetings and groups	November–March	120 students	*Attitude:* % who believe that passing classes in 9th grade matters % who indicate they will ask for help when they need it *Skills:* % who can identify resources for tutorial help % who can identify their barriers to learning *Knowledge:* % who know credits necessary to graduate % who know where and when to seek help for tutoring	*Achievement Related (AR):* Homework completion rate % Attending tutoring regularly *Achievement (A):* Compare academic improvement: Classes passed at quarter to classes passed at semester	Students will improve rate and accuracy of homework completion Students will improve academically (GPA)

Principal's signature _____   Date _____

Date of staff presentation _____   Prepared by _____

Needs Assessment Survey

BMG High School

Counseling Department

Student Input About the School Counseling Program

Instructions: Please complete this survey to help the school counseling program plan future services. Mark the number representing the degree of agreement you have with each statement. Thank you for your help.

	Strongly Disagree	Disagree	Agree	Strongly Agree
ACADEMIC DEVELOPMENT				
I think it is important for me to:				
1. Maintain, review, and revise a four-year academic plan to successfully complete my high school graduation requirements.	1	2	3	4
2. Develop and follow a four-year academic plan to match my evolving career and educational goals.	1	2	3	4
3. Understand how graduating from high school will better prepare me for continuing education and entry level jobs.	1	2	3	4
4. Realize how my decisions and actions lead to specific outcomes.	1	2	3	4
5. Value learning beyond my high school education.	1	2	3	4
6. Develop and use listening skills in a variety of academic and social situations.	1	2	3	4
7. Develop and use organizational and time management skills for success in school and in future employment.	1	2	3	4
8. Have resources/technology available to me to complete schoolwork and accomplish academic goals.	1	2	3	4

(Continued)

Needs Assessment Survey (Continued)

	Strongly Disagree	Disagree	Agree	Strongly Agree
ACADEMIC DEVELOPMENT				
9. Develop and use study skills necessary to take, organize, and use my notes effectively.	1	2	3	4
10. Understand the importance of setting up short- and long-term goals.	1	2	3	4
CAREER DEVELOPMENT				
1. Understand how life situations and circumstances influence the achievement of my career goals.	1	2	3	4
2. Identify positive motivating factors and roadblocks to achieving my academic and career goals.	1	2	3	4
3. Review and incorporate my personal learning styles, interests, strengths, and weaknesses in relation to educational and career planning.	1	2	3	4
4. Research career opportunities that relate to my interests, abilities, and lifestyle choices.	1	2	3	4
5. Have access to occupational resources to assist in my career planning.	1	2	3	4
6. Identify appropriate choices during high school that will lead to marketable skills for entry level employment or for advanced education.	1	2	3	4
7. Demonstrate positive attitudes, behaviors, and skills necessary to obtaining and maintaining a full-time or part-time job.	1	2	3	4
8. Be aware of career opportunities available at various postsecondary institutions.	1	2	3	4
9. Take the required steps toward transitioning from high school to				

postsecondary education, advanced training programs, and/or the world of work.	1	2	3	4
10. Explore experiences available to me that will help define and clarify my career interest areas.	1	2	3	4

PERSONAL/SOCIAL DEVELOPMENT

1. Have an understanding of my own growth and development.	1	2	3	4
2. Recognize and accept my personal strengths and weaknesses.	1	2	3	4
3. Possess and maintain a consistent positive self-image.	1	2	3	4
4. Use appropriate ways to express my feelings when coping with sadness, stress, and conflict.	1	2	3	4
5. Demonstrate appropriate anger management, self-control, and conflict resolution skills in a variety of settings.	1	2	3	4
6. Demonstrate responsible behaviors when interacting with my peers.	1	2	3	4
7. Demonstrate the ability to relate to and work successfully with individuals of different gender, culture, and/or disabilities.	1	2	3	4
8. Accept, respect, and appreciate differences in people.	1	2	3	4
9. Develop healthy relationships with my parents, siblings, friends, adults, coworkers, and girlfriend/boyfriend.	1	2	3	4
10. Use good communication skills in a variety of group situations.	1	2	3	4

Appendix B

Summary of School Counseling Outcome
Research Articles and Findings

RESEARCH DOMAIN	OUTCOME RESEARCH ARTICLES	FINDINGS
School Counseling Programs	Sink, C. A., & Stroh, H. R. (2003). Raising achievement test scores of early elementary school students through comprehensive school counseling programs. *Professional School Counseling, 6*(5), 350–365.	Completed a statewide study to determine whether the presence of a comprehensive developmental guidance (CDG) program impacted students' academic achievement test scores. Early elementary-age students who attended the same school for three or more years did better academically when there was a CDG program, even if the program was not fully implemented. Additionally, students who remained in the same school for multiple years with a well-implemented CDG program obtained higher achievement test scores than students who attended schools without such programs.
School Counseling Programs	Lapan, R. T., Gysbers, N. C., & Petroski, G. F. (2001). Helping seventh graders be safe and successful: A statewide study of the impact of comprehensive guidance and counseling programs. *Journal of Counseling and Development, 79,* 320–330.

Lapan, R. T., Gysbers, N. C., & Sun, Y. (1997). The impact of more fully implemented guidance programs on the school experiences of high school students: A statewide evaluation study. *Journal of Counseling and Development, 75,* 292–302. | In middle and high schools with more fully implemented CDG programs, students reported earning higher grades, having better relationships with teachers, and feeling greater satisfaction with school. Students in these schools were also more likely to report that education was relevant to later life, school was safe, and at the high school level, that career and college information was accessible. |

RESEARCH DOMAIN	OUTCOME RESEARCH ARTICLES	FINDINGS
Meta-analyses and Research Summaries	Whiston, S. C., & Sexton, T. L. (1998). A review of school counseling outcome research: Implications for practice. *Journal of Counseling and Development, 76,* 412–426.	Summarized 50 outcome studies published between 1988 and 1995 and found modest research support for interventions in the areas of career planning, group counseling, social skill training, and peer counseling.
Meta-analyses and Research Summaries	Gerler, E. R., Jr. (1985). Elementary school counseling research and the classroom learning environment. *Elementary School Guidance and Counseling, 20,* 39–48.	Completed a review of school counseling interventions at the elementary school level with a focus on teacher consultations, counseling, and classroom guidance interventions. Found that classroom guidance was related to improvement in elementary school students' behaviors.
Meta-analyses and Research Summaries	St. Clair, K. L. (1989). Middle school counseling research: A resource for school counselors. *Elementary School Guidance and Counseling, 23,* 219–226	The results of this review indicated that (1) an academic skills workshop can increase middle school students' grades, (2) a short nontraditional career workshop can alter middle school students' occupational stereotypes, and (3) a four-months-long human relations training for middle school students can reduce referrals for disciplinary problems.
Meta-analyses and Research Summaries	Wilson, N. S. (1986). Counselor interventions with low-achieving and underachieving elementary, middle, and high school students: A review of the literature. *Journal of Counseling and Development, 64,* 628–634.	Focused on interventions with low-achieving students and their parents to determine whether school counseling interventions were effective in boosting academic achievement as measured by grade point average. Summary information suggested that counseling interventions can have positive effects on academic achievement with this population.

RESEARCH DOMAIN	OUTCOME RESEARCH ARTICLES	FINDINGS
Meta-analyses and Research Summaries	Prout, S. M., & Prout, H. T. (1998). A meta-analysis of school-based studies of counseling and psychotherapy: An update. *Journal of School Psychology, 36,* 121–136.	Completed a meta-analysis of counseling and psychotherapy in school settings and concluded that there was strong evidence that these interventions are effective in this context (effect size = .97). They found that school-based psychotherapy has demonstrable beneficial effects on student well-being but did not find significant improvements in academic achievement. Because this meta-analysis only had 33 studies, the findings must be interpreted with caution, however.
Meta-analyses and Research Summaries	Baker, S. B., Swisher, J. D., Nadenichek, P. E., & Popowicz, C. L. (1984). Measured effects of primary prevention strategies. *Personnel and Guidance Journal, 62,* 459–464.	A meta-analysis that considered primary prevention efforts in school found a moderate effect size of .55.
Academic Achievement: Family Interventions	Henderson, A. T., & Berla, N. (1995). *A new generation of evidence: The family is critical to student achievement.* Washington, DC: Center for Law and Education.	Reviewed research about the effects of family interventions on school problems and concluded that when schools provide support and counseling for families, there are related increases in achievement, attendance, graduation rates, and postsecondary education enrollment.

RESEARCH DOMAIN	OUTCOME RESEARCH ARTICLES	FINDINGS
Academic Achievement: Family Interventions	Esters, P., & Levant, R. F. (1983). The effects of two-parent counseling programs on rural low-achieving students. *School Counselor, 31,* 159–166. James, R., & Etheridge, G. (1983). Does parent training change behavior of inner-city children? *Elementary School Guidance and Counseling, 18,* 75–78.	Parent counseling and consultation has been shown to positively impact student motivation, classroom behavior, and achievement.
Academic Achievement: Family Interventions	Bundy, M. L., & Poppen, W. A. (1986). School counselors' effectiveness as consultants: A research review. *Elementary School Guidance and Counseling, 21,* 215–222.	Reported that Adlerian parent consultation and parent effectiveness training can increase student academic performance, student motivation, and parent-child relationship quality.
Academic Achievement: Classroom Interventions	Carns, A. W., & Carns, M. R. (1991). Teaching study skills, cognitive strategies, and meta-cognitive skills through self-diagnosed learning styles. *School Counselor, 38,* 341–346.	Designed a curriculum intervention to increase 4th grade students' awareness of learning styles and metacognitive skills, with resultant increases in self-efficacy. Students who engaged in this intervention showed marked improvement in their academic achievement as measured by the California Test of Basic Skills.

RESEARCH DOMAIN	OUTCOME RESEARCH ARTICLES	FINDINGS
Academic Achievement: Classroom Interventions	Gerler, E. R., & Herndon, E. Y. (1993). Learning how to succeed academically in middle school. *Elementary School Guidance and Counseling, 27*(3), 186–197.	Conducted a study to evaluate the effectiveness of a 10-session, multimodal guidance unit called "Succeeding in School," which was designed to improve academic performance. Students improved their awareness of how to succeed in school after the intervention, but teacher ratings of academic achievement were not significantly different from pretest to posttest.
Academic Achievement: Classroom Interventions	Lee, R. S. (1993). Effects of classroom guidance on student achievement. *Elementary School Guidance and Counseling, 27*, 163–171.	Conducted a study to replicate Gerler and Herndon's (1993) work. Used the same materials to examine the effects of the classroom guidance intervention on academic achievement. Teachers completed pre- and posttest ratings on students' academic achievement in math, language arts, and conduct. Significant differences were found between the treatment and control groups on the pre- and posttest math scores suggesting that this curriculum can positively influence academic achievement in math.
Academic Achievement: Classroom Interventions	Stevahn, L., Johnson, D. W., Johnson, R. T., & Schultz, R. (2002). Effects of conflict resolution training integrated into a high school social studies curriculum. *Journal of Social Psychology, 142*(3), 305–331.	Integrated conflict resolution materials into a high school social studies curriculum and found that students learned both the conflict resolution and the academic content more than students who didn't receive the integrated content and were able to apply the procedures they learned more successfully.

RESEARCH DOMAIN	OUTCOME RESEARCH ARTICLES	FINDINGS
Academic Achievement: Classroom Interventions	Rathvon, N. W. (1991). Effects of a guidance unit in two formats on the examination performance of underachieving middle school students. *School Counselor, 38,* 294–304.	Compared students who received test preparation materials in small-group and classroom formats with students who received no information and found no differences among the three groups.
Academic Achievement: Small-Group Interventions	Hoag, M. J., & Burlingame, G. M. (1997). Evaluating the effectiveness of child and adolescent group treatment: A meta-analytic review. *Journal of Clinical Child Psychology, 26*(3), 234–246.	Conducted a meta-analytic review of 49 studies about group counseling. Determined that group counseling interventions can have a moderate impact on academic achievement factors (effect size = .51, standard deviation = 24, $p = .06$).
Academic Achievement: Small-Group Interventions	Shechtman, Z. (2002). Child group psychotherapy in the school at the threshold of a new millennium. *Journal of Counseling and Development, 80,* 257–384.	Completed a review of research about child group psychotherapy and noted that group counseling interventions for addressing school achievement need to include a social and emotional component in addition to the educational remediation in order to be most effective.
Academic Achievement: Small-Group Interventions	Wilson, N. S. (1986). Counselor interventions with low-achieving and underachieving elementary, middle, and high school students: A review of the literature. *Journal of Counseling and Development, 64,* 628–634.	Found that directive counseling and behavioral counseling had positive effects on academic achievement with underachieving students in a small-group setting. There was a greater impact on academic achievement for the small-group intervention than for individual counseling.

RESEARCH DOMAIN	OUTCOME RESEARCH ARTICLES	FINDINGS
Academic Achievement: Small-Group Interventions	Brigman, G., & Campbell, C. (2003). Helping students improve academic achievement and school success behavior. *Professional School Counseling, 7,* 91–98.	These results provided very strong support for the conclusion that school counseling interventions that focus on the development of cognitive, social, and self-management skills can result in sizable gains in student academic achievement. They utilized groups to augment the classroom curriculum materials in Student Success Skills with students who needed that support and found that they were able to have a significant impact on academic achievement, even with students who had been considerably underachieving.
Academic Achievement: Individual Interventions	Casey, R. J., & Berman, J. S. (1985). The outcome of psychotherapy with children. *Psychological Bulletin, 98,* 388–400. Prout, H. T., & DeMartino, R. A. (1986). A meta-analysis of school-based studies of psychotherapy. *Journal of School Psychology, 24,* 285–292.	Meta-analyses of research about the impact of psychotherapy and counseling have often found evidence that individual interventions can positively impact achievement (Casey & Berman), grade point average (ES = .58), and cognitive abilities (ES = .66) (Prout & DeMartino).
Academic Achievement: Individual Interventions	Edmondson, J. H., & White, J. (1998). A tutorial and counseling program: Helping students at risk of dropping out of school. *Professional School Counseling, 1*(4), 43–51.	A comprehensive drop-out prevention program involving both counseling and tutoring significantly assisted at-risk students in improving school achievement, self-esteem, and classroom behavior.

RESEARCH DOMAIN	OUTCOME RESEARCH ARTICLES	FINDINGS
Career Development: School Interventions	Lapan, R. T., Gysbers, N. C., & Petroski, G. F. (2001). Helping seventh graders be safe and successful: A statewide study of the impact of comprehensive guidance and counseling programs. *Journal of Counseling and Development, 79,* 320–330. Lapan, R. T., Gysbers, N. C., & Sun, Y. (1997). The impact of more fully implemented guidance programs on the school experiences of high school students: A statewide evaluation study. *Journal of Counseling and Development, 75,* 292–302.	In their statewide studies of comprehensive developmental counseling (CDG) programs, they found that students in schools with more fully implemented CDG programs reported more access to career and college information.
Career Development: Classroom Interventions	Hershey, A. M., Silverberg, M. K., Haimson, J., Hudis, P., & Jackson, R. (1999). *Expanding options for students: Report to Congress on the national evaluation of school-to-work implementation.* Princeton, NJ: Mathematical Policy Research.	Found that partnering with community members, industry, and businesses to provide internships and early career opportunities was very effective for students' career development.

RESEARCH DOMAIN	OUTCOME RESEARCH ARTICLES	FINDINGS
Career Development: Classroom Interventions	Baker, S. B., & Taylor, J. G. (1998). Effects of career education interventions: A meta-analysis. *Career Development Quarterly, 46*, 376–385.	This meta-analytic review found that curriculum-based career interventions had a moderate effect overall with a mean effect size of .34. They did not specifically identify any career education interventions in a group format.
Career Development: Classroom Interventions	Schlossberg, S. M., Morris, J. D., & Lieberman, M. G. (2001). The effects of a counselor-led guidance intervention on students' behaviors and attitudes. *Professional School Counseling, 4*, 156–164.	Curriculum designed to educate high school students about goal setting, problem solving, career exploration, and school resources significantly improved student behavior, attitude, and knowledge in these areas.
Career Development: Classroom Interventions	Savickas, M. L. (1990). The Career Decision-Making Course: Description and field test. *Career Development Quarterly, 38*, 275–284.	Found that the 10th grade Career Decision-Making Course based on Crites's model enhanced students' career planning and reduced career decision problems.
Career Development: Classroom Interventions	Baker, H. E. (2002). Reducing adolescent indecision: The ASVAB Career Exploration Program. *Career Development Quarterly, 50*(1), 359–370.	Conducted an independent evaluation of the ASVAB Career Exploration Program with high school students and found that participation in the program lowered certain kinds of career indecision and increased career exploration knowledge.
Career Development: Classroom Interventions	Peterson, G. W., Long, K. L., & Billups, A. (1999). The effect of three career interventions on the educational choices of eighth grade students. *Professional School Counseling, 3*(1), 34–42.	Found that the level of career interventions administered to middle school students had a direct impact on students' abilities to understand their educational choices and the relationship between academic choices and careers.

RESERCH DOMAIN	OUTCOME RESEARCH ARTICLES	FINDINGS
Career Development: Classroom Interventions	Fouad, N. A. (1995). Career linking: An intervention to promote math and science career awareness. *Journal of Counseling and Development, 73,* 527–534.	Found that middle school students demonstrated improved knowledge and performance in math and science courses after participating in a math and science career awareness intervention.
Career Development: Classroom Interventions	Luzzo, D. A., & Pierce, G. (1996). Effects of DISCOVER on the career maturity of middle school students. *Career Development Quarterly, 45,* 170–172.	The DISCOVER program was shown to lead to more age-appropriate decision making in middle school students.
Career Development: Classroom Interventions	Drodge, E. N., & Sumarah, J. C. (1990). The effects of the computer-based program, Career Search, on the vocational maturity of grade nine students. *Canadian Journal of Counselling, 24,* 26–35.	The Career Search intervention did not impact the vocational maturity of 9th graders.
Career Development: Classroom Interventions	Jones, L. K., Sheffield, D., & Joyner, B. (2000). Comparing the effects of the career key with self-directed search and job-OE among eighth grade students. *Professional School Counseling, 3*(4), 238–250.	Career inventories have been found to be of value as part of career guidance programs designed to meet ASCA standards, although school counselors should not rely too heavily on them.
Career Development: Classroom Interventions	Mosconi, J., & Emmett, J. (2003). Effects of a values clarification curriculum on high school students' definitions of success. *Professional School counseling, 7*(2), 68–79.	Implemented a values clarification curriculum with high school students and found that, compared with control group students, those who participated were able to expand their definition of success and to define success in unique terms.

RESEARCH DOMAIN	OUTCOME RESEARCH ARTICLES	FINDINGS
Career Development: Individual Interventions	Jones, L. W., & Spokane, A. R. (1988). Career-intervention outcome: What contributes to client gain? *Journal of Counseling Psychology, 35,* 447–462. Whiston, S. C., Sexton, T. L., & Lasoff, D. L. (1998). Career intervention outcome: A replication and extension. *Journal of Counseling Psychology, 45,* 150–165.	Meta-analyses of career counseling programs found that these interventions assisted a diverse range of students, including students from minority families, students who are gifted, students who have learning disabilities, and students from low-income families. Individual career interventions, delivered mainly through planning and advising, seemed to be the most effective way to impact student career outcomes.
Research Linking Career Development to Academic Achievement	Evans, J. H., & Burck, H. D. (1992). The effects of career education interventions on academic achievement: A meta-analysis. *Journal of Counseling and Development, 71,* 63–68.	Did a meta-analysis of research about the impact of career education interventions on academic achievement. Found minimal effects for career education (mean effect size = .16) on academic achievement as measured by GPA. Found that research indicated that career education has slightly larger effects on academic achievement for younger students and when integrated into math and English classes.
Social and Emotional Functioning: School Interventions	Embry, D. D., Flannery, D. J., Vazsonyi, T. T., Powell, K. E., & Atha, H. (1996). PeaceBuilders: A theoretically driven, school-based model for early violence prevention. *American Journal of Preventive Medicine,* Supplement to 12(5), 91–100.	The PeaceBuilders program, which focuses on reducing aggressive behavior and increasing social competence with students grades K–5, showed increases in prosocial behavior and decreases in teacher-reported aggressive behavior, with greater impact for those who were initially lower in skills at the beginning of the study.

RESEARCH DOMAIN	OUTCOME RESEARCH ARTICLES	FINDINGS
	Flannery, D. J., Vazsonyi, A. T., Liau, A. K., Guo, S., Powell, K. E., Atha, H., et al. (2003). Initial behavior outcomes for the Peacebuilders universal school-based violence prevention program. *Developmental Psychology, 39*(2), 292–308.	
	Vazsonyi, A. T., Bellison, L. M, & Flannery, D. J. (2004). Evaluation of a school-based, universal violence prevention program: Low-, medium-, and high-risk children. *Youth Violence and Juvenile Justice, 2,* 185–206	
Social and Emotional Functioning: School Interventions	Newman-Carlson, D., & Horne, A. M. (2004). BullyBusters: A psychoeducational intervention for reducing bullying behaviors in middle school students. *Journal of Counseling and Development 82,* 259–267.	Research indicates that teachers' self-reported ability to manage problematic behaviors before escalation improved as a result of the BullyBusters intervention and that related disciplinary referrals and classroom management problems decreased. This intervention was designed to change teacher knowledge and behavior rather than focus on students.
Social and Emotional Functioning: School Interventions	Robinson, S. E., Morrow, S., Kigin, T., & Lindeman, M. (1991). Peer counselors in a high school setting: Evaluation of training and impact on students. *School Counselor, 39,* 35–40.	Peer counselors gain significant knowledge and skills as a result of their training.

RESEARCH DOMAIN	OUTCOME RESEARCH ARTICLES	FINDINGS
	Morey, R. E., Miller, C. D., Rosen, L. A., & Fulton, R. (1993). High school peer counseling: The relationship between student satisfaction and peer counselors' style of helping. *School Counselor, 40,* 293–300.	
Social and Emotional Functioning: School Interventions	Bowman, R. P., & Myrick, R. D. (1987). Effects of an elementary school peer facilitator program on children with behavior problems. *School Counselor, 19,* 369–377.	Students' attendance, grades, attitudes, and classroom behaviors improved as a result of peer intervention services.
	Diver-Stamens, A. C. (1991). Assessing the effectiveness of an inner-city high school peer counseling program. *Urban Education, 26,* 269–284.	
	Tobias, A. K., & Myrick, R. D. (1999). A peer facilitator–led intervention with middle school problem behavior students. *Professional School Counseling, 3*(1), 27–33.	
Social and Emotional Functioning: School Interventions	Sprinthall, N. A., Hall, J. S., & Gerler, E. R., Jr. (1992). Peer counseling for middle school students experiencing family divorce: A deliberate psychological education model. *Elementary School Guidance and Counseling, 26*(4), 279–295.	Peer counseling for middle school students experiencing a family divorce produced positive results for peer helpers and the students receiving support.

RESEARCH DOMAIN	OUTCOME RESEARCH ARTICLES	FINDINGS
Social and Emotional Functioning: School Interventions	Carty, L., Rosenbaum, J. N., Lafreniere, K., & Sutton, J. (2000). Peer group counseling: An intervention that works. *Guidance and Counseling, 15*(2), 2–8.	Completed a 4-year longitudinal study of peer counseling and the effects on adolescent development. Their findings indicated that students who received peer counseling services scored significantly higher on coping and social skills scales.
Social and Emotional Functioning: Family Interventions	Henderson, A. T., & Berla, N. (1995). *A new generation of evidence: The family is critical to student achievement.* Washington, DC: Center for Law and Education.	Family interventions regarding social and emotional functioning produced lower special education referrals, fewer behavioral problems, and decreases in disciplinary events.
Social and Emotional Functioning: Family Interventions	Eder, K. C., & Whiston, S. C. (2006). Does psychotherapy help some students?: An overview of psychotherapy outcome research. *Professional School Counseling, 9*(5), 337–343.	Concluded that the meta-analyses of research about psychotherapy with children and adolescents indicated that oppositional defiant disorder and conduct disorder were most effectively remediated with functional family therapy, multisystemic therapy, and/or parent management training and that attention deficit hyperactivity disorder can be positively impacted by parent management training. They also concluded that anxiety, fear, and phobias in children and adolescents are most effectively treated through systematic desensitization, modeling, reinforced practice, and cognitive behavior therapy and that depressive symptoms are most effectively treated through cognitive-behavioral therapy.

RESEARCH DOMAIN	OUTCOME RESEARCH ARTICLES	FINDINGS
Social and Emotional Functioning: Classroom Interventions	Grossman, D. C., Neckerman, H. J., Koepsell, T. D., Liu, P., Asher, K. N., Beland, K., et al. (1997). Effectiveness of a violence prevention curriculum among children in elementary school. *Journal of the American Medical Association, 227*(20), 1605–1611.	Findings from a study of the Second Step violence prevention curriculum were that observed physically aggressive behavior decreased significantly in playground and cafeteria settings and that observed neutral/ prosocial behavior increased significantly in the same settings.
Social and Emotional Functioning: Classroom Interventions	Henderson, P. A., Kelby, T. J., & Engebretson, K. M. (1992). Effects of a stress-control program on children's locus of control, self-concept, and coping behavior. *School Counselor, 40,* 125–130.	Classroom instruction about stress reduction techniques helped improve student self-concept, sense of locus of control, and appropriate coping strategies.
Social and Emotional Functioning: Classroom Interventions	Kiselica, M. S., Baker, S. B., Thomas, R. N., & Reedy, S. (1994). Effects of stress inoculation training on anxiety, stress, and academic performance of adolescents. *Journal of Counseling Psychology, 41,* 335–342.	A stress reduction program helped high school students reduce anxiety and stress-related symptoms.
Social and Emotional Functioning: Classroom Interventions	Cheek, J. R., Bradley, L. J., Reynolds, J., & Coy, D. (2002). An intervention for helping elementary students reduce test anxiety. *Professional School Counseling, 6*(2), 162–165.	Found evidence to support a school counseling intervention that helped elementary students reduce test anxiety and improve test scores.

RESEARCH DOMAIN	OUTCOME RESEARCH ARTICLES	FINDINGS
Social and Emotional Functioning: Classroom Interventions	Schaefer-Schiumo, K., & Ginsberg, A. P. (2003). The effectiveness of the Warning Signs program in educating youth about violence prevention: A study with urban high school students. *Professional School Counseling, 7*(1), 1–9.	The Warning Signs curriculum did not show significant differences in experimental vs. control groups in educating urban high school students about potential violence in themselves and others.
Social and Emotional Functioning: Classroom Interventions	Morse, C. L., Bockoven, J., & Bettesworth, A. (1988). Effects of DUS02 and DUS02-revised on children's social skills and self-esteem. *Elementary School Guidance and Counseling, 22*, 199–205.	The Developing Understanding of Self and Others-2 (DUSO-2) curriculum materials did not significantly impact student self-esteem or social skills. When studies do not find an effect for an intervention, it's important to remember that there may be no finding because the assessment instruments didn't effectively measure outcomes, because the intervention wasn't well implemented, or because the intervention didn't do what was intended.
Social and Emotional Functioning: Classroom Interventions	Ciechalski, J. C., & Schmidt, M. W. (1995). The effects of social skills training on students with exceptionalities. *Elementary School Guidance and Counseling, 29*(3), 217–223.	Found that social skills training increased the social attractiveness of gifted and special needs students but did not impact student self-esteem or school behaviors.
Social and Emotional Functioning: Classroom Interventions	DeRosier, M. E. (2004). Building relationships and combating bullying: Effectiveness of a school-based social skills group intervention. *Journal of Clinical Child and Adolescent Psychology, 33*(1), 196–201.	Found that a social skills intervention enhanced third-grade students' self-esteem and self-efficacy and decreased social anxiety and aggressiveness.

RESEARCH DOMAIN	OUTCOME RESEARCH ARTICLES	FINDINGS
Social and Emotional Functioning: Classroom Interventions	Graham, B. C., & Pulvino, C. (2000). Multicultural conflict resolution: Development, implementation, and assessment of a program for third graders. *Professional School Counseling, 3*(3), 172–182.	Multicultural conflict resolution education provided students with more positive perspectives on conflict and helped to build related skills but did not impact on cultural understanding.
Social and Emotional Functioning: Classroom Interventions	D'Andrea, M., & Daniels, J. (1995). Helping students learn to get along: Assessing the effectiveness of a multicultural developmental guidance project. *Elementary School Guidance and Counseling, 30*, 143–154.	Found that a classroom-based multicultural understanding intervention enhanced 3rd graders' social skills and reduced arguments.
Social and Emotional Functioning: Small-Group Interventions	Borders, D. L., & Drury, S. M. (1992). Comprehensive school counseling programs: A review for policymakers and practitioners. *Journal of Counseling and Development, 70*, 487–498. Whiston, S. C., & Sexton, T. L. (1998). A review of school counseling outcome research: Implications for practice. *Journal of Counseling and Development, 76*, 412–426.	Summaries of school counseling research have found numerous studies indicating that group counseling was an effective way to support a wide range of student social and emotional development.
Social and Emotional Functioning: Small-Group Interventions	Hoag, M. J., & Burlingame, G. M. (1997). Evaluating the effectiveness of child and adolescent group treatment: A meta-analytic review. *Journal of Clinical Child Psychology, 26*(3), 234–246.	Found that groups that were oriented to counseling or therapy tended to be more effective (ES = .65) than structured or didactic psychoeducational groups (ES = .40).

RESEARCH DOMAIN	OUTCOME RESEARCH ARTICLES	FINDINGS
Social and Emotional Functioning: Small-Group Interventions	Kavale, K. A., & Forness, S. R. (1996). Social skill deficits and learning disabilities: A meta-analysis. *Journal of Learning Disabilities, 29*(3), 226–237.	Conducted a meta-analysis of 53 studies about social skills interventions with students who have learning disabilities. They found a small overall ES of .21, with student self-reporting of skills improvement higher than teacher or peer assessments.
Social and Emotional Functioning: Small-Group Interventions	Quinn, M. M., Kavale, K. A., Mathur, S. R., Rutherford, R. B., & Forness, S. R. (1999). A meta-analysis of social skill intervention for students with emotional or behavioral disorders. *Journal of Emotional and Behavioral Disorders, 7*(1), 54–65.	Reviewed 35 studies about students with emotional or behavior disorders and found that social skills training with this population had a small effect overall (ES = .19). There were larger effects for interventions that focused on specific, concrete social skills rather than global interventions.
Social and Emotional Functioning: Small-Group Interventions	Ang, R. P., & Hughes, J. N. (2001). Differential benefits of skills training with antisocial youth based on group composition: A meta-analytic investigation. *School Psychology Review 31*(2), 164–185.	Reviewed 38 studies about antisocial youth and found a stronger effect size with this population (ES = .62). They found that groups with prosocial peers produced stronger effect than those with only antisocial youth and that there were greater effects for skills observations, behavior ratings, and social adjustment.
Social and Emotional Functioning: Small-Group Interventions	Brantley, L. S., & Brantley, P. S. (1996). Transforming acting-out behavior: A group counseling program for inner-city elementary school pupils. *Elementary School Guidance and Counseling, 31*(2), 96–105.	Found that group counseling can make a significant difference in reducing acting-out behaviors in at-risk inner-city elementary students.

RESEARCH DOMAIN	OUTCOME RESEARCH ARTICLES	FINDINGS
Social and Emotional Functioning: Small-Group Interventions	Nelson, J. R., & Dykeman, C. (1996). The effects of a group counseling intervention on students with behavioral adjustment problems. *Elementary School Guidance and Counseling, 31*(1), 21–34. Shechtman, Z. (1993). School adjustment and small-group therapy: An Israeli study. *Journal of Counseling and Development, 72*(1), 77–81.	Group counseling interventions helped improve students' overall behavioral adjustment.
Social and Emotional Functioning: Small-Group Interventions	Bauer, S. R., Sapp, M., & Johnson, D. (2000). Group counseling strategies for rural at-risk high school students. *High School Journal, 83*(2), 41–51.	Cognitive-behavioral groups produced significant increases in self-esteem and academic self-concept of high school students.
Social and Emotional Functioning: Small-Group Interventions	Zinck, K., & Littrell, J. M. (2000). Action research shows group counseling effective with at-risk adolescent girls. *Professional School Counseling, 4*(1), 50–60.	Group counseling sessions were effective for reducing the at-risk behaviors of adolescent girls.
Social and Emotional Functioning: Small-Group Interventions	Reeder, J., Douzenis, C., & Bergin, J. J. (1997). The effects of small-group counseling on the racial attitudes of second grade students. *Professional School Counseling, 1*(2), 15–22.	Small-group counseling sessions helped to improve racial attitudes with elementary students.

RESEARCH DOMAIN	OUTCOME RESEARCH ARTICLES	FINDINGS
Social and Emotional Functioning: Small-Group Interventions	St. Clair, K. L. (1989). Middle school counseling research: A resource for school counselors. *Elementary School Guidance and Counseling, 23,* 219–226.	Reviewed outcome studies indicating that group cognitive-behavioral and relaxation-training interventions with middle school students can reduce teacher reports and referrals for disciplinary problems and that group counseling can improve middle school students' self-concept.
Social and Emotional Functioning: Small-Group Interventions	Riddle, J., Bergin, J. J., & Douzenis, C. (1997). Effects of group counseling on self-concepts of children of alcoholics. *Elementary School Guidance and Counseling, 31,* 192–202.	Group counseling interventions helped to improve the self-concept of children of alcoholics.
Social and Emotional Functioning: Small-Group Interventions	Gerler, J. E., Jr. (1985). Elementary school counseling research and the classroom learning environment. *Elementary School Guidance and Counseling, 20,* 39–48.	Group counseling improved elementary students' school behavior.
Social and Emotional Functioning: Small-Group Interventions	Whiston, S. C., & Sexton, T. L. (1998). A review of school counseling outcome research: Implications for practice. *Journal of Counseling and Development, 76,* 412–426.	Completed a review of outcome research and found that group-format social skills training developed adolescents' skills and reduced aggressive and hostile behavior.
Social and Emotional Functioning: Small-Group Interventions	Omizo, M.M., & Omizo, S. A. (1988c). The effects of participation in group counseling sessions on self-esteem and locus of control among adolescents from divorced families. *School Counselor, 36,* 54–60.	The results of outcome studies related to issues of divorce showed that group counseling can improve self-esteem and reduce hostility and aggression with children from divorced families.

RESEARCH DOMAIN	OUTCOME RESEARCH ARTICLES	FINDINGS
	Omizo, M. M., & Omizo, S. A. (1987b). Effects of parents' divorce and group participation on child-rearing attitudes and children's self-concept. *Journal of Humanistic Education and Development, 25*(3), 171–179.	
	Tedder, S. L., Scherman, A., & Wantz, R. A. (1987). Effectiveness of a support group for children of divorce. *Elementary School Guidance and Counseling, 18,* 102–109.	
Social and Emotional Functioning: Small-Group Interventions	Anderson, R. F., Kinney, J., & Gerler, E. R., Jr. (1984). The effects of divorce groups on children's classroom behavior and attitudes toward divorce. *Elementary School Guidance and Counseling, 10,* 70–76.	Adolescents who participated in divorce groups improved their attitudes toward divorce.
Social and Emotional Functioning: Small-Group Interventions	Omizo, M. M., & Omizo, S. A. (1987b). Effects of parents' divorce and group participation on child-rearing attitudes and children's self-concept. *Journal of Humanistic Education and Development, 25*(3), 171–179.	Reported that learning disabled (LD) students who participated in group counseling had higher levels of self-esteem.

RESEARCH DOMAIN	OUTCOME RESEARCH ARTICLES	FINDINGS
Social and Emotional Functioning: Small-Group Interventions	Williams, R. E., Omizo, M. M., & Abrams, B. C. (1984). Effects of STEP on parental attitudes and locus of control of their learning disabled children. *School Counselor, 23,* 126–133.	The STEP intervention improved parental attitudes and locus of control of their learning disabled children.
Social and Emotional Functioning: Individual Interventions	Casey, R. J., & Berman, J. S. (1985). The outcome of psychotherapy with children. *Psychological Bulletin, 98,* 388–400.	In an early meta-analysis about counseling and therapy with children and adolescents, they found an overall effect size for 75 studies of .71 on outcome measures such as social and global adjustment and cognitive skills.
Social and Emotional Functioning: Individual Interventions	Prout, H. T., & DeMartino, R. A. (1986). A meta-analysis of school-based studies of psychotherapy. *Journal of School Psychology, 24,* 285–292.	Only considered studies conducted in schools (n= 33), and found an overall effect size of .58 on outcomes such as behavior ratings, observed behaviors, problem-solving skills, grade point average, and cognitive abilities.
Social and Emotional Functioning: Individual Interventions	Stage, S. A., & Quiroz, D. R. (1997). A meta-analysis of interventions to decrease disruptive classroom behavior in public education settings. *School Psychology Review, 26(3),* 333–368.	In a meta-analysis of studies that analyzed individual interventions designed to decrease disruptive classroom behaviors (n= 99), they found an overall effect size of -0.78 (the negative number indicates that the behaviors decreased after the intervention, which is the intended direction).
Social and Emotional Functioning: Individual Interventions	Littrell, J. M., Malia, J. A., & Vanderwood, M. (1995). Single-session brief counseling in high school. *Journal of Counseling and Development, 73,* 341–458.	Determined that single-session brief counseling helped with the social/emotional adjustment of high school students. These students were able to reduce their concerns about problems and move closer to their goals.

RESEARCH DOMAIN	OUTCOME RESEARCH ARTICLES	FINDINGS
Social and Emotional Functioning: Individual Interventions	Littrell, J. M. (1998). *Brief counseling in action.* New York: Norton.	Conducted numerous studies indicating that brief counseling can be effective in a wide variety of situations.
Research Linking Social and Emotional Functioning with Academic Achievement	Wentzel, K., & Caldwell, K. (1997). Friendships, peer acceptance, and group membership: Relations to academic achievement in middle school. *Child Development, 68,* 1198–1209.	Found that students who were socially skilled were more successful academically and those who had social, emotional, or behavioral difficulties were less likely to achieve in school.

References

American School Counselor Association. (2003). *The ASCA National Model: A framework for school counseling programs.* Alexandria, VA: Author.

American School Counselor Association. (2004). *The ASCA National Model workbook.* Alexandria, VA: Author.

Anderson, R. F., Kinney, J., & Gerler, E. R., Jr. (1984). The effects of divorce groups on children's classroom behavior and attitudes toward divorce. *Elementary School Guidance and Counseling,* 70–76.

Ang, R. P., & Hughes, J. N. (2001). Differential benefits of skills training with antisocial youth based on group composition: A meta-analytic investigation. *School Psychology Review 31*(2), 164–185.

Ary, D., Jacobs, L. C., & Razavieh, A. (2002). *Introduction to research in education* (6th ed.). Belmont, CA: Wadsworth/Thomson Learning.

Association for Supervision and Curriculum Development. (2006). Planning and organizing for curriculum renewal. Retrieved August 21, 2006, from http://www.ascd.org [Click on Education Topics and then Standards].

Aubrey R. F. (1982). Program planning and evaluation: Road map of the 1980s. *Elementary School Guidance and Counseling, 17,* 52–60.

Baker, H. E. (2002). Reducing adolescent indecision: The ASVAB Career Exploration Program. *Career Development Quarterly, 50*(1), 359–370.

Baker, S. B. (1993). Action research in school counseling. *ASCA School Counselor, 41,* 67–68.

Baker, S. B., Swisher, J. D., Nadenichek, P. E., & Popowicz, C. L. (1984). Measured effects of primary prevention strategies. *Personnel and Guidance Journal, 62,* 459–464.

Baker, S. B., & Taylor, J. G. (1998). Effects of career education interventions: A meta-analysis. *Career Development Quarterly, 46,* 376–385.

Bandura, A., Barbaranelli C., Caprara G. V., & Pastorelli, C. (1996). Multifaceted impact of self-efficacy beliefs on academic functioning. *Child Development, 67,* 1206–1222.

Bauer, S. R., Sapp, M., & Johnson, D. (2000). Group counseling strategies for rural at-risk high school students. *High School Journal, 83*(2), 41–51.

Bloom, B. S., Englehart, M. B., Furst, E. J., Hill, W. H., & Krathwohl, O. R. (1956). *Taxonomy of educational objectives: The classification of educational goals. Handbook 1: The cognitive domain.* New York: Longman.

Borders, D. L., & Drury, S. M. (1992). Comprehensive school counseling programs: A review for policymakers and practitioners. *Journal of Counseling and Development, 70,* 487–498.

Bowman, R. P., & Myrick, R. D. (1987). Effects of an elementary school peer facilitator program on children with behavior problems. *ASCA School Counselor, 369–377.*

Brantley, L. S., & Brantley, P. S. (1996). Transforming acting-out behavior: A group counseling program for inner-city elementary school pupils. *Elementary School Guidance and Counseling, 31*(2), 96–105.

Brigman, G., & Campbell, C. (2003). Helping students improve academic achievement and school success behavior. *Professional School Counseling, 7*(2), 91–98.

Brigman, G., & Webb, L. (2004). *Student Success Skills: Classroom Manual.* Boca Raton, FL: Atlantic Education Consultants.

Bronson, R. C., Gurney, J. G., & Land, G. H. (1999). Evidence-based decision making in public health. *Journal of Public Health Management, 5,* 86–97.

Brown, D., & Trusty, J. (2005). The ASCA National Model, accountability, and establishing causal links between school counselor activities and student outcomes. *Professional School Counseling, 9*(1), 13–15.

Bully Busters. (2006). Retrieved August 21, 2006, from www.researchpress .com/product/item/5192/

Bundy, M. L., & Poppen, W. A. (1986). School counselors' effectiveness as consultants: A research review. *Elementary School Guidance and Counseling, 21,* 215–222.

Burch H., & Peterson, G. (1975). Needed: More evaluation, not research. *Personnel and Guidance Journal, 53,* 563–569.

Burtnett, F. (1993, April 28). Move counseling off the back burner of reform. *Education Week, 32,* 22.

Campbell, C. A., & Brigman, G. (2005). Closing the achievement gap: A structured approach to group counseling. *Journal for Specialists in Group Work, 30,* 1–16.

Campbell, C. A., & Dahir, C. A. (1997). *The national standards for school counseling programs.* Alexandria, VA: American School Counselor Association.

Carey, J. C., & Dimmitt, C. (2006). Resources for school counselors and counselor educators: The National Center for School Counseling Outcome Research. *Professional School Counseling, 9,* 416–420.

Carey, J. C., Dimmitt, C., Hatch, T. A., Lapan, R. T., & Whiston, S. C. (in press). Report of the National Panel for Evidence-Based School Counseling: Outcome research coding protocol and evaluation of Student Success Skills and Second Step. *Professional School Counseling.*

Carns, A. W., & Carns, M. R. (1991). Teaching study skills, cognitive strategies, and metacognitive skills through self-diagnosed learning styles. *ASCA School Counselor, 38,* 341–346.

Carty, L., Rosenbaum, J. N., Lafreniere, K., & Sutton, J. (2000). Peer group counseling: An intervention that works. *Guidance and Counseling, 15*(2), 2–8.

Casey, R. J., & Berman, J. S. (1985). The outcome of psychotherapy with children. *Psychological Bulletin, 98,* 388–400.

Center for School Counseling Outcome Research. (2004). *Center for school counseling outcome research.* Retrieved December 8, 2004, from http:// umass.edu/schoolcounseling

Cheek, J. R., Bradley, L. J., Reynolds, J., & Coy, D. (2002). An intervention for helping elementary students reduce test anxiety. *Professional School Counseling, 6*(2), 162–165.

Chwalisz, K. (2003). Evidence-based practice: A framework for twenty-first-century scientist-practitioner training. *Counseling Psychologist, 31*(5), 497–528.

Ciechalski, J. C., & Schmidt, M. W. (1995). The effects of social skills training on students with exceptionalities. *Elementary School Guidance and Counseling, 29*(3), 217–223.

Cohen, J. (1988). *Statistical power analysis for the behavioral sciences* (2nd ed.). Hillsdale, NJ: Lawrence Erlbaum.

Committee for Children. (2006). *Second Step violence prevention.* Retrieved September 11, 2006, from www.cfchildren.org/cfc/ssf/ssf/ssindex/

Cooper, H., Lindsay, J. J., Nye, B., & Greathouse, S. (1998). Relationships among attitudes about homework, amount of homework assigned and completed, and student achievement. *Journal of Educational Psychology, 90,* 70–83.

Creswell, J. W. (2002). *Educational research: Planning, conducting, and evaluating quantitative and qualitative research.* Upper Saddle River, NJ: Merrill/Prentice Hall.

Curcio, C. C., Mathai, C., & Roberts, J. (2003). Evaluation of a school district's secondary counseling program. *Professional School Counseling, 6*(4), 296–303.

Dahir, C. A., & Campbell, C. C. (1997). *Sharing the vision: The national standards.* Alexandria, VA: American School Counselors Association.

Dahir, C. A., & Stone, C. D. (2003). Accountability: A M.E.A.S.U.R.E of the impact school counselors have on student achievement. *Professional School Counseling, 6,* 214–221.

D'Andrea, M., & Daniels, J. (1995). Helping students learn to get along: Assessing the effectiveness of a multicultural developmental guidance project. *Elementary School Guidance and Counseling, 30,* 143–154.

Darling-Hammond, L. (1998). Teacher learning that supports student learning. *Educational Leadership, 55*(5), 6, 6b–6c.

Deaton, C. (2001). Outcomes measurement and evidence-based nursing practice. *Journal of Cardiovascular Nursing, 15,* 83–86.

DeRosier, M. E. (2004). Building relationships and combating bullying: Effectiveness of a school-based social skills group intervention. *Journal of Clinical Child and Adolescent Psychology, 33*(1), 196–201.

Dimmitt, C., Carey, J., McGannon, W., & Henningson, I. (2005). Identifying a school counseling research agenda: A Delphi study. *Counselor Education and Supervision, 44,* 214–228.

Diver-Stamens, A. C. (1991). Assessing the effectiveness of an inner-city high school peer counseling program. *Urban Education, 26,* 269–284.

Dodge, K. A., & Coie, J. D. (1987). Social-information-processing factors in reactive and proactive aggression in children's peer groups. *Journal of Personality and Social Psychology, 53*(6), 1146–1158.

Drodge, E. N., & Sumarah, J. C. (1990). The effects of the computer-based program, Career Search, on the vocational maturity of grade nine students. *Canadian Journal of Counselling, 24,* 26–35.

Dufour, R. (2004). What is a professional learning community? *Educational Leadership, 61*(8), 6–11.

Easton, J. Q., & Engelhard, G. (1982). A longitudinal record of elementary school absence and its relationship to reading achievement. *Journal of Educational Research, 7*(5), 269–274.

Eder, K. C., & Whiston, S. C. (2006). Does psychotherapy help some students?: An overview of psychotherapy outcome research. *Professional School Counseling, 9*(5), 337–343.

Edmondson, J. H., & White, J. (1998). A tutorial and counseling program: Helping students at-risk of dropping out of school. *Professional School Counseling, 1*(4), 43–51.

Education Trust. (1999). *Transforming school counseling.* Retrieved May 21, 2006, from www2.edtrust.org/EdTrust/Transforming+School+Counseling/main

Education Trust. (2001). *Achievement in America.* Retrieved May 21, 2006, from www.edtrust.org/edtrust/

Education Trust. (2005). *Transforming school counseling initiative* (TSCI). Retrieved August 21, 2006, from www2.edtrust.org/EdTrust/Transforming+School+Counseling

Elias, M. J., Zins, J. E., Weissberg, R. P., Frey, K. S., Greenberg, M. T., Haynes, N. M., et al. (1997). *Promoting social and emotional learning: Guidelines for educators.* Alexandria, VA: Association for Supervision and Curriculum Development.

Embry, D. D., Flannery, D. J., Vazsonyi, T. T., Powell, K. E., & Atha, H. (1996). PeaceBuilders: A theoretically driven, school-based model for early violence prevention. *American Journal of Preventive Medicine, 12*(5 Supplement), 91–100.

Esters, P., & Levant, R. F. (1983). The effects of two-parent counseling programs on rural low-achieving students. *ASCA School Counselor, 31,* 159–166.

Evans, J. H., & Burck, H. (1992). The effects of career education on academic achievement: A meta-analysis. *Journal of Counseling and Development, 71,* 63–68.

EZAnalyze. (2006). *Data analysis software for educators.* Retrieved October 13, 2006, from www.ezanalyze.com/

Fairchild, T. N. (1993). Accountability practices of school counselors: 1990 national survey. *ASCA School Counselor, 40,* 363–374.

Fairchild, T. N., & Seeley, T. J. (1995). Accountability strategies for school counselors: A bakers' dozen. *ASCA School Counselor, 42,* 377–392.

Fairchild, T. N., & Zins, J. E. (1986). Accountability practices of school counselors: A national survey. *Journal of Counseling and Development, 65,* 196–199.

Ferrance, E. (2000). *Themes in education: Action research.* Northeast and Islands Regional Educational Laboratory at Brown University. Retrieved August 21, 2006, from www.alliance.brown.edu/pubs/themes_ed/act_research.pdf

Flannery, D. J., Vazsonyi, A. T., Liau, A. K., Guo, S., Powell, K. E., Atha, H., et al. (2003). Initial behavior outcomes for the PeaceBuilders universal school-based violence prevention program. *Developmental Psychology, 39*(2), 292–308.

Fouad, N. A. (1995). Career linking: An intervention to promote math and science career awareness. *Journal of Counseling and Development, 73,* 527–534.

Fowler, F. J. (1995). *Improving survey questions: Design and evaluation.* Thousand Oaks, CA: Sage.

Gerler, E. R., Jr. (1985). Elementary school counseling research and the classroom learning environment. *Elementary School Guidance and Counseling, 20,* 39–48.

Gerler, E. R., Jr., & Herndon, E. Y. (1993). Learning how to succeed academically in middle school. *Elementary School Guidance and Counseling, 27*(3), 186–197.

Gillies, R. M. (1993). Action research for school counselors. *ASCA School Counselor, 41,* 69–72.

Graham, B. C., & Pulvino, C. (2000). Multicultural conflict resolution: Development, implementation, and assessment of a program for third graders. *Professional School Counseling, 3*(3), 172–182.

Grossman, D. C., Neckerman, H. J., Koepsell, T. D., Liu, P., Asher, K. N., Beland, K., et al. (1997). Effectiveness of a violence prevention curriculum among children in elementary school. *Journal of the American Medical Association, 227*(20), 1605–1611.

Gysbers, N. C., & Henderson, P. (2000). *Developing and managing your school guidance program* (3rd ed.). Alexandria, VA: American Counseling Association.

Hatch, T. (2002). *The ASCA national standards for school counseling programs: A source of legitimacy or of reform?* (Doctoral dissertation, University of California, Riverside, 2002). *Dissertation Abstracts International, 63,* 2798.

Hatch, T. (2004a). Measuring one thing—well. *ASCA School Counselor, 41*(3), 23.

Hatch, T. (2004b). Writing school counselor action plans and sharing results: A two-pronged flashlight approach. In T. Hatch & L. Holland (Eds.), *National Model workbook* (pp. 108–118). Retrieved November 22, 2006, from www.trishhatch.com/Documents/Hatch_National_Model_work book.pdf

Hatch, T. (2005, June), *Data made easy: Using data to effect change.* Paper presented at the American School Counselor Association, Orlando, FL.

Hatch, T., & Bowers, J. (2002). The block to build on. *ASCA School Counselor, 39*(5), 12–17.

Hatch, T., Holland, L., & Meyers, P. (2003). When it's time to change. *ASCA School Counselor, 41*(3), 18–22.

Hayes, R. L., Dagley, J. C., & Horne, A. M. (1996). Restructuring school counselor education: Work in progress. *Journal of Counseling and Development, 74,* 378–384.

Hayes, R. L., Nelson, J. L., Tabin, M., Pearson, G., & Worthy, C. (2002). Using school-wide data to advocate for student success. *Professional School Counseling, 6*(2), 86–95.

Henderson, A. T., & Berla, N. (1995). *A new generation of evidence: The family is critical to student achievement.* Washington, DC: Center for Law and Education.

Henderson, P. A., Kelby, T. J., & Engebretson, K. M. (1992). Effects of a stress-control program on children's locus of control, self-concept, and coping behavior. *ASCA School Counselor, 40,* 125–130.

Heppner, P., Kivlighan, D., Jr., & Wampold, B. (1992). *Research design in counseling.* Pacific Grove, CA: Brooks/Cole.

Hershey, A. M., Silverberg, M. K., Haimson, J., Hudis, P., & Jackson, R. (1999). *Expanding options for students: Report to Congress on the national evaluation of school-to-work implementation.* Princeton, NJ: Mathematical Policy Research.

Hoag, M. J., & Burlingame, G. M. (1997). Evaluating the effectiveness of child and adolescent group treatment: A meta-analytic review. *Journal of Clinical Child Psychology, 26,* 234–246.

Hoagwood, K., & Erwin, H. D. (1997). Effectiveness of school-based mental health services for children: A 10-year research review. *Journal of Child and Family Studies, 6,* 435–451.

Holcomb, E. L. (2004). *Getting excited about data* (2nd ed.). Thousand Oaks, CA: Corwin Press.

House, R. M., & Martin, P. J. (1998). Advocating for better futures for all students: A new vision for school counselors. *Education, 119,* 284–291.

Howard, P. J. (2006). *The owner's manual for the brain: Everyday applications from mind-brain research* (3rd ed.). Austin, TX: Bard Press.

Humes, C. (1972). Accountability: A boon to guidance. *Personnel and Guidance Journal, 51,* 21–26.

Hursh, D. (1995). Developing discourses and structures to support action research for educational reform: Working both ends. In S. E. Noffke & R. B. Stevenson (Eds.), *Educational action research: Becoming practically critical* (pp. 141–153). New York: Teachers College Press.

Isaacs, M. L. (2003). Data-driven decision making: The engine of accountability. *Professional School Counseling, 6*(4), 288–295.

James, R., & Etheridge, G. (1983). Does parent training change behavior of inner-city children? *Elementary School Guidance and Counseling, 18,* 75–78.

Jeynes, W. H. (2002). The relationship between the consumption of various drugs by adolescents and their academic achievement. *American Journal of Drug and Alcohol Abuse, 28*(1), 15–21.

Johnson, C. D., & Johnson, S. K. (1991). The new guidance: A system approach to pupil personnel programs. *CACD Journal, 11,* 5–10.

Johnson, R. S. (2002). *Using data to close the achievement gap: How to measure equity in our schools.* Thousand Oaks, CA: Corwin Press.

Jones, L. K., Sheffield, D., & Joyner, B. (2000). Comparing the effects of the career key with self-directed search and job-OE among eighth grade students. *Professional School Counseling, 3*(4), 238–250.

Jones, L. W., & Spokane, A. R. (1988). Career-intervention outcome: What contributes to client gain? *Journal of Counseling Psychology, 35,* 447–462.

Kavale, K. A., & Forness, S. R. (1996). Social skill deficits and learning disabilities: A meta-analysis. *Journal of Learning Disabilities, 29*(3), 226–237.

Keene, K. M., & Stewart, N. R. (1989). Evaluation: Rx for counseling program growth. *ASCA School Counselor, 37,* 62–66.

Kemmis, S., & McTaggart, R. (2000). Participatory action research. In N. Denzin & Y. Lincoln (Eds.), *Handbook of qualitative research* (2nd ed., pp. 567–605). Thousand Oaks, CA: Sage.

Kemmis, S., & Wilkinson, M. (1998). Participatory action research and the study of practice. In B. Atweh, S. Kemmis, & P. Weeks (Eds.), *Action research in practice: Partnerships for social justice in education* (pp. 21–36). London and New York: Routledge.

Kerlinger, F. N. (1972). *Behavioral research: A conceptual approach.* New York: Holt, Rinehart & Winston.

Kiselica, M. S., Baker, S. B., Thomas, R. N., & Reedy, S. (1994). Effects of stress inoculation training on anxiety, stress, and academic performance of adolescents. *Journal of Counseling Psychology, 41,* 335–342.

Kratochwill, T. R., & Shernoff, E. S. (2003). Evidence-based practice: Promoting evidence-based interventions. *School Psychology Quarterly, 18*(4), 389–408.

Kuranz, M. (2003). Connecting school counseling to the current reality. *Professional School Counseling, 6*(3), ii–v.

Lapan, R. T. (2001). Results-based comprehensive guidance and counseling programs: A framework for planning and evaluation. *Professional School Counseling, 4,* 289–299.

Lapan, R. T., Gysbers, N. C., & Petroski, G. F. (2001). Helping seventh graders be safe and successful: A statewide study of the impact of comprehensive guidance and counseling programs. *Journal of Counseling and Development, 79,* 320–330.

Lapan, R. T., Gysbers, N. C., & Sun, Y. (1997). The impact of more fully implemented guidance programs on the school experiences of high school students: A statewide evaluation study. *Journal of Counseling and Development, 75,* 292–302.

Lee, R. S. (1993). Effects of classroom guidance on student achievement. *Elementary School Guidance and Counseling, 27,* 163–171.

Lee, V. V., & Goodnough, G. E. (2007). Creating a systemic, data-driven school counseling program. In B. T. Erford (Ed.), *Transforming the school counseling profession* (2nd ed.). Columbus, OH: Pearson Merrill Prentice Hall.

Littrell, J. M. (1998). *Brief counseling in action.* New York: Norton.

Littrell, J. M., Malia, J. A., & Vanderwood, M. (1995). Single-session brief counseling in high school. *Journal of Counseling and Development, 73,* 341–458.

Love, N. (2002). *Using data/getting results: A practical guide for school improvement in mathematics and science.* Norwood, MA: Christopher-Gordon.

Luzzo, D. A., & Pierce, G. (1996). Effects of DISCOVER on the career maturity of middle school students. *Career Development Quarterly, 45,* 170–172.

Macintyre, C. (2000). *The art of action research in the classroom.* London: David Fulton.

Mahoney, J. L., Cairns, B. D., & Farmer, T. W. (2003). Promoting interpersonal competence and educational success through extracurricular activity participation. *Journal of Educational Psychology, 95*(2), 409–418.

Manz, C. (2002). *The power of failure: 27 ways to turn life's setbacks into success.* San Francisco: Berrett-Koehler.

Marchant, G. J., Paulson, S. E., & Rothlisberg, B. A. (2001). Relations of middle school students' perceptions of family and school contexts with academic achievement. *Psychology in the Schools, 38*(6), 505–519.

McGinnis, E., & Goldstein, A. P. (1997). *Skillstreaming the elementary school child: New strategies and perspectives for teaching prosocial skills.* Champaign, IL: Research Press.

McNiff, J. (1988). *Action research: Principles and practice.* New York: Routledge.

McTighe, J., & Wiggins, G. (2004). *Understanding by design: Professional development workbook.* Alexandria, VA: Association for Supervision and Curriculum Development.

Militello, M., Carey, J., Dimmitt, C., Lee, V., & Schweid, J. (2006). Identifying exemplary school counseling practices: Ten domains that describe the work of counselors in schools that have outstanding performance in college preparation, application, and placement with low-income students. Manuscript submitted for publication.

Mills, G. E. (2000). *Action research: A guide for the teacher researcher.* Upper Saddle River, NJ: Merrill.

Morey, R. E., Miller, C. D., Rosen, L. A., & Fulton, R. (1993). High school peer counseling: The relationship between student satisfaction and peer counselors' style of helping. *ASCA School Counselor, 40,* 293–300.

Morse, C. L., Bockoven, J., & Bettesworth, A. (1988). Effects of DUSO2 and DUSO2-revised on children's social skills and self-esteem. *Elementary School Guidance and Counseling, 22,* 199–205.

Mosconi, J., & Emmett, J. (2003). Effects of a values clarification curriculum on high school students' definitions of success. *Professional School Counseling, 7*(2), 68–79.

Myrick, R. D. (1984). Beyond issues of school counselor accountability. *Measurement and Evaluation in Guidance, 16,* 218–222.

Myrick, R. D. (1993). *Developmental guidance and counseling.* Educational Media Corporation: Minneapolis, MN.

National Commission on Excellence in Education. (1983). *A nation at risk.* Washington, DC: U.S. Government Printing Office.

National Council of Teachers of Mathematics. (2006). Overview of principles and standards for school mathematics. Retrieved July 15, 2006, from www.nctm.org/standards/overview.htm

National Governors' Association. (1991). *From rhetoric to action: State progress in restructuring the education system.* Washington, DC: Author.

Nelson, J. R., & Dykeman, C. (1996). The effects of a group counseling intervention on students with behavioral adjustment problems. *Elementary School Guidance and Counseling, 31*(1), 21–34.

Newman-Carlson, D., & Horne, A. M. (2004). BullyBusters: A psychoeducational intervention for reducing bullying behaviors in middle school students. *Journal of Counseling and Development 82,* 259–267.

No Child Left Behind Act of 2001, Pub. L. No. 107–110. (2001).

Ogawa, R. T. (1992). Institutional theory and examining leadership in schools. *International Journal of Educational Management, 6*(3), 14–21.

Ogawa, R. T. (1994). The institutional sources of educational reform: The case of site based management. *American Educational Research Journal, 31,* 519–548.

Oliver, L. W., & Spokane, A. R. (1988). Career-intervention outcome: What contributes to client gain? *Journal of Counseling Psychology, 35,* 447–462.

Omizo, M. M., & Omizo, S. A. (1987a). The effects of eliminating self-defeating behavior of learning-disabled children through group counseling. *ASCA School Counselor, 34,* 282–288.

Omizo, M. M., & Omizo, S. A. (1987b). Effects of parents' divorce and group participation on child-rearing attitudes and children's self-concept. *Journal of Humanistic Education and Development, 25*(3), 171–179.

Omizo, M. M., & Omizo, S. A. (1988). The effects of participation in group counseling sessions on self-esteem and locus of control among adolescents from divorced families. *ASCA School Counselor, 36,* 54–60.

Paisley, P. O., & Hayes, R. L. (2003). School counseling in the academic domain: Transformation in preparation and practice. *Professional School Counseling, 6*(3), 198–204.

PeaceBuilders. (2006). Retrieved June 20, 2006, from www.peacebuilders .com

Peterson, G. W., Long, K. L., & Billups, A. (1999). The effect of three career interventions on the educational choices of eighth grade students. *Professional School Counseling, 3*(1), 34–42.

Poynton, T. A., & Carey, J. C. (2006). An integrative model of data-based decision making for school counseling. *Professional School Counseling, 10,* 121–130.

Protheroe, N. (2001). Improving teaching and learning with data-based decisions: Asking the right questions and acting on the answers. *ERS Spectrum, 19*(3), 4–9.

Prout, H. T., & DeMartino, R. A. (1986). A meta-analysis of school-based studies of psychotherapy. *Journal of School Psychology, 24,* 285–292.

Prout, S. M., & Prout, H. T. (1998). A meta-analysis of school-based studies of counseling and psychotherapy: An update. *Journal of School Psychology, 36,* 121–136.

Quinn, M. M., Kavale, K. A., Mathur, S. R., Rutherford, R. B., & Forness, S. R. (1999). A meta-analysis of social skill intervention for students with emotional or behavioral disorders. *Journal of Emotional and Behavioral Disorders, 7*(1), 54–65.

Rathvon, N. W. (1991). Effects of a guidance unit in two formats on the examination performance of underachieving middle school students. *ASCA School Counselor, 38,* 294–304.

Reeder, J., Douzenis, C., & Bergin, J. J. (1997). The effects of small group counseling on the racial attitudes of second grade students. *Professional School Counseling, 1*(2), 15–22.

Reynolds, S. E., & Hines, P. L. (2001). *Vision-to-action: A step-by-step activity guide for systemic educational reform* (6th ed.). Bloomington, IN: American Student Achievement Institute.

Riddle, J., Bergin, J. J., & Douzenis, C. (1997). Effects of group counseling on self-concepts of children of alcoholics. *Elementary School Guidance and Counseling, 31,* 192–202.

Ritter, D. R. (1978). Effects of a school consultation program upon referral patterns of teachers. *Psychology in the Schools, 15,* 239–243.

Robie, B. D., Gansneder, B. M., & Van Hoose, W. H. (1979). School guidance and counseling program outcomes and measures for their assessment. *Measurement and Evaluation in Guidance, 12,* 147–165.

Robinson, S. E., Morrow, S., Kigin, T., & Lindeman, M. (1991). Peer counselors in a high school setting: Evaluation of training and impact on students. *ASCA School Counselor, 39,* 35–40.

Rowan, B., & Miskel, C. G. (1999). Institutional theory and the study of educational organizations. In J. Murphy & K. Seashore Louis (Eds.), *Handbook of research on educational administration* (2nd ed., pp. 359–384). San Francisco: Jossey-Bass.

Rowell, L. L. (2005). Collaborative action research and school counselors. *Professional School Counseling, 9*, 28–36.

Rowell, L. L. (2006). Action research and school counseling: Closing the gap between research and practice. *Professional School Counseling, 9*, 376–384.

Sackett, D. L., Straus, S. E., Richardson, W. S., Rosenberg, W., & Haynes, R. B. (2000). *Evidence-based medicine; How to practice and teach EBM* (2nd ed.). Edinburgh, Scotland, UK: Churchill Livingstone.

Savickas, M. L. (1990). The Career Decision-Making Course: Description and field test. *Career Development Quarterly, 38*, 275–284.

Schaefer-Schiumo, K., & Ginsberg, A. P. (2003). The effectiveness of the Warning Signs program in educating youth about violence prevention: A study with urban high school students. *Professional School Counseling, 7*(1), 1–9.

Schlossberg, S. M., Morris, J. D., & Lieberman, M. G. (2001). The effects of a counselor-led guidance intervention on students' behaviors and attitudes. *Professional School Counseling, 4*, 156–164.

Schmidt, J. (1996). Assessing school counseling programs through external reviews. *ASCA School Counselor, 43*, 114–123.

Schmidt. J. (2003). *Counseling in schools: Essential services and comprehensive programs* (4th ed.). Boston: Allyn & Bacon.

Sexton, T. L., Schofield, T. L., & Whiston, S. C. (1997). Evidence-based practice: A pragmatic model to unify counseling. *Counseling and Human Development, 4*, 1–18.

Shadish, W. R., Cook, T. D., & Campbell, D. T. (2002). *Experimental and quasi-experimental designs for generalized causal inference.* Boston: Houghton Mifflin.

Shechtman, Z. (1993). School adjustment and small-group therapy: An Israeli study. *Journal of Counseling and Development, 72*(1), 77–81.

Shechtman, Z. (2002). Child group psychotherapy in the school at the threshold of a new millennium. *Journal of Counseling and Development, 80*, 257–384.

Shlonsky, A., & Gibbs, L. (2004). Will the real evidence-based practice please stand up? Teaching the process of evidence-based practice to the helping professions. *Brief Treatment and Crisis Intervention, 4*(2), 137–153.

Sink, C. A., & Stroh, H. R. (2003). Raising achievement test scores of early elementary school students through comprehensive school counseling programs. *Professional School Counseling, 6*(5), 350–365.

Sink, C. A., & Stroh, H. R. (2006). Practical significance: The use of effect sizes in school counseling research. *Professional School Counseling, 9*(5), 401–411.

Slavin, R. E. (2006). *Educational psychology: Theory and practice* (8th ed.). Boston: Allyn & Bacon.

Smith, J., & Niemi, R. G. (2001). Learning history in school: The impact of course work and instructional practices on achievement. *Theory and Research in Social Education, 29*(1), 18–42.

Sprinthall, N. A., Hall, J. S., & Gerler, E. R., Jr. (1992). Peer counseling for middle school students experiencing family divorce: A deliberate psychological education model. *Elementary School Guidance and Counseling, 26*(4), 279–295.

Stage, S. A., & Quiroz, D. R. (1997). A meta-analysis of interventions to decrease disruptive classroom behavior in public education settings. *School Psychology Review, 26*(3), 333–368.

St. Clair, K. L. (1989). Middle school counseling research: A resource for school counselors. *Elementary School Guidance and Counseling, 23,* 219–226.

Stevahn, L., Johnson, D. W., Johnson, R. T., & Schultz, R. (2002). Effects of conflict resolution training integrated into a high school social studies curriculum. *Journal of Social Psychology, 142*(3), 305–331.

Stone, C. B., & Dahir, C. A. (2006). *The transformed school counselor.* Boston: Lahaska Press.

Stringer, E. T. (1996). *Action research: A handbook for practitioners.* Thousand Oaks, CA: Sage.

Task Force on Evidence-Based Interventions in School Psychology. (2003). *Coding and procedures manual.* Madison, WI: Author.

Tedder, S. L., Scherman, A., & Wantz, R. A. (1987). Effectiveness of a support group for children of divorce. *Elementary School Guidance and Counseling, 18,* 102–109.

Thomas, S. (2005). The school counselor alumni peer consultation group. *Counselor Education and Supervision, 45,* 16–29.

Thompson, D. W., Loesch, L. C., & Seraphine, A. E. (2003). Development of an instrument to assess the counseling needs of elementary school students. *Professional School Counseling, 7*(1), 35–39.

Tobias, A. K., & Myrick, R. D. (1999). A peer facilitator-led intervention with middle school problem-behavior students. *Professional School Counseling, 3*(1), 27–33.

Tyra, B., & Meyers, P. (2003). Give your student support team a SPARC. *ASCA School Counselor, 40*(3), 30–33.

Valentine, J. C., & Cooper, H. (2003). *What Works Clearinghouse study design and implementation assessment device* (Version 1.0). Washington, DC: U.S. Department of Education.

Van Horn, M. L. (2003). Assessing the unit of measurement for school climate through psychometric and outcome analyses of the school climate. *Educational and Psychological Measurement, 63*(6), 1002–1019.

Vazsonyi, A. T., Bellison, L. M, & Flannery, D. J. (2004). Evaluation of a school-based, universal violence prevention program: Low-, medium-, and high-risk children. *Youth Violence and Juvenile Justice, 2*(2), 185–206.

Wang, M. C., Haertel, G. D., & Walberg, H. J. (1993). What helps students learn? *Educational Leadership, 51*(4), 74–80.

Watts, H. (1985). When teachers are researchers, teaching improves. *Journal of Staff Development, 6*(2), 118–127.

Wentzel, K., & Caldwell, K. (1997). Friendships, peer acceptance, and group membership: Relations to academic achievement in middle school. *Child Development, 68*(6), 1198–1209.

Whiston, S. C. (1996). Accountability through action research: Research methods for practitioners. *Journal of Counseling and Development, 74,* 616–623.

Whiston, S. C. (2002). Response to the past, present, and future of school counseling: Raising some issues. *Professional School Counseling, 5,* 148–157.

Whiston, S. C., & Sexton, T. L. (1998). A review of school counseling outcome research: Implications for practice. *Journal of Counseling and Development, 76,* 412–426.

Whiston, S. C., Sexton, T. L., & Lasoff, D. L. (1998). Career intervention outcome: A replication and extension. *Journal of Counseling Psychology, 45,* 150–165.

Wiggins, J. D. (1985). Six steps toward counseling program accountability. *National Association of Secondary Principals Bulletin, 69,* 28–31.

Williams, R. E., Omizo, M. M., & Abrams, B. C. (1984). Effects of STEP on parental attitudes and locus of control of their learning disabled children. *ASCA School Counselor, 31,* 126–133.

Williams, S., & McGee, R. (1994). Reading attainment and juvenile delinquency. *Journal of Child Psychology and Psychiatry, 35,* 442–459.

Wilson, N. S. (1986). Counselor interventions with low-achieving and underachieving elementary, middle, and high school students: A review of the literature. *Journal of Counseling and Development, 64,* 628–634.

Wilson, S. J., Lipsey, M. W., & Derzon, J. H. (2003). The effects of school-based intervention programs on aggressive behavior: A meta-analysis. *Journal of Consulting and Clinical Psychology, 71,* 136–149.

Wirt, F. M., & Kirst, M. W. (1997). *The political dynamics of American education.* Berkeley, CA: McCutchan.

Wirt, F. M., & Kirst, M. W. (2001). *The political dynamics of American education* (2nd ed.). Berkeley, CA: McCutchan.

Zinck, K., & Littrell, J. M. (2000). Action research shows group counseling effective with at-risk adolescent girls. *Professional School Counseling, 4*(1), 50–59.

Index